TO BE MET AS A PERSON

TO BE MET AS A PERSON
The Dynamics of Attachment in Professional Encounters

Una McCluskey

KARNAC

LONDON   NEW YORK

For Juliet Koprowska and Douglas Haldane

Copyright Acknowledgements

Chapter 6 is based on a previously published paper 'A preliminary study of the role of affect attunement in adult psychotherapy' by Una McCluskey, Derek Roger and Poppy Nash in *Human Relations*, Volume 50 No 10, pp 1261-1273, Sage Publications, © The Tavistock Institute, 1997. Reprinted by permission of Sage Publications Ltd.

Published in English in 2005 by
H. Karnac (Books) Ltd.
6 Pembroke Buildings, London NW10 6RE

© Una McCluskey, 2005

The rights of Una McCluskey to be identified as the author of this work have been asserted in accordance with §§ 77 and 78 of the Copyright Design and Patents Act 1988

British Library Cataloguing in Publication Data

A C.I.P. for this book is available from the British Library

ISBN 1 85575 326 x

www.karnacbooks.com

Printed by Hobbs the Printers, Totton, Hampshire

Contents

8 Third experiment: an experiment designed to test whether secure attachment style correlates with empathic attunement and whether empathic attunement can be improved with training

9 The process of obtaining a reliable measure for goal-corrected empathic attunement

10 Results of the Third Experiment

11 Patterns of functional and dysfunctional careseeking-caregiving partnerships

12 Interactions between therapists and patients and their roots in infancy

Appendix 1

Appendix 2

Appendix 3

Appendix 4

Acknowledgments

First, of all, I wish to acknowledge Ian Sinclair, University of York. He has been consistently interested in and supportive of this work. I am grateful for his time, his constant searching after clarity, his knowledge of statistics, and his commitment to the truth. I wish to acknowledge Dorothy Heard and Brian Lake, whose work on the dynamics of attachment in adult life has been inspirational, and who have offered me unstinting support and encouragement.

My thanks also to the other members of the University of York Attachment Research Group which over the years has included Liza Bingley Miller, Celia Downes, Carol-Ann Hooper, Juliet Koprowska, Ian Sinclair, and Dorothy Stock Whitaker. All have offered their intellectual curiosity, knowledge, help and comments. I wish to acknowledge the support and influence of the late Jock Sutherland and Megan Browne, OBE, the former in the role of trainer in a Group Analytic programme at the Scottish Institute of Human Relations, the latter as my tutor on the Diploma in Social Work at the University of Edinburgh. They introduced me to the work of the British Object Relations School and the work of John Bowlby.

I thank my colleagues and friends in the Systems Centered Training and Research Institute who have been supportive of my work, particularly Yvonne Agazarian. In addition I would like to thank Rich Armington, Fran Carter, Susan Cassano, Susan Gantt, and Eileen Jones. I would like to thank Anna-Lena Sundlin for encouraging me to publish my work and my friend Maria Bourboulis, who kept convincing me to carry on writing.

My thanks to colleagues in the Northern Attachment Seminar, a group that has been meeting several times a year at the University of York since the mid-1980s, particularly, P.O. Svanberg, Gary Burns, Errolyn Bruce and Sue Richardson.

My appreciation is also for the colleagueship and long standing friendship of Douglas Haldane, Mary Peacey and Sally Wassell. My thanks go to my friends Una Fleming and John Fleming who have accompanied me on this journey over many years and who have provided me with a much appreciated rock of friendship in the West of Ireland and in Rome. My thanks go finally to the colleagues who supplied clinical material without which I could not have embarked on this work.

Foreword

Bringing research to a wider readership than is reached by academic journals is especially worthwhile when the research in question is as relevant as this to routine professional interpersonal encounters. Writing for all practitioners in health and social care, Dr Una McCluskey introduces us to the concept of 'empathic attunement', and develops the notion that this is evaluated by the achievement of the goals of each party (hence 'goal-corrected').

Beyond the technical issues of developing experiments and measures lie the practical processes that professionals, of various sorts, use in their routine work with clients. In following Dr McCluskey through her experiments the reader gains an understanding of the components of effective professional interaction.

Probably the most exciting 'take-home message' from this book is that the function of professional care-giving is the product of both the professional and the client (or patient), but that the carer can profoundly influence this by their response to the other. These findings are most evident in the detailed analysis of videotaped encounters described in chapter 11: using simultaneous images of both care-giver and client, Dr McCluskey has been able to show the effect on the interaction of different sorts of 'attunement' in care-giver behaviour.

This is a serious book which repays careful study. Empathic attunement, far more than being a catchy phrase, represents a set of learnable skills and attitudes, justified by a body of evidence set out here, the practice of which is highly likely to enhance the quality of all sorts of helping encounters.

Peter D Campion, PhD, FRCGP
Professor of Primary Care Medicine, York Hull Medical School.

Preface

This book presents a theory of interaction in adult life when the dynamics of careseeking and caregiving are elicited. It should be of interest to all those who work in the caring professions, such as GPs, social workers, mental health workers, psychotherapists, counsellors, nurses, psychologists, occupational therapists, physiotherapists, art therapists, those working in the field of pastoral care and others. Careseeking is usually the trigger for caregiving.

The book is based both on a series of empirical experiments designed to identify the process of empathic attunement between adults and on a detailed analysis of interaction between careseekers and caregivers. I have developed a key concept which describes the process of effective interaction between caregivers and careseekers and have called this process 'goal-corrected empathic attunement' (GCEA).

The first part of the book introduces the concept and seeks to ground it in research on psychotherapy, on the interactions between mothers and infants, particularly the work of Daniel Stern, and the theory of attachment developed by John Bowlby and Mary Salter Ainsworth and extended by Dorothy Heard and Brian Lake. The hypothesis that I am putting forward is that adult psychotherapy can be understood as an attachment-eliciting activity which arouses the dynamics of attachment in clients who come for help.

When careseeking is aroused in adults, like infants they require attunement to affect and affect regulation from a sensitive caregiver. In addition, however, they also require an empathic response. When successful, careseeking will shut down and the ever present instinctive exploratory system will resume. In this way the need of the careseeker and the response of the caregiver are goal-corrected. It is this process that I call goal-corrected empathic attunement. Once exploration is activated, the person seeking help is available to make use of their own and the other's problem solving capacities. The process of effective caregiving is a continuous process of 'rupture and repair' of the connection to the affect and concerns of the careseeker.

The process of arriving at a theory of caregiving in adult life started for me when I first saw the perturbation studies carried out by Lynne Murray and Colwyn Trevarthen. These studies involved mother-infant dyads communicating with each other through a live video link. The videos I saw started with both mother and infant animated and enjoying each other. The live connection between infant and mother was then broken without their knowledge. A video replay of an earlier 'conversation' was inserted into what had been a live connection. What I noticed was the effect on the infants of losing contact with their mothers. I was struck by the immediate collapse of animation, the fact that they instantly turned their head away from the video screen, and their look of sadness. These were two month old infants. Equally dramatic was that all activity in terms of self-expression and exploration came to an abrupt end.

During my many years' practice as a social work educator, I had noticed similar behaviours and expressions to those I had just observed on video. The context for my observations was the teaching of interviewing skills to social work students or working on interpersonal skill development with qualified professionals. I noticed these expressions (albeit in less dramatic form) in those role-playing clients when the therapist or worker, in my view 'lost touch', 'dropped them' or backed away' from their affect and the particular issue they were trying to communicate. I read Daniel Stern's work on affect attunement and misattunement between mothers and infants and began to wonder whether I had been observing misattunement in the adult context. I began to wonder whether it would be possible to catch such behaviours on video as they happened between clients and therapists in the real world. I became curious about the nature of the processes I was observing in both infants and adults; what they were and what they meant.

I became interested in whether other therapists, educators, or students noticed the same interactive phenomena that I was noticing, and set up a series of experiments to find out. In the course of exposing the phenomena to outside observation, my understanding of the processes that I had been noticing deepened and became more complex. In reality the experiments and my reading interacted so that I became clearer over time about what I was looking for and how to interpret what I was finding. In practice, the way that I went about opening up the ideas to outside observation made it possible for me to test aspects of the concept of GCEA as I went along, such as its hypothesised link with exploration and interaction. I was able to compare measurements of GCEA against the impact of both training and attachment status, and was able to assess whether some students were better at GCEA than others.

My first experiment therefore set out to see whether affect attunement which had been observed in infant-caregiver interactions could indeed be reliably identified in adult psychotherapy. To do this I divided video taped recordings of therapeutic sessions into 1.5 minute segments and asked a panel of experts and students to rate the episodes as 'attuned' or 'not attuned'. The results indicated that there was a high level of agreement between the experts on some of the excerpts shown and not on others. However, the agreement achieved between the students and the experts was no better than chance. Analysis of the data suggested that, in making their judgements, the experts paid attention to the interaction, and also associated empathic attunement with exploration; the students paid attention to neither and appeared more influenced by the behaviour of the therapist.

I then set out to see whether students would do better if given instructions to pay attention to the interaction. I created two matched groups, an experimental group and a control group. Each group received the same instructions they had been given in the first experiment but the experimental group was also given instructions to pay attention to the interaction between therapist and client when making their ratings. I used three excerpts, of which one was judged 'attuned' by 100% of the experts, and another as 'non attuned' by 80% of them. I based my results on these latter two excerpts on the assumption that the experts were 'correct'. The results showed that the experimental group made significantly more correct identifications than the control group. The qualitative analysis revealed that the students who made correct ratings also noted whether the client had engaged in or was prevented from exploration.

The results of the first and second experiments supported the idea of GCEA in adult psychotherapy as being interactive and associated with exploration. I then wished to see if it was associated with the subjective experience of the careseeker and caregiver, and the attachment style of the therapist. In addition I wished to see whether students could improve their ability to interact in an attuned way with training.

I therefore designed a third experiment which would take place at two points in time and which would allow GCEA to be measured objectively by an outside observer, and subjectively by both careseekers and caregivers. It would then be possible to test: (i) whether the measures of GCEA correlated with each other and were thus reliable; (ii) whether the GCEA ratings correlated with the attachment style of the caregiver; (iii) whether those caregivers provided with training improved more than those who were not, as judged by these measures; and (iv) if students consistently differed from each other in terms of the measures of GCEA.

I found: (i) a highly significant correlation between the two subjective scores for GCEA, and a significant correlation between the objective measure of GCEA and the two subjective measures; (ii) a significant correlation between a score for 'secure attachment' and the objective score for GCEA; (iii) a significant training effect as measured by the objective GCEA score. (iv) a significant training effect as measured by the objective GCEA score. As far as I know this is the first time an attempt has been made to measure social work students' performance against a theory of effective caregiving and which has related the results to measures of personality style in ways that make sense.

The second part of the book relates to more recent work which has involved extensive analysis of the detail of interaction between 'careseekers' and 'caregivers', accomplished through a frame-by-frame analysis of videotaped adult one-to-one interaction in a variety of settings. The outcome of this analysis has been the identification of five typical careseeking behaviours and five typical caregiving responses which together create nine patterns of careseeking/caregiving interactions.

Each of these nine patterns is accompanied by distinct vitality affects that are visible on the faces of both parties and are illustrated in the book through the use of video images captured in real time. Two of these patterns are associated with effective caregiving and seven are associated with ineffective caregiving. It is hoped that readers will find these patterns and the research that underpins them useful in making sense of their experience either as a helper or as someone seeking help and that they will inspire further research and reflection in this very important field. One of the unique contributions of this research is to highlight that when the goals of the interaction have been successfully met this is known subjectively and is visible though the vitality affects expressed non-verbally by both parties.

Those in the field of child care, child psychotherapy and play therapy have been exposed to a wealth of research coming from the attachment field. Therapists working with adults have been looking to attachment research to help them make sense of processes between adult couples and how early styles of interaction with caregivers affect the pattern of relationship developed between partners or spouses. Research generated by neuroscientists which has been helped by advances in technology, particularly brain imaging, has brought to our attention not only the importance of interaction with another human being for brain development but also the crucial timing for certain kinds of interaction, which coincide with the development of attachment processes in infancy.

This book sets out a framework for thinking about the way adults interact with one another, particularly when they are anxious, under stress or frightened (these being the states that arouse the dynamics of attachment and which are usually present when people have reason to see health personnel, social workers, psychotherapists, pastoral counsellors). At these times, people need a response that puts them in touch with their competence to act; a response which reactivates their emotional, physical, intellectual capacity: a response which allows them to make use of the resources available to them, including people on whom they can rely, and their spiritual, aesthetic and financial resources. Above all, the response needs to be felt as related to the individual: sensitive, alert and focussed on well-being.

Adults as well as infants communicate the state they are in to others through words, non-verbal expressions, posture and vitality affects (the level of liveliness or deadness communicated through the body). Professional helpers respond to these messages, particularly vitality affects, in ways that trigger patterns of interaction that quickly take on a life and habit of their own. Changing these patterns involves being willing to see something different in the face of the other or to hear something different in the tone of their voice from what one thinks is there; it involves staying present to the actual experience of the other and not reacting defensively.

Training offered to those involved in the medical, social, pastoral or psychotherapy professions rarely addresses the complexities of the form in which careseeking is expressed. Most professional training courses have counselling or skills based laboratories or observed fieldwork practice as standard. However, this type of training mainly operates without a theory of interaction and without seeing the relevance of research into early careseeking and caregiving as laying down habitual context-specific patterns of behaviour and therefore relevant for understanding styles of careseeking and caregiving in adult life. Interviewing skills, divorced from an understanding of personality development and organisation and the dynamics aroused in the intimate act of helping another human being, fail to get to the heart of what professional helpers needs to learn: that the dynamics of caregiving and careseeking are highly complex, have their roots in early infancy and require an understanding in their own right.

The patterns of effective and ineffective caregiving should help practitioners to understand and identify the processes they encounter in their everyday working lives.

The experience of being met as a person is known subjectively and is visible to those who witness it. Caregivers who can respond with compassion and intelligence and who can support the intelligence and good sense of those who seek their care, however distressed and with whatever bewildering an array of careseeking behaviours, will experience the joy and pleasure of meeting and being met by a fellow human being. It is worth it.

CHAPTER ONE

The dynamics of careseeking and caregiving

We are born with the expectation of being met as a person
(Sutherland, 1993)

Introduction

Every doctor, therapist, educationalist, social worker, organisational consultant, knows when an interview or session has 'gone well'. They feel enlivened, energised and physiologically nourished in some way. Their whole system is involved, not just their emotional or intellectual capacities; it feels like a complete, what we call 'good', experience. Conversely, we have all experienced the opposite. We have had encounters, either as caregivers ourselves or we have approached someone for help such as a GP or consultant, and have come away dissatisfied and distressed. What are these dynamics about? Is there a correlation between the affect experienced by the person seeking help and the person approached for help? As therapists, educators, consultants or clinicians, how seriously should we take our experience of the encounter as an indicator of how successful the consultation was from the point of view of the person seeking help?

This book presents a way of understanding the interactions between professional caregivers and the people who come to them for help. It is directed at all those who provide therapeutic help to individuals or who have to negotiate and manage interviews with people when they are anxious or under stress, particularly when the nature of the consultation raises issues of threat to livelihood, health and well-being.

A key concept presented in the book is that of goal-corrected empathic attunement (GCEA). Goal-corrected empathic attunement implies that when individuals approach others whom they consider have the resources, or access to the resources, to help them, the ensuing interaction is mutually regulated in ways that are experienced by both as either satisfactory or unsatisfactory. Satisfactory interactions are experienced when both parties achieve the goal of their respective, separate but interdependent instinctive biologically based systems of careseeking and caregiving.

The concept of goal-corrected empathic attunement (GCEA), which is described and presented in this book, has been developed within the context of psychotherapy. GCEA is also found in forms of caregiving outwith the context of psychotherapy. Indeed, one of the advantages of the theory of interaction being presented here is that it seeks to ground psychotherapy in psychological theories derived from other fields.

The aim of this book is to help us make sense of the feelings we have both when we are successful and we are unsuccessful in providing help for other people when they are in what one would describe as a 'state'. It also addresses our own or others' experiences of feeling frustrated and defeated by attempts to achieve a compassionate and intelligent response when we are frightened and anxious. The idea is to take the reader through some of the early research in psychotherapy which looked at just this issue. Such research provides the base for a close look at attachment theory and what extended attachment theory in particular suggests is going on between adults when they engage in careseeking/caregiving relationships. The central core of the book is a series of experiments that explore the role of empathic attunement in effective caregiving.

Many of us, whether or not we see ourselves in the role of caregiving, actually do perform that function when someone asks us for help. We may be parents, teachers, psychotherapists, counsellors, medical doctors, nurses, occupational therapists, physiotherapists, social workers, clergy, debt managers, organisational consultants, or members of the general public offering a service. When people are anxious and seek help what they need is a non anxious response that understands and acts on the nature of their request accurately, leaving them in a settled and satisfied state. All of us have observed when these encounters go smoothly and have marvelled at the skill of the caregiver involved. Some people seem to be naturally 'good' at responding to the various ways in which distress and anxiety manifest themselves; others clearly get involved or respond in ways which make matters worse, either by ignoring the distress, or becoming hostile and defensive.

This book sets out a framework for thinking about the way we interact with one another, particularly when we – or they – are anxious, under stress or frightened. At these times what we need is a response that puts us in touch with our competence to act; with our emotional, physical and intellectual capacity. A response which enables us to identify people we can rely on, as well as our spiritual, financial and aesthetic resources. And if we are severely incapacitated this response must also feel related to us, be sensitive, alert and responsible and above all focused on our well-being.

A person who is frightened will to some extent regress to an earlier stage of development; they will not be in touch with their full capacity in the here and now. They will also behave towards the person they are seeking help from in ways that are familiar and habitual to them and which may or may not work. This book will present ideas based on attachment theory, on research into infant and child development and on extended attachment theory that provide pointers for how adults will seek help when in crisis, frightened or in distress. The book will also present some preliminary research that provides some evidence for these views and provide pointers for future research.

From the viewpoint being presented in this book, adults who seek help when frightened, in pain or facing threat to their lives will adopt one of four typical stances: (i) they will have confidence in their strategies for getting help and be clear and direct in their communication; (ii) they will have no confidence that their needs will be addressed and attended to and so will only seek help *in extremis* and then in a way that minimises the extent of their problem, thereby giving inadequate information to the potential caregiver; (iii) they will be uncertain, half hopeful, half sceptical, and therefore communicate in contradictory and ambiguous ways; or (iv) they will be bewildered, unclear, uncertain and disorganised about the state they are in and what would relieve it, fearing any response could potentially make things worse, thus avoiding seeking help in the first place and being frightened/angry when in a caregiving context .

As caregivers, responding to these different strategies for getting help and the different forms of relating through which such strategies are mediated, is a challenge. Training offered to those involved in the medical, social, pastoral or psychotherapy professions rarely addresses the complexities of the form in which careseeking is expressed. Most professional training courses have counselling or skills-based laboratories or observed fieldwork practice as standard. However, this type of training mainly operates without a theory of interaction and without seeing the relevance of research into early careseeking and caregiving as laying down habitual, context-specific patterns of behaviour, and therefore relevant for understanding styles of careseeking and caregiving in adult life.

Typically taught to young professionals in training are the skills of listening, observing, clarifying, negotiating, empathy and goal-setting. However, these skills, divorced from an understanding of personality development and organisation and the dynamics aroused in the intimate act of helping another human being, fail to get to the heart of what one needs to learn: that the dynamics of caregiving and careseeking are highly complex, have their roots in early infancy and require an understanding in their own right. This is what this book addresses.

When I was in my early twenties, I accompanied my mother to see a consultant cardiologist in Fitzwilliam Square in Dublin, about the possibility of her having an operation to replace three malfunctioning valves. She came out from the consultation in considerable distress. From what I could gather she was told she was not ill enough to warrant the risk of the operation. She was very frustrated, depressed and in despair. I do not know whether she conveyed any of this to the cardiologist or whether he had any clue that she saw the operation as her only hope of survival and wanted to have it whatever her chances. From what I know of her she would have been polite, deferential and would have accepted his advice with good grace and a smile, would have thanked him for his time and paid his exorbitant fee. I had come from Scotland where I was working, and my mother had travelled at some inconvenience and distress from the south of Ireland to Dublin for this consultation. It lasted about twenty minutes. Neither of us thought to seek a further word on the subject, to go back into the building and discuss the choices and the risks of having the operation more fully. She died six months later aged fifty-five.

This is an account of a desperate attempt to get help in the light of an extremely dangerous medical condition. It is an example of both failed careseeking and failed caregiving. A more skilled careseeker may have negotiated that consultation better; a more skilled caregiver may have looked behind my mother's elegant, well-dressed appearance and gentle manner and seen the desperation of a woman who felt she was losing control of her life. Part of my mother's careseeking style was to support the other's claim to know what was best; an effective caregiver in this instance would have had to have the skills necessary to deflect such flattery, to override the fragility of her physical appearance and tackle her directly about the risks she was willing to take.

Should caregivers fail to meet the needs of careseekers, the latter cannot reach the goal of careseeking, and commonly become frustrated and then depressed. What happens when each partner is failing to reach their goals, and what is happening to their careseeking and caregiving systems is increasingly being researched and understood in both non-human primates and in human beings.

(Heard and Lake, 1997, p.5)

It is with this arena of interaction, that between careseeker and caregiver that is the concern of this book.

In the early seventies, after qualifying in social work at Edinburgh University, I worked for five years in an innovative department of child and family psychiatry in Fife (Haldane et al, 1980). Staff in this department were either trained in psychodynamically oriented therapeutic work or were interested in such work. This meant that there was an emphasis on the meaning of the interactions taking place between therapists and clients. There was an interest in how clients were responding to the therapeutic interventions by the therapists and the impact of such interventions on the clients' lives. The relationship formed between therapist and client was seen as a very important aspect of the work and probably a key factor in any meaningful change.

The relationship was understood to have meaning particularly for the client who was seeking help, and the therapist saw it as an integral part of their job to try and be as aware as possible of this aspect of the working relationship. Within a psychodynamic framework for working, attention was paid to the feelings that were aroused in therapists by their clients and thought was given to the possibility that these feelings may be unconsciously projected by the clients into the therapists as a way of communicating aspects of their experience too painful to know about, assimilate or put into words.

The work of the psychodynamically trained therapist is to be tuned into these affects and processes and to try to conceptualise their meaning. The psychodynamically trained therapist understands the process of ongoing therapeutic work to be the unravelling and working through of this material with the client in ways that make sense to the client and feel helpful. I was very interested in this work and both received and took part in providing psychodynamic supervision for staff, much helped by the writings of Michael Balint (Balint and Balint, 1961), Janet Mattinson (Mattinson, 1975) and Donald Winnicott (Winnicott, 1958a; Winnicott, 1971a; Winnicott, 1971; Winnicott, 1967;

Winnicott, 1958b; Winnicott, 1971b). The clients we were working with were families where the children or adolescents were providing cause for concern either to their parents, school, GPs, or from other agencies, professionals such as probation officers or educational psychologists.

Even though the work was stressful and demanding, the department was a very satisfying place to work. The culture was thoughtful and reflective and the work was subject to constant study and research, much of which was written up. It was in this working context that I came across and worked with other social work colleagues dealing with the same client group. The point of contact was often over a referral of one of the families they were working with. It was striking how seemingly unaware they were of the emotional dynamics of the family and how little support there was for such understanding within the organisation that they worked for. It was equally noticeable that this lack of awareness seemed to affect their capacity to consider engaging the family in resolving their problems in the here and now.

My colleagues often seemed to respond by considering one of two alternatives: refer the family on to another department (such as ours) or place one or more of the children in residential or foster care. The emphasis on separating children from parents often coincided with a lack of awareness that the child and family needed to know what this separation was about, why it was happening, how long it would be for and whether and how they would all come together after the period of separation was over. The idea of the referral to another department, or the separation being part of a planned process that the social worker was overseeing, that had a beginning, a middle and an end that anticipated the post intervention period, was generally absent. Just as these social workers seemed blind to the meaning of relationships within families and the impact of separation on family members, so they seemed equally blind to the impact of their own behaviour on the families who came to social services for help.

They seemed to react to the pain and distress being presented to them by going into flight, a flight that put distance between themselves and the person seeking help rather than coming closer to the person or family to work at whatever needed to be done. It seemed hard for them to think that they or their behaviour might mean something to the families, or that they might have something to offer in the way of help with the family relationships.

This happened in the early to mid nineteen seventies. It highlights the difference between organisational structures which support the task of caregiving and which strive to understand the dynamics of careseeking and caregiving, and organisational structures that do not, and the effect of this on individual members of staff in terms of their response to complex emotions and behaviour. There have been several studies since which support this observation that organisational structures impact on professional functioning and well-being, and on the capacity of professional carers to collaborate effectively with colleagues and provide a relevant and thoughtful service for their clients. Examples are the work of Janet Mattinson and Ian Sinclair, (Mattinson and Sinclair, 1979; and others (Agass, 2000; Brearley, 2000; Woodhouse and Pengelly, 1986). These and other studies demonstrate the crucial importance of understanding the impact of emotionally difficult and disturbing work on the thought processes and behaviour of the professional carers involved.

At the level of policy, the importance of professional collaboration, interagency functioning and collaborative interdisciplinary training at pre- and post- professional qualification has been emphasised over the years in a number of government inquiries. The current green paper *Every Child Matters* (2003) aims to bring together health and social services staff in schools and local children's centres. Government plans to set up children's trusts by 2006 designed to amalgamate social care, health, education and other services are precisely in order to address the failures in communication between services that numerous inquiries, and more particularly that into Victoria Climbie's death, have made so tragically clear. What all policies need to be watchful of, however, is that any attempt to improve interprofessional collaboration must be grounded in an understanding of the dynamics of communication between careseekers and caregivers in the first place; in a knowledge of the way emotions are communicated, registered and understood, and of the different ways in which professionals and others so quickly become defensive in the context of any form of communication which is infiltrated by anxiety.

Starting towards the end of the seventies and continuing through the eighties up to the present day, there has been a movement away from the idea that professional caregivers need certain conditions which support their work towards the idea that what is needed is more effective monitoring and clearer procedures. It has become as if good practice can be encapsulated in good procedures and the able practitioner need only follow them. The concept and practice of purchaser and provider in health and social services exemplifies this assumption, where the professional caregiver is bought to provide a tightly defined service within strictly defined time limits.

On a visit to a social services office in my capacity as consultant to a family therapy team I found the social workers completely demoralised; they were low in numbers in terms both of referrals to their service and in new recruits of staff to their team. Even their own regular members were attending their fortnightly meetings in haphazard fashion. Their description of their most recent reorganisation was that the teams were now so structured that they rarely met their colleagues from other teams; the office was dead at 5 p.m. in the evening, where previously they would have stayed on and chatted with their colleagues – they now do their work and go home.

The work was so compartmentalised, they told me, that before they saw a client they had to establish a contract for service with them by post and then wait for them to make the appointment at the office – home visits are a rarity. It could take three weeks or longer to actually make face-to-face contact with someone who has presented to the duty team in an emergency. Most self-referrals fall by the wayside – they did not show up for appointments and the view of the social work staff was that they were not responding quickly enough.

The sense of alienation from the core of their work, from direct contact with people wanting help was palpable. And of course what is obvious to the reader from the way this service is organised and delivered is that there is a complete absence of the idea (in the minds of the managers) that the dynamics aroused by careseeking might be worth taking into account and paying some attention to when organising a service, and that if careseekers are met by an impersonal response from potential caregivers it might well influence how they feel about pursuing their request for help. The experience that we had in the department of child and family psychiatry in Fife referred to earlier confirmed that clients sought help reluctantly, rarely followed through on first request for help and needed highly responsive staff who could effect home visits – otherwise these usually desperate people dropped from the sight of social workers, GPs and others. From what we now know of attachment behaviour, insecure careseeking styles will tend to be avoidant and avoidant ambivalent in relation to perceived caregivers, so these observations make sense.

The process of refining and defining procedures for good practice clearly arises from the observation and analysis of past mistakes and has the objective of taking the best practice and ensuring that this becomes the standard. However, the need to ensure proper standards of care for sick and vulnerable people should be informed by an understanding of the properties or nature of the relationship struck or formed between careseekers and their caregivers. This relation-ship is crucial to the communication of the nature of the service required and the provision of that service. It mediates the transfer of information not only from users of social to social work staff about issues of child care and protection, but also from patients to orthopaedic surgeons about the nature of the pain and disability being experienced, or between patients and nurses about the need for more painkillers.

These and other examples represent careseeking in a context of anxiety, pain, and distress. How the caregiver responds is crucial in terms of whether the careseeker feels understood; feels that their intelligence, sensitivities and imagination are respected as sources of relevant information and therefore can proceed safely to explore more complex dimensions to the issue(s) that they are concerned about: whether that is a recent heart attack and the potential consequences; discovery of abuse of a child by a trusted other; or complex emotional states being explored in psychotherapy.

Caregivers who are working to procedures alone may well give a service that satisfies the auditors and the inspectors of quality controls, but they may not be quite so focused on the effect of their behaviour or the response they are getting from the careseeker. Indeed they may be oblivious to the fact they are getting less than half the story and losing trust and confidence. This, in the long run, is going to cost time and money, it keeps the unsatisfied careseeker returning in one form or another in order to find the conditions which will support their recovery.

The dynamics of caregiving and careseeking being presented in this book are those pertaining to the actual interactions taking place between the careseeker and the caregiver. The studies and experiments presented examine the actual dynamics of that relationship; how we can understand the interactions between careseeker and caregiver which shape that relationship and influence whether it is successful or otherwise.

Origins of interest in attunement in therapy

I first set out to study affect attunement in the context of adult psycho-therapy. I did so from a sense that it was an important area of study. I have over thirty years experience of working with people in couple relationships, families or groups and also have considerable experience of working with trainee social workers at post-graduate level.

There is a particular phenomenon that has exercised me constantly over these years. This is the frequency and regularity with which therapists withdraw from the affect being expressed by their clients. Sometimes the affect is expressed verbally by the client; sometimes non-verbally. This withdrawal takes the form of either (i) carrying on as if totally oblivious to the information coming through about the affective state the person is in, or the affect they wish to communicate; or (ii) distracting them from the direction they are heading, either by asking unrelated questions or introducing a change of subject. In addition, I have noticed, that as clients bring in what they consider to be affectively significant material they often tend to glance at the face of the interviewer, then look away. This movement I have captured on video many, many times. In my view it fits the phenomena of social referencing described by Klinnert (Klinnert *et al.*, 1983) which describes how a one-year-old infant placed in an ambiguous situation will check the expression on their mother's face (affect) to determine whether they should proceed in a direction that seems unsafe or stay where they are.

My practice as consultant/trainer is to stop the therapist at the points in the session where they failed to respond to the communication of affect. I have therefore accumulated a great deal of information about what was happening for the therapist at that time, what they were experiencing and thinking, what they wanted to do and what was getting in the way of them doing it. Questions I would generally ask the therapist were: did you see the expression on his/her face just now?; did you notice the tone in the voice?; did you notice the way he looked at her when she or he said that?; did you hear what she said just now? I have never had any therapist say to me that they had not noticed what I was drawing their attention to. For some it was less vivid than others; for some they needed me to retrace what had happened and give a verbal description (or if it had been videoed, then a video replay) of the movement or expression of the careseeker, but once this happened they were aware they had seen what I was referring to.

Having stopped the session and had a discussion with the therapist about what they had missed, why they had backed away from it, whether they thought if we re-ran that sequence they could pick it up if it happened again and if so how they might do that, I then got to see what happened next. When they changed the way they responded to the client's affect, I noticed three things: a) there were changes in the client's vitality affects, their sense of liveliness and involvement, and this was often accompanied by a change of colour and muscle tone in the face; b) the client pursued the conversation in a direction congruent with the affect that they had communicated (even though sometimes this affect was expressed non-verbally, in context one got a sense of where they were going); c) the therapist became more involved, seemed to be more alive and engaged and purposeful, as if engaged in something they experienced as real. Those were my observations of the therapist and the effect of a change of strategy. If one thinks about it in attachment terms the change in strategy required the caregiver to shift from behaviour that put distance between themselves and the care-seeker to one that promoted emotional proximity between them.

I was also observing the client. What I noticed was that once the therapist had backed away from the client's affect, the client would change tack, sometimes in such a subtle way that it was hardly recog-nisable. This seemed to be in the service of going along with the direction being pursued or suggested by the therapist. I have also never seen a client insist that they stick with the affective meaning of what they were saying, or suggest that it be pursued by the therapist in lieu of the direction being presented to them by the therapist. This observation of the careseeker's behaviour seems to fit the mental organisation associated with the insecurely attached child (Target and Fonagy, 1998). Target suggests that the way that caregivers relate to the affective component of the child's experience of reality corresponds with the caregiver's own attachment status. I return to these ideas more fully in the next chapter.

I am not saying that I think clients never return to their own pathway at some point in the future and that therapists always divert them away; rather I believe clients do make many attempts to get the therapist to attend to their deepest emotional concerns and that thera-pists do in the end mostly respond, but that the process may take longer than it need and not be understood as well as it might.

In the Spring of 1993, I attended a one-day conference at the University of York on attachment issues in working with children, led by Mary Sue Moore, and saw the videos of the perturbation studies carried out by Murray and Trevarthen (Murray and Trevarthen, 1986). These made an enormous impact on me. I saw the process of attune-ment between happy and contented mother and infant couples and I saw the direct effect on the infant of non attunement. I was absolutely riveted by the immediacy with which the infant withdrew eye contact, turned their head away and looked down at the floor or looked away. I began to wonder about the role of attunement in careseeking/care-giving relationships and the effects of misattunement and non-attunement on the development of the relationship itself. This prompted me to read the work of Daniel Stern (Stern, 1985). For me, Stern's work supported the theory of Ronald Fairbairn (Fairbairn, 1952) with which I was very familiar and which was contrary to the view of child development held by Melanie Klein and others. Fairbairn maintained that infants were person-seeking from the start. Stern's review of the literature on infant development and his own research seemed to confirm this thesis.

A few months later I wrote a paper with a colleague entitled 'Pre-verbal communication: the role of play in establishing rhythms of communication between self and other', (McCluskey and Duerden, 1993). We wrote at the end of that paper:

> To understand what is required in therapy we need to capture the detail of the process of communication between people when they feel they are being understood and communicating well. Maybe like Stern and others we need to film it and play it back in slow motion so that we can examine the detail of the interaction – capture the ebb and flow – amplify and name the processes for ourselves, so that we can recognise and learn them. As social workers or therapists we need to understand more about not only the context of therapy: purpose, predictability, reliability; the processes of attachment, loss, transference and counter transference, but also the mechanics of communication. The work of the naturally good enough mother in Winnicott's phrase needs to be analysed.
>
> (McCluskey and Duerden, 1993, p.26)

I started the research presented in this book as a consequence of the work for that paper. That being the case I set out primarily to study attunement in careseeking caregiving situations between adults in a therapeutic context.

The preliminary work involved getting the views of my peers and trainees on excerpts of clinical practice; I wanted to know whether they would agree with my judgement that in one instance the therapist was attuned to the client's affect and in the other that the therapist was not attuned.

Because my understanding of the function of the concept of affect attunement has changed and developed during the course of the research, it provides a particular challenge as to how to present the key ideas and concepts. My current position, which developed through the reading and empirical work for this book, is that the concept of affect attunement that I started off with is insufficient to describe the process of effective caregiving responses. Through the empirical work I went on to develop the concept of goal-corrected empathic attunement. I locate this concept within three intellectual domains: the psycho-biological theory of attachment; earlier research into the process of counselling and psychotherapy; and the field of developmental psychology.

This was not always my position. I started out in my first experi-ment (chapter six) with the concept of affect attunement as defined by Stern (1985): "Affect attunement ... is the performance of behaviours that express the quality of feeling of a shared affect state without imitating the exact behavioural expression of the inner state" (p.143). The definitions of affect attunement that I used for my first experiment were: "attunement is a way of communicating to the other that one has recognised the affect they are experiencing. Attunement conveys to the other that one has a feeling sense inside of what it feels like to be them right now". By the end of that experiment I understood that the activity of affect attunement on its own was insufficient to describe the processes that activated the biologically based instinctive exploratory system. I understood that the process of affect attunement captured just a fraction of the interactive process associated with successful care-giving responses.

However, I did not always find myself updating my terms, even when my understanding of the concept had shifted. For some time into the study I continued to use the term 'affect attunement' when in fact I should have been using the term 'empathic attunement'. As far as this book is concerned I use the term 'affect attunement' in chapter six when I describe my first experiment. I shift from using the term 'affect attunement' to using 'empathic attunement' in chapter seven, when I describe my second experiment.

Structure of the book

This book presents a theory of careseeking and caregiving in adult life. As already mentioned, the central concept in the book is that of *goal-corrected empathic attunement*. It became clear to me in the course of the research that empathic attunement is goal-corrected. This means that when the caregiver attunes successfully to the communication of the careseeker, then careseeking behaviour temporarily shuts down. The subjective experience is one of relief or of feeling settled and the instinctive exploratory system within the careseeker functions normally. What contributes to successful caregiving responses is attention to the vitality affects being communicated by the careseeker. These indicate what is happening to various instinctive systems within the careseeker during the interaction. The careseeker does actually provide non-verbal information through their vitality affects to the caregiver about the accuracy, usefulness, redundancy or uselessness of their response. I develop this idea fully in chapters eleven and twelve.

I locate empathic attunement as a necessarily component of effective caregiving – attunement to affect without empathy is insufficient, as is empathy devoid of an emotional connection with the other.

Our understanding of empathy needs to be expanded so that our attention as parents or educationalists is focused on the conditions necessary for sustained empathy. All of us are capable of 'empathic moments'. For those of us working with the excluded, the disadvantaged, the traumatized, the abused, 'empathic moments' are not enough; what is required is sustained empathy and this can only happen in a context that understands the emotional dynamics of caregiving and can support and sustain the caregiver him- or herself at the core of their being.

The first four chapters provide the building blocks for constructing and presenting the concept of goal-corrected empathic attunement. They draw particularly on attachment theory, studies of interaction between parents, infants and children, and concepts of empathy. However, they also cover some of the more general research in psychotherapy.

The three subsequent chapters present the empirical studies designed to identify the elements and processes involved in the concept of goal-corrected empathic attunement and test various hypotheses. They are concerned to see whether (i) the phenomenon of affect attunement could be identified in adult psychotherapy; (ii) it referred to an interactive process and was associated with exploration; (iii) the attachment status of 'caregivers' affected their ability to engage in goal-corrected empathic attunement (GCEA); (iv) 'caregivers' who were given training would improve their performance in GCEA. Chapter ten presents the results of this experiment. Chapter eleven describes patterns of interaction associated with effective and ineffective caregiving and illustrates the vitality affects that accompany successful and unsuccessful interaction. Chapter twelve concludes the book with a summary of the research.

CHAPTER TWO

Research on the process of interaction in adult psychotherapy

To good old British empiricists it has always seemed self-evident that the mind, uncorrupted by past experience, can passively accept the imprint of sensory information from the outside world and work it into complex notions; that the candid acceptance of sense-data is the elementary or generative act in the advancement of learning and the foundation of everything we are truly sure of. Alas, unprejudiced observation is mythical too. In all sensation we pick and choose, interpret, seek and impose order, and devise and test hypotheses about what we witness. Sense data are taken, not merely given: we *learn* to perceive.

(Medawer, 1962, p.133)

Introduction

On the whole psychotherapy is a private treatment paid for out of personal income. Because of its relative under-representation in the public services there have been few large-scale, publicly funded research projects into its effectiveness. Most notable of these was the work of the Chicago group in the 1940s and 50s, of which Carl Rogers was a leading figure. In the United Kingdom, the Department of Health commissioned a review of psychotherapy research driven by the current interest in evidence-based provision of services. This was published by Roth and Fonagy (1996) under the title 'What works for whom?: a critical review of psychotherapy research'.

The review by Roth and Fonagy reflects what was actually happening in the field of psychotherapy. The picture that emerges is not that of a unitary form of treatment. Rather there is a cluster of psychotherapies, psychodynamically oriented therapies, cognitive behavioural therapies – interpersonal, systemic, integrative, group, family and so on. I quote at length from Roth and Fonagy's introductory chapter to show the scale of the problem and the issues involved.

> ... there is considerable cross-fertilisation between treatment approaches, in terms of both theory and technique. Currently, for example, there is a degree of convergence among clinicians rooted in psychoanalytic practice and those whose interests lie primarily in cognitive-behavioural techniques. While the latter are increasingly interested in non-conscious processes and the impact of the psychotherapeutic relationship, the former have shown more concern about the nature of knowledge representation and the significance of cognitive factors that may account for slow progress within psychotherapy. Ultimately, theoretical orientations will have to be integrated, since they all approximate models of the same phenomenon: the human mind in distress. For the moment, however, integration may well be counter-productive, as theoretical coherence is the primary criterion for distinguishing false and true assertions in many psycho-therapeutic domains.
>
> (Roth and Fonagy, 1996, pp.11–12)

In practice, integration is not common, psychotherapy research is generally small scale, conducted by a few researchers collaborating together in universities. Sometimes this is done in conjunction with clinically active colleagues who are motivated to understand why what they do seems to work or fail to work. For this reason the literature on psychotherapy is rather diverse. What we know is that there is a vast range of different psychotherapeutic paradigms. The register of the United Kingdom Council of Psychotherapy recognises eight distinct psychotherapy sections (e.g. psychoanalytic and psychodynamic psychotherapy section, hypnotherapy section, family, marital, sexual therapy section), between them representing in the region of 60 organisations, each with their own particular orientations to theory and practice.

While I understand the reasoning behind the statement of Roth and Fonagy quoted above, I find their reluctance to seek general theories unsatisfactory. It seems to me that the essence of psychotherapy should be that it is an effective response provided by one or more persons to another human being in distress who is seeking help. Psychotherapy is a response to careseeking. For each individual the dynamics of careseeking and caregiving go back to infancy. A theory of careseeking and caregiving is most naturally grounded in research in this area (infancy). A key concern of this book is to see whether such a theory can be provided.

As a beginning, this chapter sets out to see whether traditional psychotherapy research has looked to the field of infant development to help understand the processes involved in the early careseeking/caregiving relationships in order to elucidate careseeking/caregiving behaviours in adult life. I am also interested in whether the researchers have considered the possibility that an understanding of the dynamics of careseeking and caregiving would help to understand the process of psychotherapy itself.

At the same time I am interested in what psychotherapy researchers have discovered about the process that goes on between careseekers and caregivers. This is a traditional concern in the field of counselling and psychotherapy, where those who study what is known as 'process' are interested in the interaction between therapist and client and the relationship formed between them. Process is a word that carries several meanings. It sometimes refers to interaction, sometimes to relationship, sometimes to both verbal and non-verbal sequences of behaviour, sometimes to only one dimension of interaction. This chapter presents the work of key researchers in this rather broad field over the past 50 years.

The literature on this question is vast so I have selected my sample based on the following criteria:

(i) eminence and contribution to the field;
(ii) research that covered the major traditions of counselling, psychotherapy and psychoanalysis;
(iii) major centres of funded research.

I will start with the work of the Chicago school of psychotherapy research. I will then examine the work of Carkhuff and Berenson who represent a more counselling tradition. Finally I will look at the work of Lester Luborsky who comes from a psychoanalytic background. He has taken the concept of transference and developed ways of exploring its manifestation and resolution in the therapeutic process.

The idea of transference comes as we know from early experiences of relationship and how these experiences are projected onto others. Early experience of relationship clearly arises in the context of careseeking and caregiving.

The work of these authors covers a time period of about 50 years and can be located within different decades. I will present them chronologically, starting with the Chicago group, continuing with Carkhuff and Berenson, and ending with the work of Luborsky.

The work of the Chicago Group: 1940–1960

Carl Rogers is often seen as a proponent of counselling (he tends to use the word counsellor where others would use the word therapist) and as being outside the more traditional psychoanalytic schools. I include his work under psychotherapy because his definition of the goal of therapy includes change at the level of the structure of the personality.

> During therapy the concept of self is revised to assimilate basic experiences which have previously been denied to awareness as threatening, the person becomes more realistic, he integrates previously denied experience.
>
> (Rogers, 1953, p.419)

Awareness and integration of previously excluded material would certainly fall within the goal of psychotherapy.

In 1942, Rogers published a complete account of a tape-recorded counselling process. All interventions by client and counsellor were marked and all interventions by the counsellor were annotated by Rogers. What is clear from the account itself, the annotations and the remarks made by him, is that Rogers sees the response of the therapist as crucial in terms of facilitating or inhibiting the client's exploration of his feelings and concerns. For example:

S10 I have a good ear for harmony then. But when I'm blocked, I seem to lose that, as well as my dancing ability. I feel very awkward and stiff.

C11 M-hm. So that both in your work and in your recreation you feel blocked.

S11 I don't want to do anything. I just lie around. I get no gusto for any activity at all.

C12 You just feel unable to do things, is that it?

S12 Well, I actually feel pressure on me just like that (pointing to abdomen) as near as I can refer to it, uh-pressing right on my dynamo, as you might say.

(Rogers, 1942, p.269)

Rogers annotated this sequence thus: "C11, C12. Good instances of entirely non-directive responses which simply recognise the feeling being expressed, make conversation easy, and enable the client to continue to explore his attitudes." While Rogers notes sequence, he is basically concentrating on the nature of the therapist's response. He also picked up on the importance of the atmosphere created between therapist and client and attributed this to the therapist. He writes that there are four definite qualities that "characterise the most helpful counselling atmosphere":

(i)   a warmth and responsiveness on the part of the counsellor which makes rapport possible, and which gradually develops into a deeper emotional relationship;

(ii) permissiveness in regard to expression of feeling – the client comes to feel that all feelings and attitudes may be expressed;

(iii) a clear structure in terms of time boundaries and what types of actions are permitted during the session;

(iv) freedom from any type of coercion or pressure.

(Rogers, 1942, pp.87–89)

While atmosphere is something that one would normally assume to be the product of interaction, Rogers puts it down to the behaviour of the therapist, how the therapist is conducting him or herself, and the setting of structure in terms of time boundaries.

Fred Fiedler (1953) also took the view that the dominant party to the therapeutic encounter is the therapist:

… the relationship is created by the therapist; all psychotherapies have as their effective core the interpersonal relationship rather than specific methods of treatment; and the therapist's conveyed feelings rather than his methods are the prerequisites to the formation of a therapeutic relationship.

(Fiedler, 1953, p.297)

Fielder's study was carried out on a sample of 16 cases and looked at several hours from the beginning, middle and end parts of therapy. Some cases extended into the hundredth or two hundredth hour of treatment (see page 311). Given this broad range of sampling, Fiedler found that the patient is almost immediately aware of the therapist's feeling towards him. He also found that "in order to have a patient who expresses his feelings freely, one must be a therapist who has favourable attitudes towards his patient" (p.313).

His observations of 'successful' and 'unsuccessful' therapists led him to the view that the differences between therapists were not necessarily intellectual, but could also be based on emotion, in terms of their feelings for their patients. He explored what feelings are found in 'good' therapists and what feelings are found in 'bad' therapists. He found that 'good' therapists see their patients as similar to themselves (see Fielder, 1953, pp.296–315).

Fielder carried out various studies that suggested that he saw the therapist as the pivotal figure in the therapeutic process. For instance he carried out a study on whether the therapeutic relationship is primarily a function of the therapist's competence or of the therapist's method and orientation. He also set out to challenge the assumption that therapists trained by different schools create different kinds of relationships (better/worse).

He explored this by asking a number of therapists of various degrees of reputed competence from different schools to take part in a project aimed at discovering 'what they considered to be the ideal therapeutic relationship. Two different sets of statements were used and three different types of therapists co-operated. The therapists were drawn from the psychoanalytic, non-directive, and Alderian schools, as well as some who considered themselves to be eclectics; several non-therapists also co-operated. He found that (i) therapists of different schools see the same elements in the relationship as important, and that differences in school and method do not lead them to attempt the creation of a relationship which differs in essence from those which therapists of other schools seek to create; (ii) non-therapists described the ideal therapeutic relationship in terms no different from those of therapists, indicating that the therapeutic relationship is not unique to psychotherapy but can be found – or at least imagined – by those who have never experienced therapy; (iii) therapists who were reputed to be experts agreed more with experts of different schools than with non-experts within their own school.

Fiedler (1953) goes on to provide further evidence that "the therapist plays the determining part in shaping the relationship" (p.302). He got judges to rate therapists working with different patients and also had them re-rate the therapists with the same patient but using a different therapeutic session. His findings suggested that therapists are quite stable from patient to patient and are not affected by differences in the content of the hour or differences between patients.

Rogers and Dymond describe a massive programme of research into Client-Centred Therapy undertaken at the University of Chicago in the early 1950s:

> It studied the progress of 80 individuals – clients, "drop-outs" and controls over a period ranging from a few months to four years. It involved the administration of a six-hour battery of tests on more than two hundred occasions to these individuals, the recording of well over a thousand therapeutic interviews, and the transcription of many of these interviews for further research and analysis.
>
> (Rogers and Dymond, 1954, p.413)

It is interesting that in spite of this detailed attention to *interaction* Rogers seemed to stick with the idea that the process was predictable and the outcome inevitable provided the therapist behaved in certain ways:

> ...whether by chance, by insight into personality, by scientific knowledge, by artistry in human relationships, or by a combination of all these elements, we have learned how to initiate a describable process, which appears to have a core of sequential, orderly events and which tends to be similar from one client to another. We know at least something of the attitudinal conditions for getting this process under way. We know that if the therapist holds within himself attitudes of deep respect and full acceptance for this client as he is, and similar attitudes towards the client's potentialities for dealing with himself and his situations; if these attitudes are suffused with sufficient warmth, which transforms them into the most profound type of liking or affection for the core of the person: and if a level of communication is reached so that the client can begin to perceive that the therapist understands the feelings he is experiencing and accepts him at the full depth of that understanding, then we may be sure that the process is already initiated.
>
> (Rogers, 1953, pp.44–45)

Rogers maintained that there was a predictable pattern to the way in which issues were presented for exploration and that this pattern was affected by the therapist's response to the client.

An example of research focusing on the processes operating *within* the psychotherapeutic session is work on the changing levels of client defensiveness during the progression of therapy. Seeman and Raskin (1953, p.213) refer to a 'measure of defensiveness', a concept developed by Hogan (1948) and applied by Haigh (1949). Apparently, Haigh compared the defensive behaviour of the first and second halves of therapy and found a decrease in defensiveness in the latter half of therapy. When the measure of defensiveness was compared with positive measures for the same group of cases (e.g. self acceptance, insight), the correlations between the measures indicated that, on average, defensiveness reduces as statements of self acceptance and insight increase.

It is interesting that researchers were noticing that when therapy was successful the level of client defensiveness in relation to the therapist lowered in the second half of therapy. A reduction in defensiveness was linked with relaxation of attitudes to self and others. I would suggest that a reduction in defensiveness must indicate that the therapist is relating in a way that does not arouse defensiveness in the client, or that they can respond to the client in such a way as to make it less necessary for the client to defend themselves.

There is interesting research from the field of child development that throws light on defensiveness which I will return to in the next chapter of this book. I will also suggest in that chapter that the effect of process in potentially strengthening and affirming a sense of self is something that can be achieved outside psychotherapy in the interaction of mother and infant. Rogers himself felt no need to derive his conclusions from such a developmental hypothesis. Instead he pursued a purely inductive approach:

> We endeavour to describe, study, and understand the basic process which underlies therapy, rather than warp the process to fit our clinical needs or our preconceived dogma or the evidence from some other field.

> (Rogers, 1953, p.45)

Given such views, it was never likely at this point that psychotherapy research would have looked to ethology, biology, information processing or general systems thinking to make sense of the processes being observed. They were more likely to be influenced by the research going on in psychology at that time, which among other things was concerned with deriving valid measurements of various individual characteristics (such as defensiveness, self acceptance, self perception etc.).

In conclusion, therefore, one can say of the early researchers of the Chicago group that they were highly attentive to process and outcome, and the individual characteristics of the therapist that facilitated a positive outcome. The researchers were interested both in the process of change and in the nature of what was being changed – i.e. personality structure. In addition they also developed measures for rating the outcome of therapy. However, while they were studying interaction they tended (i) to study the individual behaviour and personality characteristics of the therapist as the dominant person and not interaction *per se*, and (ii) they were decidedly against locating the study of therapeutic process outwith the therapeutic encounter itself and therefore by definition had no interest in seeking to understand the dynamics of psychotherapy by examining the processes involved in the interactions taking place between infant careseekers and their caregivers.

From a focus on the individual to a focus on interaction: 1960–1980

For reasons of brevity, I have chosen to concentrate in this section on two main authors, Carkhuff and Berenson, the former being a major name associated with the psychotherapy research of this period.

These researchers took the view that all helping interactions had a 'for better' or 'for worse' effect upon the person being helped. Like Rogers[1] they thought that what facilitates these interactions in the direction of 'for better' is the existence of certain core dimensions attributable to the person who is helping, which were: a) empathic understanding; b) positive regard; c) genuineness; and d) concreteness or specificity of expression. They saw these, rather than techniques, as the keys to success.

1. The core conditions necessary for successful psychotherapy according to Rogers:
    (i)   The presence of a relationship – 'two persons are in psychological contact';
    (ii) The state of the client – the client should be in a state of vulnerability or anxiety – incongruence;
    (iii) The state of the therapist – the therapist should be within the confines of this relationship, a congruent, genuine, integrated person;
    (iv) The therapist must experience acceptance of the client;
    (v)   The therapist must experience empathy for the client;
    (vi) The client must experience the therapist's empathy and acceptance.
                                   (Rogers 1957 in Kirschenbaum & Henderson 1990, p.224)

We find, for example, that the helper's final, not his initial, level of empathic understanding is related to patient improvement in therapy ... the implication is that ultimately the helper's effectiveness is related to his continuing depth of understanding rather than his ability to 'technique it' during early phases of therapy. Indeed too much empathy too early in therapy may have a deleterious effect upon patient development because it may create too much tension and anxiety in the helpee.

(Carkhuff and Berenson, 1969, cited in
Carkhuff and Berenson, 1977, p.8)

This view of empathy and its nature links in an important way with what I was putting forward in chapter one of this book. Carkhuff and Berenson worked out five levels of therapist behaviour for each of these core dimensions, expressing the view that level 3 was the "minimally facilitative or effective level of functioning". The five levels actually demonstrate a deepening process of communication and interaction that they feel is necessary to facilitate change. They track the reciprocal interaction between therapists and clients and they identify the nature and variety of the affective communication between clients and therapists.

Carkhuff and Berenson put a primary emphasis on the helper's capacity to facilitate exploration. They make the point that exploration is not an end in itself but without it nothing else meaningful can happen:

We need to be able to train helpers to respond fully to the helpee's frame of reference. These responses need to be a great deal more than simple-minded reflections. The helper's ability to respond must take him fully into the helpee's experience, not only to facilitate helpee exploration but also to teach the helpee how to explore.

(Carkhuff and Berenson, 1977, p.153)

That Carkhuff and Berenson were tuned in to interaction is evident from the following quotation:

The accuracy of the helper's responsiveness is dependent upon the helper's listening skills. The level of the helper's listening skills is dependent on the helper's observation skills and the level of the helper's observation skills is dependent upon the helper's attending skills. Responding is much much more than a verbal exchange. Responding incorporates the complexities of attending: attending involves physical, emotional, and intellectual attending, observing and listening.

(Carkhuff and Berenson, 1977, p.155)

While interaction is clearly the vehicle of the exploratory process the dominant focus is on the skill of the therapist.

Carkhuff and Berenson produced valuable work in terms of addressing the process of change and also examining what facilitates change. They build on the work of the Chicago group. What they offer in addition to the work of the early researchers is a much more carefully thought out review of the elements of affect intensity, empathy and responsive interaction. The communication of affect from the therapist to the client and the client to the therapist is highlighted.

What these researchers notice is the fact that the way the therapist responds to the expression of affect in turn affected the level of exploration that developed between them. They note the effect of the level of affect intensity displayed by the therapist in *response* to the client's presentation of affect (see pages 8–18, Carkhuff and Berenson 1977). They do not seek a theoretical explanation to account for why this should be so. I suggest that these researchers point us to the fruitfulness of researching infant/caregiver interactions. The communication of affect is largely non-verbal and therefore reaches back to the earliest forms of communication in infancy. This is not a route that the researchers took themselves; instead they concentrate on detailed analysis of interaction and the effect of therapist responsiveness on the client's exploratory process.

I will now turn briefly to the work of psychotherapy researchers during the past twenty years, noting in particular the work of Lester Luborsky.

Psychotherapy research: 1980–2000s

In the 1980s there was a return to the study of the therapeutic relationship to see what in the relationship itself contributed to clients getting better or getting worse, following a period of therapy (see McLeod, 1994, p.142). During this period there has been a proliferation of research instruments designed to measure the psychotherapeutic process itself.

McLeod (1994) lists the problems with the study of psychotherapeutic process, starting with the fact that the word itself means different things to different researchers. According to him there are at least four definitions of the term 'process' in use:

(i) Process is a general condition that exists in a therapeutic relationship, for example, an emotional climate of warmth and acceptance.

(ii) A process consists of a sequence of behaviours or actions engaged in either by the counsellor, the client or both together.

(iii) Process refers to aspects of the experience of either the client or the counsellor.

(iv) Process refers to contractual aspects of therapy such as frequency, length or number of sessions. (p.142)

McLeod (1994) concludes,

However process is understood or defined, there is a general agreement that it comprises a highly complex and elusive set of phenomena. (p.143)

Lester Luborsky (Graff and Luborsky, 1977; Luborsky and Crits-Christoph, 1988; Luborsky *et al.*, 1994) developed the concept of "The Core Conflictual Relationship Theme", as a result of trying to trace the basis for his clinical judgements. He came to the view that most of his judgements were based on attending to the patient's accounts of narratives of interaction either with him-/herself or with other people. He then noticed that there was a recurring theme to these interactions. He identified three components to these narratives: a) what the patient wanted from the other person; b) how the other person reacted; and c) how the patient reacted to their reactions. Luborsky linked his perception of pattern with the presence and manifestation of transference phenomena. In his 1994 paper he describes the method he arrived at for gaining reliable ratings of the CCRT. His aim was to use the system to test Freud's propositions in relation to transference. He used judges to rate transcripts, the transcripts were marked off in relation to the units being analysed, and the units themselves were rated in line with pre-defined categories.

Luborsky's work has been very influential and much referenced, (Allison, 1994). His work is aimed at testing hypotheses that inform his clinical diagnosis and intervention. The theoretical framework informing the research is steeped in an object relations interactional model of personality development. As such it is highly relevant to the thesis being presented here. Luborsky is examining the way transference presents over time. He sees transference as having its origins in the past. I will suggest in chapter three that there is now ample research from the field of child development to cast light on the interactive patterns that develop between infants and their caregivers, and the variation of these patterns based on caregiver sensitivity and responsiveness ...

Finally in order to conclude this section I will quote briefly from another contemporary researcher who I consider representative of much current work in this field, in that he is using modern technology to observe and record the verbal and non-verbal process taking place between therapist and client. His work is in the area of affect attunement that I will introduce into the book in the next chapter; it is highly associated with infant/caregiver interactions.

Anstadt and his colleagues in Germany (Anstadt, Merten, Ullrich, and Krause, 1997) completed a rigorous study of 11 brief therapies carried out by therapists of different modalities – cognitive behaviourist, psychodynamic, client centered.[2] They used Luborsky's concept of the Core Conflictual Relationship Themes (CCRTs) as a baseline for judging outcome and used the instruments developed by Friesen and Ekman (1984, 1986) – Facial Action Coding System (see also Ekman, 1975, 1979, 1993) to assess the expression of emotion by both parties. They found that therapists who compensate for emotional expression have better outcomes. Such a therapist might, for example, respond with an expression of surprise, or sadness, or distress to an account that the client produced without much emotion.

This seems to imply that the therapist who can catch the underlying emotion and surface it, or who can bring in the emotions of surprise or curiosity, is more effective than one who responds with the same affect that is being expressed by the patient. This also links with the work of Berenson and Carkhuff referred to earlier. For example, these researchers stress the need to raise arousal levels on some occasions and lower them on others. This is something that has been researched by developmental psychologists and which I will introduce in my next chapter.

While this work (Anstadt et al., 1997) in particular is aware of the research on the infant/caregiver relationship (such as the interplay of

2. The therapists were required to have worked with at least 150 cases, have five years experience and training responsibilities in their field. All treatments were video recorded using a split screen technique. The researchers were testing the hypothesis that affective facial behaviour of therapists and patients in terms of whether the therapist mirrored the expression of affect presented by the patient or compensated for the affect in the first session would be predictive of treatment outcome.

facial emotional expressions between caregivers and babies on the developing relationship between them) they do not look to this relationship to provide a paradigm for understanding the processes involved in caregiving/careseeking relationships in adulthood, of which psychotherapy is one form. They do not conceptualise adult psychotherapy as a careseeking/caregiving process which activates the dynamics of attachment and thereby all the associated secure, insecure and turbulent relationship patterns that such a context is likely to elicit (see Heard and Lake, 1997).

Conclusion

What all studies on process have in common is a wish to try to get at what are the important features of therapy – how does it work, what do clients say or remember they found helpful,[3] what kinds of issues come up and is there a pattern to their resolution that relates to therapist or client behaviour? What all of them do is to get right into the detail of the interaction that is taking place between therapist and client. Between them they represent a vast amount of careful and detailed work that takes as its reference point the unit of interaction itself or concepts related to the interactive process, such as the effect on here and now interaction of experiences of relationship in the past.

Between them these researchers point to the importance of (a) the process of interaction between therapist and client; (b) enabling the client to explore their concerns; (c) responding appropriately to the level of affective arousal in the client; (d) empathic response maintained and deepened over time; and (e) the way in which relationships experienced in the past are acted out in the present in relation to the therapist so that the therapist is responded to as if they had the same attitudes and feelings towards the client as someone from their past.

What McLeod (1994) says is needed is a theory that will allow the interactions between these phenomena to be understood (1994, p.150). He reaffirmed this view in 1998 in his chapter on the current state of psychotherapy research (p.343).

I agree with McLeod and suggest that what has been missing in psychotherapy research is a theory of interaction. I suggest that what we need now is a theory of interaction that takes account of the biological nature of careseeking and caregiving processes and the

---

3. I am thinking of the work on significant moments (Hardy, Shapiro *et al.*, 1998).

particular dynamics aroused between caregivers and careseekers when careseeking is presented in less than straightforward ways in adult life.

There are a number of aspects of the research quoted in this chapter that I make use of in chapter five in constructing the concept of goal-corrected empathic attunement. For example, I make use of (i) the observations of attunement to affect, and affect regulation; (ii) the quality of empathic response; (iii) the role of defensiveness in relationship; (iv) how experience of relationships in early childhood both filters what one sees and responds to in the here and now, and affects how one processes that information. But before I do this I need to set the research covered in this chapter in the larger context of developmental processes in infants and young children, and then set these in the context of an instinctively based biological theory of attachment between caregivers and careseekers.

It seems to me that most psychotherapy research has not had a theory of caregiving based on an understanding of developmental processes and that this information was not available to the profession until recently. An exception has been research based on the ideas of Freud. He had his own theory of personality development from which he evolved therapeutic technique and practices. This aspect of Freud's work has, however, had much less influence on research than on practice. Much of the work since his time has focused on aspects of therapeutic technique, dimensions of psychotherapy or outcome.

Much of dynamic psychotherapy has been based on reconstructed accounts of early childhood development, based on what adults remember, and what they present as problems and concerns. We now have a wealth of research on what actually happens interactively between caregivers and careseekers at the earliest stages of development. It seems plausible to assume that a better understanding of the processes that lead the human infant to seek help from another person, and what happens to the growth of that infant when this process goes well or badly, may be relevant to the processes we observe in the adult domain when a distressed adult seeks help in a psychotherapeutic context.

In my next chapter I will present evidence from the world of infant research to support a theory of effective caregiving within adult psychotherapy based on infant/caregiver interactions.

CHAPTER THREE

Infant/caregiver interactions: the process of affect identification, communication, and regulation

... although psychoanalysis is avowedly a developmental discipline it is nowhere weaker, I believe, than in its concepts of developmental ...

(Bowlby, 1988, p.66)

Introduction

Psychodynamic psychotherapy has traditionally seen a link between experiences of relationship in early life, and problems with relationships, or dysfunctional relationships, in adult life. The centrality of the relationship between therapist and client in terms of personality change and development has been confirmed. However, as we have seen, few researchers have taken seriously the nature, purpose and function of the dynamics of interaction between careseekers and caregivers.

During most of the time that research was being conducted into the adult psychotherapeutic process little was done on researching the actual happenings that take place between infants and their caretakers. Bowlby was one of the few practising adult psychoanalysts and child psychiatrists who was researching this area. He made connections between the *actual experience* that children have with those who look after and care for them, how they process that experience, and the effects on later relationships in adult life.

Some psychotherapists have now become interested in attachment theory as a paradigm for psychotherapeutic practice and research. However, most still rely on the theoretical constructions of experienced clinicians who have formed their views on human development from working with children or adults who have suffered abuse and or neglect in childhood. Even though most psychotherapeutic trainings now require a pre-clinical year or more, devoted to 'normal' infant observation, understanding of these observations is still influenced by the theoretical paradigm favoured by the particular training institute in question. The most influential of the psychoanalytic frameworks used by training institutes in general, whether they be adult or child focused, is the work of Melanie Klein and Wilfred Bion. While Roth and Fonagy (1996) take the view that each individual psychotherapeutic paradigm needs to be theoretically coherent, there is currently an interest in something like a theory of interaction that would go some way to making sense of the helping relationship.

This chapter sets out to explore the interactions that take place between infants and their caregivers and the effect of these on the developing pattern of relationship established between them. I start with a paper by Gyorgy Gergely. In this paper Gergely, who is himself a developmental psychologist, provides a bridge from the world of psychoanalysis to the world of observation and experiment. He basically points out the impossibility of the position of Klein and Mahler, both prestigious figures in the field of child and adult psychotherapy, in relation to their understanding of child development.

Not all psychoanalysts shared Freud's – or even Klein's – view of infant development. Ronald Fairbairn (1952) and others saw the infant as person-seeking from the start of life and presumed the development of a dynamic mental structure in response to actual experience with caregivers. The work of the object relationists is supported by the psychobiologists and infant researchers, who explore amongst other things the regulation and communication of affective states, and the way that this process is embedded in infant/caregiver interactions. This work reflects Bowlby's requirement that theory should be bedded in what actually happens in infancy and in a theory of interaction in adult life that could inform the psychotherapeutic process.

From deduction to construction:
from Melanie Klein to Gyorgy Gergely

The image of the biological newborn needing 'socialisation' to become a person does not apply when attention turns to evidence for complex psychological expressions in the responses of contented healthy newborns to people who take them as persons with intentions and feelings of companionship, and who feel pleasure when the infant responds.

(Trevarthen *et al.*, 1998, p.16)

Over the last twenty-five years there has been an explosion of research into infant development. This work has relied on observation and experiment, often in the infant's natural environment, and has used cine video and audio equipment, including spectrographs, to get at the fine nuances of interaction, both verbal and non-verbal, taking place between infants and their caregivers. This work has produced evidence that contradicts previously held beliefs within such diverse fields as psychoanalysis and cognitive psychology about the way that infants make sense of the world and the way they relate to and respond to people and inanimate objects. The title of the book *The Scientist in the Crib* by Alison Gopnik *et al.* (Gopnik *et al.*, 1999) captures the way that infants are now regarded.

In 1992 Gyorgy Gergely published a remarkable article that bridges the world of adult psychoanalysis and infant research. In it he considered the difference between Mahler and Melanie Klein in relation to their understanding of the origins of defensive splitting and projection, and discusses the scientific evidence for both concepts. Klein believed that children were born with an innate death instinct, which meant that they were continually threatened by destruction, and in response to which they split off these aggressive impulses and projected them into an external object. This object or objects then become target(s) of feared, fantazised persecutory attacks. Mahler did not believe in an innate death instinct. She located the origin of defensive splitting in a much later phase of development, in what she termed the rapprochement crisis, which starts somewhere between 18 months and two years. The mother is seen as 'all good' or 'all bad' in relation to the dual experiences of both longing for the mother and fearing engulfment.[4]

---

4. See page 16 of article for a full description.

Gergely devotes most of his article to outlining the assumptions about child development inherent in the concept of defensive splitting and projection. Because this work gets to the heart of the difference between theoretical reconstructions of childhood experience and experimentally derived information about the process of development, I will summarise Gergely's observations and use his work as a bridge via which I can bring in some of the relevant research on infant development.

To arrive at the formulation of defensive splitting and projection, Gergely suggests that both Klein and Mahler imply a differentiated representation of self and other as:

   (i) separate physical objects;

  (ii) causal agents or recipients of actions;

 (iii) separate minds with non-identical intentional states:

 (iv) objects that retain their identity while being represented as objects of different (and ambivalent attitudes).

(Gergely, 1992, pp.18–19)

According to Gergely, for Klein's theory of defensive splitting to hold up the newborn infant would have to be capable of all the above. While Mahler, by locating the origin of defensive splitting later in the child's development, avoids these particular assumptions, according to Gergely she holds that

during the first weeks of life, the infant is surrounded by a "quasi-solid stimulus barrier", an "autistic shell which [keeps] the external stimuli out" [Mahler *et al.*, 1975].

(Gergely, 1992, p.15)

Though Mahler and Klein differed from each other in the way that Gergely outlines, they both represent a significant influence on the way individual dynamics are still understood by adult psychotherapists and group analysts in the United Kingdom. They also both differ from the object relations school of psychoanalysis spearheaded by Ian Suttie (1935, 1988) and expressed most fully by Ronald Fairbairn (1952). What distinguished Fairbairn and his followers from other psychoanalytic theorists of the time (and now) was that he saw the infant as *person seeking* from the start of life, as opposed to pleasure seeking or seeking relief from unpleasant instinctual drives. What has emerged through the studies of the developmental psychologists is that the view of the infant engaging with the world of people from the start is a more accurate picture of infant development than Klein's.

What all theorists in the adult domain have in common is a wish to understand the mechanisms by which disturbed adults tend to replicate patterns of relationship with other people across a variety of situations and contexts, irrespective of the passage of time, and how they seem to maintain the character of these relationships in spite of finding them unsatisfactory in one form or another. Psychotherapy, as discussed in the last chapter, is sought out primarily as a response to distress. The expectation is that understanding something about the origins of behaviour and the mechanisms which support the repeating pattern might free one from its repetition and compulsion. All object relation theorists share the view that the origin of present difficulties in relationship are located in the past and that the mechanism by which these difficulties are maintained in the present is through the process of internalising the experience of self in these many and diverse relationships in the form of internal working models.

In other words, early relationships are internalised in such a way that they act as dynamic structures within the person; these are activated by and influence the pattern of current relationships. Depending on the severity of the pain involved in the original gestalt of relationships as experienced by the person, they are more or less open (permeable) to influence and change based on current experience of relationships. Fairbairn (1952) called these dynamic relationship structures 'internal objects'; Bowlby (1979) called them "internal working models"; Heard and Lake (1997) call them 'internal working models of the experience of relationships' in order to differentiate them from the fact that we create internal working models of all experience; Daniel Stern (1985) calls them "experiences of relationships that are generalised".

What these dynamically orientated psychotherapists have in common is a view that the person is a surveyor of their experience of relationship from the start, that images of the self and other operating together are stored and remembered for their predictive and adaptive value and used to guide and interpret subsequent relationships. They understand interpersonal behaviour as based and predicated on experience. This is what accounts for repetition of disturbed relationship patterns across the life cycle.

What the developmental psychologists are able to do is to provide the evidence for the way in which young infants relate to the world of people and objects, and for how they actively participate in responding to and regulating not only their own and others affective responses, but also the way in which they apply reason and logic to the manipulation and perception of physical objects. Before examining the role of affect attunement in the identification, regulation and communication of affective states and the way that it is embedded in infant/caregiver interactions, I will present a short account of two experiments designed to show how infants make sense of the expression of affect, expect some order and consistency to its expression and expect affect and behaviour to be congruent.

Gergely and Peter Fonagy (1998) developed an Emotion Action Task that involves presenting one-year-old infants with video images of adults relating to an object. The infant is exposed to several different sequences. The first one involves a picture of the adult being pleased to see the object and then reaching out for it and drawing it towards her. The actor holds the affect for a few moments so that the infant can absorb it, before reaching for the object. The test involves several variations on this scenario.

The sequences the infant sees are: (i) positive emotion followed by congruent action; (ii) positive emotion followed by incongruent action; (iii) negative emotion followed by congruent action; (iv) negative emotion followed by incongruent action. So for example the last video sequence is the actor showing displeasure towards the object to the point of displaying an expression of disgust, and then following this by reaching out to the object, hugging it to them and displaying pleasure. What Gergely and Fonagy have found is that the infant categorises the person as irrational if the gestures are incongruent with the emotion in the voice *if the congruent display comes first in the sequence of viewing*. They gauge this on the basis of the span of attention given to the different episodes by the infant and the infant's expressions of puzzlement and confusion. Gergely (1996) provides evidence that non-verbal infants are aware of lack of congruence between the affect being displayed on a person's face and the emotion that they are experiencing.

Affect regulation is linked with caregiving from the start of life

The emotional expressions of the infant and their caretaker function to allow them to mutually regulate their interaction.

(Edward Z. Tronick, 1989, p.112)

In 1983, Hofer wrote:

> ... hidden within the interactions between infant and mother, we and others have found a number of processes by which the mother serves as an external regulator of the infant's behaviour, its autonomic physiology, and even the neurochemistry of its maturing brain.

Hofer provides evidence from numerous animal studies which show that vital physiological systems which the young are unable to regulate themselves are regulated by contact with the parent, and that the physiological effects of separation from the parent are likely to be some of the cause of the distress expressed on separation.

> Many of the more slowly developing separation responses may thus be due to withdrawal of the previous regulation supplied by the mother rather than being part of the acute emotional response to disruption of attachment.
>
> (Hofer, 1983, p.199)

Later work by Schore (1994, 2000, 2003a and 2003b) suggests that the early social environment,

> mediated by the primary caregiver, directly influences the evolution of structures in the brain that are responsible for the future socio-emotional development of the child.
>
> (Schore, 1994, p.62)

His argument is that attachment patterns between infants and caregivers take place during the phase of development when the infant is dependent on the other for the regulation of their biological and neurological systems.

> The resulting variety of affective interactions between the caregiver and the infant is imprinted into the child's developing nervous system. Different types of stimulation are embedded in these 'hidden' socio-affective interactions, and they elicit distinctive psychobiological patterns in the child. In response to such socio-environmental experiences, hormonal and neurohormonal responses are triggered, and these physiological alterations are registered within specific areas of the infant's brain which are undergoing structural maturation during a sensitive period.

Siegel suggests that

a child uses a parent's state of mind to help organise her own mental processes. The alignment of states of mind permits the child to regulate her own state of mind by direct connection with that of her parent ... The study of emotion suggests that non-verbal behaviour is a primary mode in which emotion is communicated, facial expression, eye gaze, tone of voice, bodily motion and the timing of response are each fundamental for emotional messages.

(Siegel, 1999, p.121)

Mechthild Papousek (1994) found that certain characteristics of infant-directed speech (the form of which is culturally specific in the sense of being adapted to the structure of the language of the host country) do not vary across cultures and have at least four functions:

(i) to regulate arousal and affect in infants;

(ii) to draw attention to caregiver's speech;

(iii) to guide infants in practising communicative subroutines;

(iv) to mediate linguistic information.

Caregivers use tone, pitch and rhythmic modulation (melody) of their voice to regulate the affective arousal states of their infants. Other research confirms that infants are highly responsive to caregiver affect as expressed on the face, and that their own arousal levels are affected by the interaction between them and either an emotionally available and attuned caregiver (Segal et al., 1995) or an emotionally absent (depressed) or non-attuned caregiver (Stern, 1985).

Correct identification of affect by the caregiver affects the infant's developing sense of self

Susan Vas Dias, a child psychotherapist trained at the Anna Freud Centre and with over twenty years as a consultant child psychotherapist, suggests that what is *also* going on (in addition to regulation) is that the mother is making the baby's internal emotional world intelligible to the baby. She builds on the fact that because affect is always accompanied by visceral arousal, the *experience* of affect is located in the body, therefore the infant's direct understanding of self is through the experience of affective states.

Vas Dias suggests that by attuning to the infant's feeling state and framing it in words, "Their [the caregiver's] tone will mirror the baby's affective state, the baby will feel attuned with and emotionally held, and their inner state/self validated. The labelling of the feeling state will facilitate the infant's ability to be familiar with, know, and scan how he or she is feeling ... *and (he or she) will be able to build upon this to develop their own self-narrative and internal dialogue"* (my italics). (Vas Dias, 2000, p.161). Of course when the infant's affective state is not validated, but distorted, mocked or humiliated, the later clinical presentation, according to Vas Dias, is of someone who has little self narrative, and does not experience their emotions – in other words does not have access to their core self. Such people present their silence for treatment (see Vas Dias, 2000).

Confirmation for the hypothesis of Vas Dias (that because affect is always accompanied by visceral arousal, the *experience* of affect is located in the body, therefore the infant's direct understanding of self is through the experience of affective states) comes from the work of Meltzhoff and his colleagues. This contrasts with Piaget who took the view that infants can only begin to know themselves and others after they have acquired the ability for symbolic play – somewhere between 18 and 24 months (in other words, that they access their sense of self primarily though their cognitive function). Nadel, 1999, and Andrew Meltzhoff (Meltzoff and Moore, 1977; Meltzoff, 1983; Meltzoff, 1992; Meltzoff and Moore, 1995; Meltzoff, 1999a; Meltzoff *et al.*, 1999b) discovered that infants have the capacity to know that another person is like themselves within minutes of being born.

Meltzhoff 's (1983) work on imitation (infants as young as forty-two minutes imitate facial expressions) shows that in order to imitate, the baby must understand the similarity between an internal feeling and an external face that they see. "Imitation is a behavioural measure indicating that newborns, at some measure of processing no matter how primitive, can map actions of other people onto actions of their own body" (Meltzoff, Gopnik and Rapacholi, 1999b). Gopnik *et al.* (1999) suggest that this behaviour indicates that "from the time we are born, we know quite directly that we are like other people and that they are like us" (p.30). Meltzoff and Moore (1977) proposed that *when babies imitate they are linking the visual appearance of other people to their own internal kinaesthetic and proprioceptive feelings, connecting the visible bodily actions of others and their own internal states* (my italics).

Field *et al.* (1982) have shown how two- to three-day-old babies are consitently able to frown, smile, look surprised, imitating the expressions adults show to them. When, for example, new-born babies scan live faces, they show more fluid physical movements (of their arms, legs, hands and feet) and they use their voices (Brazelton, 1974). The

Papouseks (1979) have filmed mothers and neonates greeting one another with smiles and direct eye contact. What is striking is that when the mothers were asked by the researchers to close their eyes for a period of two minutes following this type of greeting, their babies first of all looked puzzled, then distressed, then looked away.

Rovee-Collier and Fagan (1981) and Field (1981) have demonstrated that infants have the capacity to remember and anticipate consequences of their own actions. The cross-cultural work of the Papouseks' (1979) has indicated that infants are programmed to interpret a range of emotional expression on the human face and that parents are programmed to interpret the emotional response on the face of their infant.

> By three months babies co-ordinate their own expressions, gestures, and voices with the expressions, gestures and voices of other people.
>
> (Gopnik *et al.*, 1999, p.31)

Judy Dunn (1999), when discussing the ways that infants develop a sense of who they are, suggests that in the early interchanges between infant and caregiver the caregiver takes both sides of the conversation with explicit comments on what the baby wants or feels: "Oh, you are feeling hungry, I know!" or "Oh all right, we know what you want!" (1999, p.231). According to Dunn, parents frame the beginnings of intentional communication for the baby in order to make the world more intelligible to the baby and the baby more intelligible to them.

What these studies show is that infants have direct access to their own and others' affective states right from the start of life and that they respond to lively, interested interaction with fluid physical movements, expressions of pleasure and vocalisations. Infants who have first witnessed congruency between actions and emotions do not engage with (withdraw from) subsequent incongruent behaviour.

> At the age of two to three months, infants begin to give the impression of being quite different persons. When engaged in social interaction, they appear to be more wholly integrated. It is as if their actions, plans, affects, perceptions, and cognitions can now all be brought into play and focused, for a while, on an interpersonal situation. They are not simply more social, or more regulated, or more attentive, or smarter. They seem to approach interpersonal relatedness with an organising perspective that makes it feel as if there is now an integrated sense of themselves as distinct and coherent bodies, with control over their own

actions, ownership of their own affectivity, a sense of community, and a sense of other people as distinct and separate interactants. And the world now begins to treat them as if they are complete persons and do possess an integrated sense of themselves.

(Stern, 1985, p.69)

How caregivers communicate to infants that they understand their affective state: the process of affect attunement

Stern (1985) refers to affect attunement as "the acts and processes that let other people know that you are feeling something very like what they are feeling" (p.138). "How can you get 'inside of ' other people's subjective experience and then let them know that you have arrived there, without using words?" (p.138). Caregivers communicate to their infants that they are on their wavelength, so to speak, through what Stern (1985) calls cross-modal attunement.

> For there to be an intersubjective exchange about affect, then, strict imitation alone won't do. In fact, several processes must take place. First, the parent must be able to read the infant's feeling state from the infant's overt behaviour. Second, the parent must perform some behaviour that is not a strict imitation but nonetheless corresponds in some way to the infant's overt behaviour. Third, the infant must be able to read this corresponding parental response as having to do with the infant's own original feeling experience and not just imitating the infant's behaviour. It is only in the presence of these three conditions that feeling states between one person can be knowable to another and that they can both sense, without using language, that the transaction has occurred.
>
> (Stern, 1985, p.139)

This is attunement to vitality affects. It is done in such a way that, for instance, the tone and pitch of an infant's vocalisations are matched by the rhythm and intensity of the mother's hand movements. A sense of vitality and enjoyment communicates itself to observers; the pair are clearly in tune. At the other end of the scale, Stern provides examples of misattunement or non-attunement. These are painful to watch and involve either a lack of awareness of the baby's affect and intention, as in the case of a psychotic or extremely depressed caregiver, or a lack of willingness to engage with the baby for other reasons.

Stern describes observing an encounter which induced a feeling of angry tension in the observers, as the mother carried on with excited play (more in tune with her own needs), unaware of her infant's reluctance (Stern, 1985, pp.197–8). What the observers saw the infant doing was mis-time her responses by a fraction, or use brief gaze aversion, just at the highest pitch of her mother's excitement. What is particularly significant is that the infant's strategy was to respond to her mother, rather than to initiate movements herself. The interaction had no quality of creativity to it, as understood by the caregiver and infant mutually contributing to the play. In Stern's observation, the infant was following the mother.

Stern suggests, based on observations of many such infants over time, that when they are alone one of two things seem to happen: "They cut short their potential positive excitement, most likely by activating a dis-regulating mother as the evoked companion, or they show freer access to their own pleasurable excitement and can wallow in it, as if they inhibited or somehow prevented the activation of the RIG." p.195–6

> We do not know why some infants seem able to regulate their excitement so much more successfully when alone than when interacting with a disregulating parent. Whether we are talking about inhibited evoked companions or selective generalisations, it would appear that those children who are more successful at escaping the evoked presence of a problematic parent when alone gain the advantage of being able to utilise more of themselves. At the same time, they are dealt the disadvantage of living more alone in the world.
>
> (Stern, 1985, p.196)

Beebe and Lachmann (1988 quoted in Kiersky and Beebe, 1994) argue that "these mutually regulated bi-directional interactions between infant and caretaker provide the basis for an infant's pre-symbolic representations of self, other, and self with other." They suggest that "these 'interaction structures' provide a way of determining what 'being in tune with' the mother might feel like to the infant as well as what being mis-attuned might feel like ... in this conceptual frame-work, the state of the other is perceived and expressed through moment-by-moment changes in time, space, affect, and arousal. Thus, the *timing* of communication between caretaker and child, the changing *spatial* relationship between the participants, and the degree of affective stimulation and proprioceptive *arousal* are the significant dimensions of early social exchange" (Kiersky and Beebe, 1994, p.390).

Stern (p.197) gives an example of intolerable under-stimulation. He describes the case of Susie, "a normally spunky infant, well endowed with all the capacities to appeal to and elicit social behaviour from any willing adult, plus a lot of persistence to keep trying at the faintest hint of success." Susie's mother, however, was depressed, preoccupied with a recent divorce and had not wanted Susie in the first place. Stern describes the situation where Susie was unable to spark enough so that her mother ever took over the up-regulation of excitation. In other words whatever Susie did or however vivacious she was her mother never responded in any way that would either match or increase her level of excitation. While in Susie's case her mother never actually took control of the down-regulation of excitation, Stern suggests that "her lack of responsivity acted as a drag on Susie's attempts to up-regulate".

> The actual and fantasised experiences with a self regulating other are essential for encountering the normally expected range of self-experiences, and without the other's presence and responsive behaviour, the full range simply does not develop. There is a maturational failure, a 'self-regulating-other-deficiency disease.' This is just another way of stating that only a selected portion of the whole spectrum of self experiences of excitation may get exercised during this period resulting in a permanent influence during this sensitive period upon what experiences become part of the sense of a core self.
>
> (Stern, 1985, p.198)

Affect attunement is the process by which one human being communicates to the other that they are on their wavelength. "Vitality affects therefore must be added to affect categories as one of the kinds of subjective inner states that can be referenced in acts of attunement. Vitality is ideally suited to be the subject of attunement because it is composed of the amodal qualities of intensity and time and because it resides in virtually all behaviours one can perform and thus provides a continually present (though changing) subject for attunement. Attunements can be made to the inner quality of feeling of how an infant reaches for a toy, holds a block, kicks a foot, or listens to a sound. Tracking and attuning with vitality affects permits one human to be with another in the sense of sharing likely inner experiences on an almost continuous basis. This is exactly our experience of feeling-connectedness, of being in attunement with another. It feels like an unbroken line. It seeks out the activation contour that is momentarily going on in any and every behaviour and uses that contour to keep the thread of communion unbroken" (Stern, 1985 p.55).

Stern video-taped many mother/infant pairs at two, four, six, nine, eighteen, twenty-four, and thirty-six months. He found that on showing these tapes to new or experienced groups of students they were inevitably struck by "the sense that the two individuals are conducting their interpersonal business in a similar and recognisable fashion throughout" (Stern, 1985, p.186).

Infants' responsiveness to affective interaction with caregivers and their response to loss of contact with caregivers

One of the first experiments carried out to test the hypothesis that infants (7 months) and mothers are actively engaging in meaningful communication is part of what have become known as *perturbation studies*. These studies were carried out by a number of people (Brazelton *et al.*, 1974); Trevarthen and Hubley, 1978; Trevarthen, 1979a; Tronick *et al.*, 1977; Tronick, 1989; Oster *et al.*, 1992; Gergely, 1996). I will describe the original research carried out on this subject by Lynne Murray as part of her doctoral thesis in Edinburgh. She studied perturbations in infant (6–12 weeks old)/caregiver interactions. Perturbation studies show that infants are distressed when 'out of contact' with a person with whom they have been experiencing pleasurable affective commerce. They show conclusively that infants are communicating and that their smiles and other facial expressions are not just due to the passage of wind or the fanciful imagination of devoted mothers or fathers.

Murray set up three experiments:

(i) the first involved interrupting a period of normal communication between an infant and their mother by the arrival of a researcher into the room and engaging the mother in conversation in such a way that the mother turned away from her infant;

(ii) the second perturbation required the mother to stop communicating with her infant and adopt a 'Blank' face – while continuing to look at the infant;

(iii) the third perturbation took place in the context of the mother and infant communicating with each other through video contact. This perturbation took the form of the

researchers changing the images and sounds that the
mothers and infants had of each other so that they were
seeing and hearing each other out of 'real' time.

The outcome of these three perturbations has been described at some
length by Lynne Murray (Murray, 1998).

Before I describe the infant's reactions to the perturbations I will
quote Murray's own description of the way the infant and mother were
communicating before the interruptions:

> During the periods of normal interaction the infant's gaze was
> directed to the mother's face almost all the time, and the infant
> smiled, made active gestures and 'prespeech' tonguing move-
> ments and wide shapings of the mouth.
>
> (Murray, 1998, p.131)

In her analysis of the infant's reactions to the three perturbations
described in the previous paragraph, Murray noticed the following:

1. With the first perturbation, the infant's communication
   subsided and signs of positive excitement were reduced.
   There was no increase in signs of negative affect or in the
   incidence of displacement behaviours such as fingering the
   clothes, or sucking the fist. "Although the infant gazed less
   at the mother this seemed not to be a function of active
   avoidance of her, but rather reflected the infant's interest in
   the researcher."

2. When the mother presented a 'Blank Face', "the infant very
   quickly appeared disturbed. An initial form of response
   frequently occurred that suggested protest ... active
   prespeech movements were at first sustained, if not intensified
   and frowning increased, and these behaviours occurred while
   the infant looked at mother. This phase of apparent protest
   was typically followed first by signs of distress, such as
   grimacing, or displacement activities of the hands, and
   subsequently by withdrawal, with the infant's gaze being
   averted from the mother's face and the head drooping."

3. "In the closed-circuit television experiment ... when
   confronted with the replay sequence there was a rapid
   change in behaviour that in some respects resembled the
   response to the Blank Face perturbation. Gaze was largely
   averted from the mother and was interspersed with short,

darting glances at her, and there were also signs of distress such as frowning and grimacing, and fingering of the clothes and face. However, unlike the response to the Blank Face disruption, 'prespeech' tonguing and wide open mouthing occurred less often, and the impression was not so much one of protest, but rather one of puzzlement or confusion." Further analysis revealed that frowning and looking away were associated with the video replay, while frowning and looking at the face were associated with the Blank Face perturbation.

Confirming the function of affect communication, work by Campos *et al.* (1983) found that when 10-month-old infants are exploring the surface of the visual cliff they will look to their mothers to see if they should proceed. If the mothers signal fear or anger most infants will not cross, but if the mothers present a joyful expression the infants will proceed. Infants react similarly to voice tone as to facial expression. The experiment showed that infants regulate their own behaviour, especially when presented with an ambiguous situation, by 'reading' the caregiver's face or tone of voice – this is what is known as social referencing behaviour. It confirms the work on voice tone and facial expression just referred to.

Bretherton (1990) draws on a range of research which describes the way in which mothers differ in their sensitive responsiveness towards their infants during the infant's first three months. These interactive patterns were predictive of how the mother and infant were found to be communicating at the end of the infant's first year and were linked with secure and insecure attachment patterns.

As we have seen from research quoted earlier in this chapter, face-to-face interactions between infants and adults starting as young as three months are bi-directional (mutually regulated). Infants modify their affective displays and behaviours on the basis of their appreciation of their caregiver's affective response – they respond to turn taking signals cued by the caregiver (Cohn, 1987). This mutually regulated co-ordinated behaviour has led to interaction between infant and caregivers being described as reciprocal, synchronous or coherent. Brazelton and Cramer (1990) identify synchrony, symmetry and contiguity, which organise into entrainment (i.e. long sequences of anticipated responses) as associated with attunement and security. Such reciprocal behaviours have the quality of autonomy, play and flexibility, as one and then the other contribute to the sequence of events.

Caregiver/infant interactions: the patterning of relationship

In his 1989 paper Tronick describes two infant/parent interacting dyads each playing peek-a-boo.

In the first, the infant abruptly turns away from his mother as the game reaches its 'peak' of intensity and begins to suck on its thumb and stare into space with a dull expression. The mother stops playing and sits back watching her infant. After a few seconds the infant turns back to her with an interesting and inviting expression. The mother moves closer, smiles, and says in an exaggerated voice, "Oh, now you're back!" He smiles in response and vocalises. As they finish crowing together, the infant reinserts his thumb and looks away. The mother again waits. After a few seconds the infant turns back to her, and they greet each other with big smiles.

In the second scenario, the infant turns away and does not look back at her mother. The mother waits but then leans over into the infant's line of vision while clicking her tongue to attract attention. The infant, however, ignores the mother and continues to look away. Undaunted, the mother persists and moves her head closer to the infant. The infant grimaces and fusses while she pushes at her mother's face. Within seconds she turns even further away and continues to suck on her thumb.

According to Tronick, in both instances turning away and sucking is the infant's way of calming themselves down and regulating their emotional state. In the first example the mother is able to wait until her infant has 'recovered', in the second the mother pursues the infant in an intrusive manner, is unable to respond to the signals from her infant to move away, giving rise to increasingly negative affect from the infant. If these patterns persist and become typical of the interactions between these dyads one would predict that the first pair would have a happier more open and straightforward relationship and the second would be more fraught.

The second sequence of interactions is very similar to one described by Kiersky and Beebe (1994) referring to work carried out by Beebe and Daniel Stern in 1977. They describe a sequence of "chase and dodge":

> Looking at a sample of approximately six minutes at the beginning of a videotape play session, we observed a complex and rapid sequence in which mother "chased" and infant "dodged." The mother chased by following the infant's head and body movements with her own head and body, pulling his arm, picking up to adjust his orientation or attempting to force his head in

her direction. To every maternal overture, the infant could move back, duck his head down, turn away, pull his hand from her grasp, or become limp and unresponsive. The infant exercised a virtual "veto power" over her attempts to engage him in a face to face encounter.

(Kiersky and Beebe, 1994, p.41)

Tronick (1989, p.113) has labelled *self-directed regulatory behaviours* as: looking away, self comforting, and even self stimulation. He also gives an example of an infant's goal-directed behaviour. He describes an infant reaching for something outwith its grasp. After each unsuccessful attempt he pauses, sucks his thumb, gets angry. The mother sees what he wants to do and brings the object just within his reach. The infant grasps the object and smiles. One can see what the infant's experience might be if the mother was not paying attention (was not psycho-biologically attuned), or for some reason (maybe depression, fatigue, illness) failed to respond so that the infant had repeated experiences of failure in reaching his or her goals and of having their affective intentions disregarded. The infant would begin to learn that his affective message did not seem to impact on other people. "Other-directed and self-directed regulatory behaviours are part of the infant's normal repertoire for coping with sadness, uncontrolled anger, and the extremes of positive affect, which can turn into distress. They enable the infant to control the potential disruptive effects of these emotions and their extremes on his or her goal-directed activities." (Tronick 1989, p.114).

Patterns of affect attunement associated with effective caregiving

Tronick and Cohn (1989) found that normal interaction between infants and caregivers was characterised by moves from affectively positive, mutually co-ordinated states to affectively negative, miscoordinated states, and back again, on a frequent basis. In his 1989 paper Tronick summarises his own observations (published in 1980) of infants who chronically experienced miscoordinated interactions: "These infants repeatedly engaged in self regulating behaviours (e.g., they turned away, had dull looking eyes, lost postural control, orally self comforted, rocked and self clasped). Cohn & Tronick (1990) came up with very interesting associations between caregiver behaviour and infant expression of affect (the infants were 7 months). For instance, mothers who were disengaged had infants who expressed more protest, mothers who were intrusive had infants who tended to look away more; mothers who were positive had infants who expressed more positive affect. Tronick (1989) sums up the situation in what Stern would call mis-attuned infant/caregiver partnerships as "the participants are stuck in affectively negative miscoordinated interactive states, and their messages calling for change are disregarded" (p.116).

The interactional states that characterise normal good enough interaction are ones that move from positive affect to negative affect and back to positive. Tronick (1989) would argue that such experience would enable the growth of more complex abilities in the infant, namely the "experience of having negative affect transformed into positive affect would enable the infant to elaborate his or her other-directed affective communicative and self-directed regulatory capacities and to use them more effectively – to be able to maintain engagement with the external environment in the face of stress … From this experience, the infant develops a representation of himself as effective, of his or her interactions as positive and reparable, and of the caretaker as reliable and trustworthy" (p.116).

It is clear from the studies quoted and the examples given that infants respond to what they are experiencing in ways that regulate their own affective states and that they seek out and enjoy positive affective interaction with caregivers. It is also the case that as they develop an interest in their physical environment they have a wish to influence it. Infants' behaviour toward people and things can be described as goal-corrected. In terms of achieving a sense of competence in their interactions with people or things, infants are dependent on help from their caregiver to interpret accurately what they communicate or signal. Failure to reach their goals causes distress and provides a void in the area of competence.

It is also the case that normal interaction moves from positive to negative to positive, so that good interactions can be described as a process of rupture and repair. I return to these points as a major building block for my theory of goal-corrected empathic attunement in chapter five. It is my view that *the self-regulatory behaviours that we observe in infants are the beginnings of the instinctive goal-corrected system for self-defence.* I will also return to this idea in chapter five. I now move on to explore whether affect attunement alone is sufficient for effective caregiving or whether something more is needed. I will also return in chapter eleven to showing the way in which we can identify 'self-regulating' and 'other-regulating' behaviours as they operate in the context of clinical consultations.

Affect attunement and empathy

Daniel Stern (1985, p.145) suggests that affect attunement is different from empathy as it occurs mostly automatically and largely out of awareness. Empathy, on the other hand, involves the mediation of cognitive processes. What the two concepts share is emotional resonance. On the basis of his review of the literature on empathy, Stern suggests that empathy consists of at least four distinct and probably sequential processes:

(1) the resonance of feeling state;
(2) the abstraction of empathic knowledge from the experience of emotional resonance;
(3) the integration of abstracted empathic knowledge into an empathic response;
(4) a transient role identification.

While Stern agrees that what empathy and affect attunement share is the initial spark, as he puts it, of emotional resonance, "... attunement takes the experience of emotional resonance and automatically recasts that experience into another form of expression. Attunement need not proceed towards empathic knowledge or response. Attunement is a distinct form of expression in its own right" (p.145). In my view this definition of attunement, i.e. "attunement takes the experience of emotional resonance and automatically recasts that experience into another form of expression", is the clearest definition that Stern offers of the act and process of attunement. It separates it from emotional resonance alone and defines it essentially as the giving of expression to the affect of the other in a way that the other can recognise as originating in and belonging in themselves.

Resonance, on the other hand, to my mind, involves accessing similar feelings to the other inside oneself that one may or may not have been conscious of. Resonance can take place intra-personally or interpersonally. This process happens almost out of consciousness and comes from being in attunement to the affective state of the other.

Affect attunement comprises two stages: stage one requires being in resonance with the feeling state of another; stage two activates a desire to communicate that one knows the affective the state of the other (cross modal matching of vitality affects, rhythm and shape) in such a way that the infant knows one knows their experience. Purposeful misattunement is the process whereby the other captures the infant's experience enough for the infant to know they are on their wavelength, and then uses this connection to divert the infant towards another affective state, e.g. from wakefulness to sleep, from not feeding to feeding, from physically or emotionally calm to distressed.

Stern thus summarises mother/infant attunement as involving some form of matching, where what is being matched is the other person's emotional state and where the matching is cross-modal (i.e. is not dependent upon using the same mode of verbal or non-verbal communication by both interactants).

What Stern shows conclusively is that we pick up the affect of other people; what we do with it, how we interpret it and how we respond to it is another matter and is largely dependent on our empathic capacity, how secure we feel and our level of arousal and well being. Empathy can be understood as our capacity to move away from ourselves as the locus of our reference for understanding emotion and sensation and see these phenomena as they might be experienced by another person, given *their* context and the information coming to them from their senses and cognition. It involves the capacity to read another's mind and put oneself in his or her shoes.

When caregiving is benign and attuned the language that accompanies the interactions between caregiver and infant is described by Lynne Murray as 'motherese' (Murray and Trevarthen, 1985). It is clearly understood by both, is a source of enjoyment, stimulation and arousal, and is interactive and goal-directed, as demonstrated by the perturbation studies experiment described earlier. What that experiment showed was the level of distress induced in the infant when they were given the 'pretend mother' or the 'absent mother' to relate to, having enjoyed the experience of live contact. Anyone who has seen the spilt-screen video images of this experiment cannot fail to be convinced that through the medium of 'motherese' infants and adults communicate in meaningful, enjoyable, vitality enhancing ways, and that when such interaction is terminated non-voluntarily from the infant's point of view the affect is one of sadness and distress.

What these studies help us to see is that careseeking and caregiving is an interactive process of great complexity. Affect regulation in the very young infant is clearly important to keep physiological arousal levels within manageable and comfortable limits. In addition, affect attunement, purposeful misattunement, non attunement and empathy are clearly involved in the process of establishing reciprocity in the caregiving relationship. Affect attunement that is not followed by empathy will lead to distrust and defensiveness. Affect attunement that *is* followed by empathy should support a feeling of being able to trust one's affective experience, one's capacity to communicate accurately and to feel secure and confident in the relationship.

> Thus, an infant's distress becomes a resonance motivating an empathic caregiver to contact the infant tenderly and to keep making changes until the infant is comfortable; i.e., the distress becomes a basic form of infant communication which says "please change what is happening" (Emde, Gaensbauer, and Harmon, 1976, pp.85–87). Conversely, the infant's pleasure becomes a process of resonant pleasure which reinforces (rewards) an empathic caregiver's maintenance and/or repetition of ongoing conditions and becomes a basic form of infant communication which says "Keep up what you are doing, I like it, [please continue]" (Emde *et al.*, 1976, p.87). Stated in another way: empathic care favors interruption of the infant's distress but opposes interruption of the infant's pleasure.
>
> (Weil, 1992, p.41)

Summary

Infants are clearly communicating with their caregivers prior to the onset of language. The pattern of communication developing between them and their caregivers is beginning to be established before the addition of speech. We now have a better idea of how the infant self is developed, and the sense they are making of congruence and incongruence between feeling and behaviour. We also know that the way infants are communicated with, the consistency, predictability, reliability and congruence of the affective messages they are receiving from their caregiver, and the way their own communications are received, are determining factors in the infant's sense of a coherent self and their expectations of interactions with others.

We can conclude from these studies that in the course of the first year infants understand three major components of emotion:

(i) that the expression of emotion is intentional and meaningful;

(ii) that people can respond to one's expression of emotion and validate one's internal experience;

iii) that one can infer the meaning of behaviour and actions from the emotional expression of others.

It is my hypothesis, to be elaborated later, that as the infant moves into the verbal domain (and even before), affect attunement from an unempathic caregiver leads to profound distress when the infant is in careseeker mode. Affect attunement that is devoid of empathy gives rise to defensiveness (self-regulatory behaviours) and inhibits exploration.

The complexity of affect attunement, it seems to me (and I am not aware of Stern writing about this), is that it can be experienced by the person being attuned to as a precursor to empathy. This is wonderful if the infant then experiences an empathic response. However, this may not be the case. Infants, as we have seen from the studies described in this chapter, will learn quickly if affect attunement is followed by painful misattunement or non attunement and will take steps to defend themselves. In addition to these two possible scenarios one has the person who has mixed experience – sometimes attunement is followed by motherese and later, when communicating verbally, by empathic responses, but at other times the access allowed by attunement is used by the caregiver to attack and hurt. The infant quickly learns adaptive strategies to cope with the contradictory responses he or she receives to expressions of careseeking. Pat Crittenden (1995) describes these patterns in detail. We need research that focuses on the attachment organisation that follows initial uninterrupted periods of empathic attunement, and what happens if this is broken and replaced by other attachment figures who, while they have the skills of affect attunement, are non-empathic and/or abusive or worse. The attachment network for children is as important to study as the single or double most important attachment figures (see article by Trevarthen 2003).

It seems to me that attachment theory, with its focus on the biological instinctive systems of caregiving and careseeking, provides an excellent conceptual framework to help make sense of diverse care-seeking and caregiving patterns, and for helping to understand the processes set in train when caregiving is dysfunctional, neglectful, ineffective or abusive.

It would be reasonable to assume that an understanding of the role of attachment difficulties in psychopathology should have implications for therapeutic interventions.

(Rutter, 1995, p.565)

In this chapter we have looked at evidence from the field of infant research which supports the view of Fairbairn and other object relations theorists that the infant is person seeking from the start of life and is not a bundle of instincts and drives from which he or she seeks relief and assuagement. The pattern of relationship that develops between infants and their caregivers is clearly influenced by the way in which each interacts with the other and seems to persist in its original pattern of organisation over time.

In the next chapter I locate caregiving in psychotherapy and allied professions in the context of attachment theory.

CHAPTER FOUR

Patterns of careseeking/caregiving relationships: research into attachment behaviour in infants and young children

Overall, attachment history does seem to contribute to the prediction of anxiety, anger, and empathy during childhood. Children with resistant attachment histories seem to be more likely than children with other histories to have problems with anxiety, perhaps in response to the constant vigilance they have developed in their early attachment relationships. Children with avoidant or disorganised/disoriented histories are most likely to show hostile, aggressive behaviour, both with parents and with peers, perhaps as a response to chronic rejection and insensitivity from their caregivers. In contrast, children with secure histories seem to have acquired a foundation for empathy from their early relationships; they take to new relationships the ability to be sensitive to another's emotional cues, as well as a pattern of dyadic affect regulation in which the one who is not distressed helps to regulate the other.

(Weinfield *et al.*, 1999, p.79)

Introduction

In the last chapter, we looked at the way in which infants are psychobiologically dependent on their caregiver for basic regulation of their affective states. Research into infant development provided evidence that infants know within moments of birth that they are like other people and can match expressions on others' faces with their own internal bodily states. Infants, when they are not hungry, tired or ill, enjoy communicating with an attuned adult who vocalises and matches, raises or lowers their level of vitality. Infants expect congruence between behaviour and emotion and are puzzled and distressed when this does not happen. When removed from contact with an adult with whom they have been sharing pleasurable affective experience they withdraw into themselves. When adults relate in unattuned and mis-attuned ways the infant will do what they can to protect themselves, even if all they can do is avoid eye contact. Non attunement to affect between caregivers and infants is extremely distressing to watch as is affect attunement that is followed by unwanted misattunement.

In addition we saw that patterns of interaction get established between infants and caregivers, and noted briefly that these patterns were predictive of how the mother and infant were found to be communicating at the end of the infant's first year and that they were linked with secure and insecure attachment patterns (Bretherton 1990). I ended the chapter noting and raising the issue of affect attunement in careseeking and caregiving, and that affect attunement, purposeful misattunement and non attunement can contribute to complex patterns of careseeking/caregiving interactions. The next step is to explore the literature on attachment theory with a view to understanding the processes of careseeking and caregiving.

My aim in this chapter is to present a brief overview of attachment theory, to show the way that attachment behaviour has been assessed, its persistence and stability, and the debate around this issue; its link with affect attunement; its transgenerational transmission from parent to infant; the patterns of caregiver/careseeker interactions associated with secure and insecure attachment status (particularly in relation to how the dyads interact while playing and how they communicate about emotion).

I will discuss the work of researchers such as Ainsworth (Ainsworth and Wittig, 1969; Ainsworth *et al.*, 1978; Ainsworth, 1991; Main, 1985, 1991, 1995; and Crittenden, 1995).

Attachment theory

Attachment theory, developed by John Bowlby (1969, 1973, 1980, 1982), describes the function of attachment behaviour (survival), the situations under which careseeking behaviour is activated (fear, distress, illness and anxiety), the object of attachment behaviour (protection through proximity with a preferred caregiver) and the conditions under which attachment behaviour is assuaged. Bowlby also introduced the concept of set goal into attachment theory. As well as acknowledging the existence of finite set goals, such as orgasm, Bowlby saw attachment behaviour as an example of a behavioural system that had a continuing set goal. In the area of attachment behaviour the goal was a certain sort of relationship to another specified individual.

Internal working models of the experience of relationship

In Bowlby's view individuals build up a set of mental representations of how their attachment-seeking behaviour has been received and responded to by their attachment figure and these are stored as templates of experience. Bowlby described them as internal working models. Heard and Lake (1997) describe them as 'internal models of the experience of relationship, (IMERS). This way of describing internal models allows for the fact that individuals have different experience of the same person – in different moods for example – so that different templates for the experience of that person are stored as predictors and guides of their present and future behaviour.

The reorganisation of these internal working models of relationship in the light of reality is the challenge for most psychotherapies. Bowlby (1991) identified communication as the key issue that psychotherapists have to struggle with, and argued, on the basis of scientific evidence, that a major block to communication intrapsychically and interpersonally is the way an infant's emotive signals have been responded to by their primary caregiver. These findings have been supported and corroborated through the work of Ainsworth (1978, 1991), Grossmann et al. (1985, 1988), Grossmann and Grossmann (1991a, 1991b), Fonagy et al. (1992, 1995a, 1995b), Main (1991, 1995, 1999), Crittenden (1995) and Emde (1990a, 1991), amongst others. One of the biggest challenges in this area comes from people who because of early trauma and abuse dissociate affect and cognition from experience (see Bacon & Richardson, 2001), or who have been deliberately directed away from own perceptions and emotions by trusted adult attachment figures (Bowlby 1988, chapter four).

Attachment classification: stable and persistent over time

Mary Salter Ainsworth (Ainsworth and Wittig, 1969) first noted in her Ganda study the different way in which mothers communicated with their children – the way that they held them talked to them, sang to them touched and stroked them – the whole way that they regarded and interacted with their infants. It was during her time with the Ganda tribe that she put forward the concept of the *Secure Base*. She also noted that the ways that children used their secure base (mother) was different depending on the quality of interaction that had been going on between them. Later in Baltimore, USA, when she set out to study attachment behaviour she incorporated home visits into the design of her research in order to capture the quality of interaction between infant and caregiver. Through her observations of infants and mothers Ainsworth noticed that effective caregiving – caregiving that would assuage careseeking – was much more than simply providing proximity to the caregiver, as Bowlby had suggested; it had to include the interactional style in which caregiving is provided (in other words what we were discussing in the last chapter).

In order to study attachment behaviour Ainsworth devised what has become known as the Strange Situation Test. This is a 20-minute test consisting of eight episodes. Mother and infant are introduced to a laboratory playroom, where they are later joined by an unfamiliar woman. While the stranger plays with the baby, the mother leaves briefly and then returns. A second separation ensues during which the baby is completely alone. Finally, the stranger and then the mother return. Ainsworth found that the infants explored the toys and the playroom more vigorously when in the presence of their mothers than after the stranger entered or while the mother was absent. Ainsworth's stroke of genius was not just to observe what the infants did while mothers were absent but to notice that they differed in their response to her when she returned. She went on to classify their responses on reunion into secure, insecure ambivalent and insecure avoidant.

The largest group were the secure, accounting for two thirds of her sample, and the smallest group was the ambivalent. The insecure group have been further classified (Main, 1985) into insecure avoidant, insecure ambivalent and disorganised. These classifications have been shown to be stable over time[5] and persist into adulthood (see Cassidy and Shaver (1999) for a full account of research into attachment behaviour and clinical implications; also Main & Cassidy (1988), Main (1991), (1995), and Bretherton (1991)). Summaries of research findings on the three types of infants (Campos *et al.*, 1983) and research on the general population (Hazan and Shaver, 1987) confirm that the secure group account for about 60% of the studied population. In spite of the many replications of the results of the SSI test, in fact the test itself has never been validated (George and Solomon, 1999).

Ainsworth found that sensitive mothers had children who were securely attached at one year; *that maternal sensitivity was the primary determinant of quality of attachment: sensitive mothers have secure children, inconsistent mothers have ambivalent children and interfering/rejecting mothers have avoidant children.* Sensitive handling refers to the caregiver's ability and willingness to perceive the infant's communications as reflected in his/her behaviour, emotional expression and vocalisations, to see and interpret them from the infant's point of view, and to respond to them promptly and appropriately according to the infant's developmental and emotional needs.' (Ainsworth *et al.*, 1974, 1978)

The adult attachment interview

In 1985 George, Kaplan, Goldwyn and Main piloted what has become known as the Adult Attachment Interview (AAI). This is an hour-long, semi-structured interview which asks for a description and evaluation of early relationships with each parent. Main (1995) describes how this interview yields four central classifications of the state of mind of the person being interviewed. When applied to parents it has been found that each classification corresponds to a pattern of infant response to the parents in the Ainsworth Strange Situation. "Parents who are coherent and collaborative in discussing their histories (classified as secure/autonomous parents) tend to have *secure* infants, parents *dismissing* of their own experiences tend to have *avoidant* infants, parents *preoccupied* by their own parents tend to have *resistant* infants, and parents suffering lapses in reasoning or discourse during the discussion of traumatic events (classified as

5. Klaus and Karin Grossmann (1991) confirm these findings, drawing on two major prospective studies that they carried on in 1976 and 1980. The 1976 study comprised newborns, the 1980 study had infants from 11 months old. They tested all their infants on the Ainsworth's Strange Situation test at 12–18 months.

unresolved/disorganised parents) tend to have *disorganised/disoriented* infants" (pp.408–9).

Main (1995) cites studies by Hamilton (1995) and Waters *et al.* (1995) who found a correspondence between the classification of adult status and the classifications made during the Strange Situation done 16 to 20 years previously, giving evidence for the stability of these patterns over time. A study by Fonagy *et al.*, (1991, 1992), showed that classifications of parental adult attachment status corresponded with the attachment status of their children, providing evidence for transgenerational transmission. Nevertheless, the most striking and uplifting fact to come out of the AAI studies is that adults who can give a fluent, coherent and reflective account of their childhood attachment relationships (whatever those relationships were like) have children of their own who are classified as secure. This finding, in my opinion, has great significance for psychotherapy and relationship-focused social work. The psychotherapeutic medium must be *par excellence* the medium through which a person can develop some level of metacognition in relation to the experiences they have had in earlier life and are having now.

Careseeker/caregiver dyads: communication patterns in relation to affect

The Grossmanns (1991a, 1991b) describe two major prospective studies carried out in 1976 and 1980. They re-analysed the videos they had of the Strange Situation Test (carried out with all the participants) to examine the communication patterns operating between infants and caregiving figures. They looked at the emotional communication of the infants and how the parents responded. What they found was that infants classified as securely attached were more direct in terms of communicating their distress to the parent and more successful at gaining comfort and support. Infants who were impaired in their mood and play behaviour during the two separations, and who had an avoidant attachment to the parent present, communicated less directly to the parent on their return.

I consider that these findings are enormously interesting and offer a focus for examining interaction in adult one-to-one psychotherapy. It may be that secure and insecure therapy dyads develop particular patterns of communication in relation to discussing affectively laden material.

Two further tests carried out by the Grossmanns revealed that children reacted differently to a play sequence involving changing emotional expressions on the part of the person playing with them (e.g. from happy to interactive to sad) if in the presence of a parent with whom they were judged secure than if in the presence of a parent with whom they were judged insecure. The play partner is dressed as a clown and goes through a series of activities with the infant in the presence of one or other parent. These activities include being happy, wanting to play with the infant, and finally crying (Grossmann and Grossmann, 1991b). When they were with the 'secure' parent they were able to reflect back the different emotions, promptly and accurately. When they were in the presence of the parent with whom they had been classified as 'insecure' the infants' response was neither prompt nor accurate. What this work shows is that infants who feel secure with their attachment figure are more autonomous, more emotionally coherent and fluent, and more flexible in terms of monitoring and responding to affect in others.

In the adult context such a pattern of communication between therapist and client should indicate that the dyad is secure and exploration is under way.

Careseeker/caregiver dyads: interaction patterns in relation to play

The Grossmanns (Grossmann and Grossmann, 1991b) also report on interactions they observed taking place between parents and infants (again 12–18 months) in a free play situation. They found that infants classified as secure communicate more subtly, with soft vocalisations, whereas infants in insecure dyads initiate interaction more often with toy presentations and loud vocalisations. They also addressed parental sensitivity in terms of reacting to the infant's emotional state and independent play activity. They found that how parents responded to their infant while the infant was playing depended on whether they had classified that parent and child couple as secure or insecure. In 'secure' couples, when the child was playing happily the parent stayed away from them and observed; if their child became bored or started to lose interest or became distressed they would intervene and offer a toy or suggestion. This usually led to a resumption of play with high interest and energy.

In contrast, in couples classified as 'insecure' the parent rarely offered a toy, stayed away from their infant when he or she showed low interest in play or was in a poor mood, but did initiate many play activities when the infant was already playing with high interest. In addition they found that mothers of avoidant infants withdrew from their infant specifically when the infant seemed sad. This usually resulted in the child ceasing to play and becoming uncertain and distressed.

It seems to me that these are extremely important observations, depicting a combination of a lack of affect attunement and empathy. In the adult context of psychotherapy where the 'third' element between the two people is not 'play' but discussion of emotional concerns, it struck me that to monitor the interaction pattern between the care-seeker (client) and the caregiver (therapist) could provide interesting clues as to whether the interaction is contributing to the maintenance of defensive careseeking.

Careseeker/caregiver dyads: interaction strategies based on secure or insecure relationships

I present the following work from Crittenden to show the coherence of the strategies developed for coping with misattunements and impingements. This work lends weight (by providing more detail) to the observations of the Grossmanns just recounted.

According to Crittenden (1995), sensitive caregiving not only ensures security in the infant but also teaches them that their behaviour is meaningful and that it has predictable effects on others. In contrast, infants classified as avoidant at one year of age will typically have experienced maternal rejection when they displayed affective signals indicative of a desire for closeness with their mothers. If these infants protest they often experience maternal anger. If caregivers are consistent in what they do, however rejecting, infants will develop an organised strategy for dealing with their attachment figure (see Main, 1995). On the other hand, "When infants cannot predict their care-giver's response they become anxious and angry ... Without a strategy for changing the probabilities of caregiver behaviour, however, these infants remain unorganised with regard to attachment" (Crittenden 1995, p.371).

Crittenden argues that by one year, infants who are labelled secure have learned the predictive and communicative value of many interpersonal signals; they have made meaning of both cognition and affect. Avoidant infants, on the other hand, have learned to organise their behaviour without being able to interpret or use affective signals; that is they have made sense of cognition but not affect. Ambivalent infants have been reinforced for affective behaviour but have not learned a cognitive organisation that reduces the inconsistency of the mother's behaviour. Infants classified as ambivalent are also referred to as resistant, because of the way that they have been observed to resist approaches from mother on her return, during the reunion phase of the Strange Situation Test.

Main (1995, p.419) describes the behaviour of the resistant infant during the 'strange situation' as follows: "mother's absence leads to exhibitions of marked distress, so that separation episodes are quickly terminated. Mother's return to the room fails to settle the baby, however, and consequently he is still crying, whining or fussing at the end of each reunion episode. To the observer, the behaviour of resistant infants can be unsettling, since neither the baby's distress nor his preoccupation with mother's whereabouts is affected by her actual return. In addition the baby may alternate between seeking to be held by mother and angrily pushing her away." It is for this reason that this pattern of behaviour has been termed both 'insecure resistant' and 'insecure ambivalent'.

> Ainsworth's home records showed that mothers of the four resist-ant infants in her sample were unpredictable, discouraging of autonomy, and insensitive to infant signals and communications. Most displayed some warmth and involvement at times ... Unlike the mothers of avoidant children, most considered them-selves highly invested in mothering. They differed from the 'avoidant' mothers by not physically or verbally rejecting their children ... Face to face interactions with their babies were marked by lack of contingent pacing and they were observed to be 'tender and careful' in how they managed their babies in only 2% of observed episodes.
>
> (Main, 1995, p.420)

Main is quoting from her knowledge of the original Ainsworth study.

These 'organised' strategies will keep the insecure avoidant child at a distance from the caregiver and thereby unable to reap the benefit of full attentive supportive care and will keep the insecure ambivalent/resistant child in a state of hypervigilence for affective cues that might signal what is going to happen next. Both types of children suffer hyper-arousal. The heart rates of the apparently avoidant infants are as elevated as those for secure infants during separation, and pre-to-post Strange Situation rises in cortisol are somewhat greater for avoidant than for secure infants (see Main 1995, p.418). As I understand Main and Crittenden, both patterns of insecure attachment depict organised if restricted responses to attachment figures. Persons in all classifications are subject to becoming disorganised if their attachment figure becomes frightening, threatening, physically or sexually abusive.

Mary Main (1995), in an extensive review of the findings from the Strange Situation, points out that "only (that majority of) infants whose mothers had been 'sensitive and responsive to infant signals and communications' in the home had shown the expected behavioural patterning. For infants whose attachment behaviour had been consistently rejected, threatening conditions (mother's absence during the strange situation) failed to activate attachment behaviour. For infants whose mothers had been unpredictable, in contrast, mother's presence failed to terminate it. Insecure infants, then, either failed to exhibit attachment behaviour in threatening conditions and actively avoided mother on reunion or else, remaining preoccupied with mother throughout the separation, failed to explore in conditions of safety." (p.449)

Main points out that because the attachment behavioural system is conceptualised as being continually alert and context sensitive, the primary propensity to seek proximity in response to threat, and to terminate proximity-seeking in conditions of safety, must still be active. Conditions listed by Bowlby which are well known to activate attachment behaviour are: "a) occurrence of alarming events; b) rebuffs by other children or adults" (1969 p 259). "In this conceptualisation, then, the infant's conditional strategy (avoidance or preoccupation) is understood to be imposed on a still-active primary strategy. Maintenance of a "minimising" (avoidant) or "maximising" (resistant) behavioural strategy is therefore likely eventually not only to become dependent on the control and manipulation of attention but also eventually to necessitate overriding or altering aspects of memory, emotion and awareness of surrounding conditions." (p.451)

I consider this to be an enormously important statement by Main and one that is outwith the scope of this book to address fully. However, what it makes me think is that insecure-attachment style not only imposes a huge strain (fatigue) on the psychobiological system but also that psychotherapeutic help attuned to the complexity of careseeking behaviour could have physical as well as psychological effects. In addition, if Main is correct, one would expect that effective psychotherapy would increase the careseeker's capacity to relate to and take in information from their surroundings and to be more effective in terms of planning for survival and developmental issues. More importantly, it may indicate the type of psychotherapeutic help required. If Main is correct in what she infers about the 'avoidant' person's capacity to remember their early experiences accurately, due to their defensive organisation, then a form of psychotherapy that does not primarily rely on remembering and making sense of one's experience may be more helpful. In this instance, Systems Centred Therapy (Agazarian, 1997) which focuses on experience in the here and now as opposed to explanation of the 'there and then' might be more useful in promoting change. I have discussed this more fully elsewhere (McCluskey, 2002; McCluskey in press). The thesis that I am building up to is that adults are likely to present with their particular careseeking style when they approach psychotherapeutic help and to maintain or return to that style if they feel anxious or threatened.

I wish to look now at research by Haft and Slade (1989) which suggests that attachment security in the caregiver corresponds with the capacity to attune to a range of emotion in careseekers, thus facilitating effective caregiving. This work supports that of Tronick (1989), Crittenden McKinsey (1995), Main (1995), and Fonagy *et al.* (1991), amongst others, and I use it as a major building block in my construction of a model of effective caregiving within the psychotherapeutic domain.

Effective caregiving: attunement to a range of affect

Haft and Slade (1989) reported the results of a study in which they found that the nature of a mother's internal affective experience powerfully influences the affects she acknowledges and attunes to in her child. They set out to see whether differences between mothers in their ability to access a variety of their own affects and experiences will influence the kinds of affects and experiences they can acknowledge in their babies.

The researchers classified attunement into low-order attunement and high-order attunement, using the affect attunement scale devised by Stern (unpublished). Using the scale the mother's attunements were rated along a continuum from negative attunement (a score of –2 or –1), to comments or communications (a score of zero), to positive attunements (a score of +1 or +2). In addition, each rater rated the quality of the attunement, i.e. the degree to which the mother entered into or shared in the infant's subjective experience. A response with a score of 1 was labelled a low-order attunement – here the mother combined her desire to share in the baby's affective experience with an intention to teach or otherwise alter his experience. On the other hand a score of 2 (rated as high-order attunement) was one where the intention was purely to share in the baby's affective experience. Responses scored in the other direction (–1 or –2) indicated mother's entry into the affective experience, but with the intent to mock or scorn the baby.

They found:

(i) Securely attached mothers' (rated on the AAI) responded to a broad range of affective experiences and could correctly assess their baby's affect, whether it was positive or negative. They evinced little psychological need to distort their babies' affect in order to protect a particular state of mind regarding attachment and attuned with an even hand to their babies' expressions of initiative, effort, exuberance, frustration, anger and need for closeness. When they did misattune, it was not in any systematic way with a bias in favour of one kind of affective experience over another.

(ii) In the preoccupied group a pattern of selective misattunement was discovered. For example, the mothers did not attune or validate their baby's expression of initiative and exuberance during play. They either totally ignored these type of expressions in their babies or misattuned to them. Ambiguous situations seemed to provoke confusion and anxiety – when the babies signalled to the mothers that they needed to know what to do the mothers tended to become anxious at their own inability to understand their babies' persistent requests for clarification. There was an unpredictable area of distortions and misattunements that occurred pervasively, in the context of both positive and negative baby affect.

(iii) The dismissing group distorted their babies' affect by misreading it primarily when it was negative and did so most consistently when the baby directed the negativity towards them and not at an object. In marked contrast to the relatively unpredictable pattern of the preoccupied group, dismissing mothers distorted and mis-attuned consistently, following a pattern that was defined by the type of baby affect displayed. Dismissing mothers were most comfortable attuning to their babies expression of exuberance, especially in the context of mastery at play. The baby's expression of autonomy and separateness seemed most comfortable for these mothers and were the preferred state for affective sharing. They seemed to reject bids from their babies for comfort and reassurance. The first line of approach was typically to use comments to override the baby's affect, as if trying to make it go away. If this was not successful and the baby continued to be distressed or angry, a misattunement would often follow. There was often a sadistic quality to these misattunements and comments.

The authors conclude that with the insecurely attached mothers there are real limitations on the kinds of subjective experiences that can be experienced and shared.

Summary

In chapter three we looked at the way in which infants arrive in the world ready to meet other people, interact with and enjoy them. We saw that the infant cannot do this on his or her own and that in order to achieve this goal he or she needs help from an attuned, sensitive and empathic caregiver who is willing to search out what the infant is communicating and then make sense of it. When the infant does not get this response he or she develops defensive strategies to cope with the emotional disturbance aroused. In the face of continued lack of attunement, or deliberate or accidental misattunement or non-attunement, the infant develops distinctive patterns of relationship with self or others. *These patterns, it seems to me, serve the function of regulating emotional and physiological arousal in the absence of a satisfactory acquittal of the original instinctive system, which was aroused.* (See article by Denham *et al.* for a discussion of emotional competence in pre-schoolers and subsequent social competence; their argument is that too much negative feedback to children requires excessive self regulation which cannot be sustained.)

When the goals of the biologically based, instinctive careseeking system have not been met then defensive behavioural strategies will be apparent in the interaction. Attachment theory helps us to understand the central place of affect regulation in the experience, monitoring and negotiation of relationships.

By locating attachment as a primary motivational system within the person, with its own function, purpose and behavioural sequences, which are activated and terminated within particular environmental conditions we now have a language that makes sense of the experiences of feeling protected or unprotected, helpless or helped, valued or dismissed, anxious or secure.

(Lieberman *et al.*, 1991)

Such a view makes it possible to consider the ways in which careseekers in psychotherapy sessions may experience the interaction between them and their therapist and offers pointers for how to understand the process of this relationship.

During the course of this chapter I have remarked on different occasions about the implications of particular pieces of research into infant/adult dyads (in terms of expressing, communicating and responding to emotion) for later manifestations of careseeking in adults, particularly within a psychotherapeutic context. I wish to summarise them here before proceeding to my next chapter.

The Grossmanns' work indicated that secure and insecure infant/parent dyads develop particular patterns of communication in relation to discussing affectively laden material. For example, in the case of infants in infant/parent dyads classified as 'insecure', when exposed to different displays of affective expression, their response to the affect was neither prompt nor accurate, indicating that they were unsure how to 'read it' or respond.

Crittenden's observations suggested that the three main types of insecurely attached infants have different ways of managing affective and cognitive information:

(i) Avoidant infants learn to organise their behaviour without being able to interpret or use affective signals.

(ii) Ambivalent infants have been reinforced for affective behaviour but have not learned a cognitive organisation that reduces the inconsistency of the mother's behaviour.

(iii) Disorganised infants, those who cannot predict their caregiver's response, become anxious and angry. Without a strategy for changing the probabilities of caregiver behaviour, these infants remain disorganised with regard to attachment.

On the other hand, infants who feel secure with their attachment figure are more autonomous, more emotionally coherent and fluent, and more flexible in terms of monitoring and responding to affect in others.

The Grossmanns' free-play work with parent/infant dyads (12–18 month) classified as secure and insecure indicated:

(i) infants in 'secure dyads' communicate more subtly, with soft vocalisations;

(ii) infants in 'insecure dyads' initiate interaction with toy presentations and louder vocalisations;

(iii) in 'secure dyads' if the child was playing happily, the parent stayed away and observed, but would intervene and offer suggestions if the child became bored or lost interest;

(iv) in 'insecure dyads' the parent rarely offered a toy, stayed away from their infant when the infant showed low interest in play or was in a poor mood and only joined in the play when the infant was playing with a high level of interest. Also, they found that with infants classified as avoidant, the parent withdrew from the infant when the infant appeared sad, resulting in the infant stopping play and seeming uncertain and distressed.

Haft and Slade's study points out that:

(i) Secure caregivers responded with an even hand to a range of affect – not privileging one type over another.

(ii) The 'preoccupied' group did not attune to or validate the infant's expression of initiate or exuberance.

(iii) The dismissing group misread affect when it was negative and were most comfortable validating exuberance and mastery at play; they rejected bids for comfort and reassurance.

Such observations suggest to me that in the adult context, therapeutic work geared towards effecting change in the way in which the client experiences themselves and others needs to be attuned to the complexity of the careseeking/caregiving pattern and the many ways in which it disguises and deflects the self and other from experiencing certain affects. I will return to this in detail in chapter eleven.

In my next chapter I present the work of Heard and Lake (1997) who have developed the construct of the attachment dynamic which takes account of instinctive goal-corrected motivational systems in addition to careseeking and caregiving, thus allowing us to hold a more complex picture of child and adult behaviour and concerns. I use their work to elucidate the process of effective caregiving within psycho-therapy and explain why I call this process goal-corrected empathic attunement. My next chapter, therefore, builds on the last chapter and this one and will conclude the theoretical section of this book.

CHAPTER FIVE

Presenting the concept of goal-corrected empathic attunement: effective caregiving within psychotherapy

Should caregivers fail to meet the needs of careseekers, the latter cannot reach the goal of careseeking, and commonly become frustrated and then depressed. What happens when each partner is failing to reach their goals, and what is happening to their careseeking and caregiving systems is increasingly being researched and understood in both non-human primates and in human beings.

(Heard and Lake, 1997, p.5)

Introduction

The documented findings that the orbitofrontal system is involved in 'emotion-related learning' (Rolls, Hornak, Wade & McGrath, 1994) and that it retains plasticity throughout later periods of life (Barbas, 1995) may also help us to understand how developmentally-based affectively-focused psychotherapy can alter early attachment patterns ... Attachment models of mother/infant psychobiological attunement may thus be used to explore the origins of empathic processes in both development and psychotherapy, and reveal the deeper mechanisms of the growth-facilitating factors operating within the therapeutic alliance

(Schore, 2000, p.39)

In this chapter we will concentrate on the transposition of the research on careseeker/caregiver dyads to the context of adult psychotherapy. In order to set the context for relating the work on attachment in infants to the adult context of psychotherapy I will start with the work of Heard and Lake, practising psychoanalytic psychotherapists who have extended the theoretical base of attachment theory to take account of the problems that clients bring to therapy. Heard and Lake (1997, 2000; Heard, 2003) have extended attachment theory to include three instinctive motivational systems other than careseeking and caregiving – sexuality, interest sharing and self-defence. I will then move on to show how I have put together the concept of goal-corrected empathic attunement, why I locate it in the interpersonal system of caregiving and careseeking and why I think it makes sense to locate it within the extended view of attachment theory – the theory of the dynamics of attachment (Heard and Lake, 1997) which provides a way of thinking about instinctive systems of interest sharing, sexuality and defence, and the vitality affects associated with each.

The attachment dynamic

According to Heard and Lake the instinctive goal-corrected complementary systems of careseeking and caregiving described by Bowlby are insufficient to describe the complexity of motivational states that inspire and direct human beings. In 1986 in a paper entitled 'The attachment dynamic in adult life' Heard and Lake argued that companionable interest sharing was a major motivational force that brought human beings together into relationship with one another. In addition to interest sharing they included a further two systems: the affectional sexual system and the system for self-defence. In 1997, in their book *The Challenge of Attachment for Caregiving*, they elucidate the way in which these five goal-corrected systems interact with one another to form what they term the attachment dynamic and provide the research basis for their hypothesis.

Heard and Lake's (1997) theory of the dynamics of attachment conceptualises the self as a system of interacting systems which has relationship with others at its core. The self is conceived as interpersonal, experienced through relationships with others or through the process of defence against the pain of relationship. Experience of relationship with attachment figures is coded within the self in the form of 'relationships as experienced' (IMEARs – Internal Models of the Experience of Attachment Relationships).

The five systems within the attachment dynamic are therefore:

   (i) the careseeking system;

  (ii) the caregiving system;

 (iii) the interest-sharing system;

 (iv) the sexual system;

  (v) the system for self-defence.

These systems operate interdependently in order to develop and maintain a sense of well being and competence. When the goals of one or more of the five systems within the attachment dynamic are not met (particularly the careseeking system) then various levels and degrees of the following can occur:

   (i) a sense of well being diminishes;

  (ii) there is a neglect of self care and care for others;

 (iii) exploration is inhibited;

 (iv) the person operates from the system for self-defence and *in extremis* will choose survival of the self at any cost.

Any system within the attachment dynamic can fail to reach its goal by being overridden by other systems within the dynamic. For example, the caregiving system is activated when help is sought from a careseeker; however if the careseeker presents in a way that stimulates anxiety in the caregiver, the caregiver may retreat into self-defence and or experience or start exhibiting careseeking behaviours themselves. This process is described by Heard and Lake (1997, 2000).

If the careseeker fails to have their careseeking needs met, the behavioural patterns which accompany careseeking cannot shut down and the system for careseeking is infiltrated by the activation of the personal defence system. In this way careseeking is then expressed by whatever behaviours have been found to evoke in the caregiver responses that assuage the pain of not reaching careseeking goals. When the caregiver is activated to provide caregiving, frustration of this goal to give care is also likely to cause distress. When the needs of the caregiver and the careseeker are met, there is satisfaction and relief in both parties.

The attachment dynamic describes an interpersonal process that takes place through two different kinds of social exchange which present usually in mixed form. These two kinds of social interactions are (i) supportive companionable and (ii) dominant versus submissive. A supportive companionable interactive stance will generally support exploratory behaviour in whichever system is activated within the attachment dynamic. A dominant versus submissive type of social interaction will generally lead to intermittent incomplete and unsatisfactory exploratory processes at the individual and interpersonal level. One can see a relationship between these two distinct forms of relating and the observations of both the Grossmanns and Haft and Slade referred to in the last chapter. The research findings from both these projects imply a 'supportive companionable' form of relating from the secure parent and infant/toddler, and within the secure parent/infant dyads. The 'dominant versus submissive' forms can be seen in the selective ways of responding to emotion, vitality, exploration and mastery from the caregiver on the one hand, and the soft or loud vocalisations from the careseeker on the other. Heard and Lake (1997) cite an evolutionary base to these distinct forms of relating, and suggest that the capacity for both forms is hard wired within us all.

The system for interest sharing introduced by Heard and Lake in 1986, and again in 1997 and 2003, finds support from the observations of Trevarthen (2001) and Trevarthen, who note the ways in which infants and caregivers are communicating to their mutual shared satis-faction from the start when the baby is relaxed, well fed and not in pain. Subsequent, infant/caregiver observations, even of the ones cited in the last chapter, provide evidence for the importance of interest sharing for emotional regulation and well-being (see the reference to insecure dyads observed by the Grossmanns). The importance of interest sharing and its place within the dynamics of attachment will be addressed in detail in a forthcoming publication by Heard, Lake and McCluskey.

The system for exploration

The system for exploration is not included within the attachment dynamic. Exploration is not activated by attachment behaviour. *The exploratory system is conceptualised as always active unless overridden by the dynamics of attachment.* According to Heard and Lake (1997) the exploratory system has both an intra-individual and interpersonal component. The intra-individual component refers to all that we do which involves creating personal meaning; the interpersonal comp-onent refers to interest sharing with peers (Heard and Lake, 1997, 2000).

In addition, while the exploratory system is not part of the attachment dynamic, Heard (2003) conceptualises it as part of the caregiving system. In other words, when caregiving is aroused, it is the caregiver's exploratory system that seeks to understand what the careseeker needs and works out what might meet those needs. A caregiver whose exploratory system is not activated to understand the needs of the care-seeker will not provide effective care.

I will now present my own research on developing the concept of goal-corrected empathic attunement.

Goal-corrected empathic attunement: a process involved in effective caregiving

> An earlier paper (Emde, 1988) reviewed how current infancy research points to the centrality of the infant/caregiving relation-ship experience and of emotional availability in the context of that experience for establishing both continuity and the potential for later adaptive change. Moreover, linking infancy research with psychoanalytic clinical theory generated a proposal about moti-vational structures. The proposal is as follows. Early-appearing motivational structures are strongly biologically prepared in our species, develop in the specific context of the infant/caregiver relationship, and persist throughout life. I have since realised that more can be said. These motivational structures can also be regarded as fundamental modes of development. As such, they are life-span processes that can be mobilised through empathy in the course of therapeutic action with adults.
>
> (Emde, 1990b, p.883)

As we have seen, attachment behaviour in very young children according to Bowlby (1969) is activated in the context of fear, distress, illness and anxiety, and results in the infant seeking proximity with their caregiver. The function of attachment behaviour is to ensure survival. Attachment behaviours continue throughout the life cycle and are activated under certain environmental conditions. Individuals build up a set of mental representations of how their attachment-seeking behaviour has been received and responded to by their attachment figure and these are stored as templates of experience – what Bowlby described as internal working models. Heard and Lake, as mentioned earlier, describe them as internal models of experience in relationship (IMERs) with particular attachment figures. The basic idea is that experience of self in relation to attachment figures is stored as models of how such relationships have worked in the past and as a basis for predicting how they might work in the future.

The idea of internal working models of self in relationship is critical for helping us to understand the nature of the psychotherapeutic relationship. In this relationship the careseeker (the client) brings to the experience their various templates of how their relationships with their earlier attachment figures have worked and this will both influence their behaviour in the therapeutic relationship and their experience of the therapist's response to them.

Careseeking is always directed towards a caregiver, and will only cease when the goal of careseeking has been met, i.e. when the caregiver gives the required response. Failures on behalf of the caregiver to adequately meet the needs of the careseeker will result in the attachment behaviour of careseeking failing to shut down. Instead it will remain active but in less visible or complete sequences of behaviour. In the therapeutic relationship one would expect to see the careseeker exhibiting attachment behaviours, demonstrating particular attachment styles (careseeking patterns), and also expressing behaviours that indicate their expectations of the responses of the therapist. Psychotherapy offers the opportunity to identify these complicated presentations of attachment behaviour and to respond in ways that will assuage careseeking and promote the exploratory system.

The psychotherapeutic relationship: an account of interactional sequences using the concept of goal-corrected empathic attunement

Careseeking behaviours will be activated in the context of psychotherapy and the careseeker (client/patient) will be motivated to have their careseeking needs met by the caregiver (therapist), who will be perceived in the therapeutic context as 'older and wiser'. One would also expect the caregiver to be activated to meet the needs of the care-seeker. A failure in this regard one would see as a failure in the caregiving system. More precisely, what is failing here (according to Heard and Lake, 2003) is the exploratory component of care-giving. The exploratory system is not part of attachment (careseeking) behaviour. The exploratory system is a separate system which is always active *unless* overridden by careseeking. It is the exploratory aspect of caregiving that is paying attention to the meaning of the many presentations of affect by the careseeker, or the meaning of the lack of affective presentation, as in the work described with extremely emotionally abused adults by Susan Vas Dias (2000).

In the adult context, if the caregiver does not attune to the affect of the careseeker, careseeking will not be assuaged, but even more importantly the careseeker will have no evidence on which to base their confidence that the caregiver would be able to support them in their exploration, discovery and potential action. In this context, affect attunement requires resonance to the feeling state of the other, and a willingness to engage with and regulate the other's state of arousal so that the careseeker is optimally placed for exploration. In addition to affect attunement, the adult caregiver working with an adult careseeker must also convey that they *understand* where the other is headed and have some resources in addition to what the careseeker has to help them get there.

Attachment theory proposes that exploratory behaviour in individuals is dependent on the accessibility of a safe base, one that can be relied on to be supportive and educative in times of crisis or threat. This is as true for the Antartic explorer as it is for any of us going about our daily business, knowing that there is somebody somewhere who could help pick up the pieces if we get into real trouble.

The other building block for the concept under discussion is empathy. For the operation of therapeutic work, attachment theory on its own is insufficient as it fails to address the nature of the support offered back at base. The instinct to survive can get a child or adult to return to a safe place when necessary. However, the reception one gets at base will determine whether one actually gathers further resources or simply recovers and resuscitates the ones one already has. What makes the difference is whether one is greeted with:

(i)   an attuned response to one's internal state of arousal;

(ii) the person attending to you not only does that but stays long enough with you in order to address that arousal state;[6]

---

6. This means dealing with it in such a way that one is helped to restore one's own internal balance (see Weil, 1992). If this is done properly with sensitivity and care then one is able to access one's cognitive and emotional intelligence (i.e. the process of affect regulation I discussed in chapter three). This alone is very useful because it puts one back in charge and in touch with one's own personal competencies.

(iii) the person responding does so empathically and can maintain an empathic stance over time and for as long as is necessary;

(iv) the person responding can put one in touch with one's own skills, resources and capacity to act and influence events.

This brings into the frame another person who can offer support. It also brings in a *relationship* with another person. This is very different to having to rely on one's own resources, as happens when all that is offered is skilled attunement. Attunement and empathy as described are not sufficient. Skilled empathy will take the other near the domain of experience and thinking of the other person, but *the process of helping the other access their own competence requires the helper to move beyond just putting the other in touch with what they know already. It requires that they help them access that which they are on the edge of knowing.*

This process requires that the helper use their own intelligence to think about the situation of the other, including what they might be thinking about, and engage to the limits of their own intellectual capacity without fear of losing to the other that which belongs to them. This is an act of emotional, imaginative and intellectual generosity which goes beyond appreciating the situation the other is in; it joins with and engages with them in opening up for exploration ideas and courses of action that neither may have articulated in quite this manner heretofore.

This fine-tuning of emotion, intelligence and imagination on the part of the therapist requires that they monitor the effect of their input on the client and adapt, adjust and arrange their responses to the verbal and non-verbal feedback they are getting. Therapists working in this way elicit feedback to their input and check what is happening for the other. They do not just rely on verbal and non-verbal signals which can be ambiguous and open to misinterpretation. The process I am describing is active and interactional. *It is a process of communicating and regulating vitality affects.*

The behaviours of caregiving and careseeking are complementary, so one would expect to be able to observe an interactional sequence of behaviours where they both, in their respective roles of caregiver and careseeker, seek to influence each other to have their respective goals met. At the conclusion of a successful sequence of interactions one would expect to observe some relief and satisfaction for both parties.

In therapy, what is communicated non-verbally by the careseeker reaches back to the earliest forms of the self, the self that was communicating and making sense of how they and others fitted together and understood each other long before language was available, and at a time of extreme physical dependence. It is into this domain that the therapist enters through empathic knowledge. Empathy of the form described here is a crucial component of effective caregiving.

> The empathic process in which therapists steep themselves in the world of the other attempting to understand how others see and experience themselves and their worlds, putting this into words and checking their understanding, appears to us to be curative. Empathy is a process of co-constructing symbols of experience. Clients' process of symbolising their experience in awareness promoted by empathic responding to their internal experience appears to us to be a universal core ingredient of the therapeutic process. Being able to name an experience first makes the previously implicit explicit, thereby providing an improved sense of facilitation and comprehension of how one knows what one is experiencing. This in and of itself provides some clarity and relief from earlier confusion.
>
> (Bohart and Greenberg, 1997, pp.5–6)

Based on the idea that attachment behaviour is always active until assuaged (cf. Bowlby, 1969; Main, 1995; described earlier, and Heard and Lake, 1986, 1997), the theory of goal-corrected empathic attunement that I am putting forward therefore refers to the activity whereby one person (the client) seeks to engage the other person (the therapist) in attending to their emotional and practical concerns in such a way that they can understand themselves better and manage their interactions with others more effectively. The therapist has to acknowledge and regulate the careseeker's emotional state, convey that they grasp the significance of the material being brought and the context within which it has arisen, the meaning it has for the client, and the direction and manner in which the client wishes to pursue it. The therapist needs to respond with attunement and empathy, plus ideas and concepts which are held together within a theoretical framework that add a dimension that the client can use to gain another perspective on themselves and what they have brought. The principles on which goal-corrected attunement work are open systems of communication between the two parties concerned, that are regulated, directed and corrected by feedback.

The therapist (caregiver) has first to manage the emotional arousal (affect regulation) of the client (careseeker) so that they are in the best state possible to think about and explore their problem. This the caregiver does through attuning to the presenting affects – the vitality affects as described by Stern (1985). This may involve 'tuning down' the client's affects in such a way as to bring them within manageable levels so that the client can think clearly. Or it may involve 'tuning up' and amplifying the client's affect so that they can begin to access their own affective experience. This can be long, painful work taking many months and even years with those who have had the extremes of mis-attunement hinted at earlier (see Vas Dias 2000; Truckle, 2000; Mollon, 2000). Secondly, the caregiver has to relate to the content so that the careseeker can re-examine their concerns from the advantage of a meta perspective. This is achieved through empathy.

The process of goal-corrected empathic attunement that I am presenting locates caregiving in the psychotherapeutic context within the theory of the dynamics of attachment (Heard and Lake, 1986, 1997).

What happens when careseeking is activated is that the exploratory system is overridden. In order to engage the client in exploratory work careseeking must be assuaged by effective caregiving. In other words, in the therapeutic context assuagement of the careseeking system will provide the conditions necessary for the exploratory system to function. Dorothy Heard has identified distinct vitality affects associated with the three stages to this process: 'relief when careseeking needs are met; enlivenment when in the process of exploration and well being when in touch with competence to act' (Heard, 1997a).

Goal-corrected empathic attunement therefore involves an open system of communication between two parties engaged in a psychotherapeutic endeavour. This in turn involves a wish to be understood and helped on the one hand, and a capacity to attune to affect, regulate arousal levels, empathise, provide thoughtful ideas and responses, together with a flexible response to non-verbal and verbal feedback on the other. The aim of empathic attunement is to facilitate the functioning of the client's exploratory system. If the blend of empathy, affect attunement and regulation of arousal levels has been successful then the exploratory system will 'kick in', signalling that the goal of the interaction has been met.

The processes that one would expect to take place are as follows: an expression of concern by the careseeker (communicated both verbally and non-verbally) is matched by the caregiver for emotional intensity and vitality (Stern's cross modal affect attunement); this is followed by further revelations by the careseeker, which are responded to in such a way by the caregiver (as described in Bohart's definition of empathy quoted earlier) that the careseeker's meaning, as well as the feeling they have about the content, is being understood; this in turn leads the careseeker to raise further concerns, which are then responded to by an expression of affect attunement by the caregiver; this results in visible assuagement on the part of the careseeker and a sense of satisfaction in the caregiver. At this point the careseeking system shuts down temporarily until a further careseeking behaviour is activated.

I would expect from the attachment literature and my own observations referred to in chapter one that most stages of this process will be accompanied by social referencing behaviours, as described by Emde (1983, 1985) and Kiersky & Beebe (1994), where the careseeker scans the caregiver's face for cues on which they make a judgement as to whether it is safe to proceed.

> Social referencing is a process whereby an individual, when confronted with a situation of uncertainty, seeks out emotional information from a significant other in order to resolve the uncertainty and regulate behaviour accordingly. In our experimental social referencing paradigms we have constructed situations of uncertainty that involve an unfamiliar toy robot, an unfamiliar person, or a glass-topped crawling surface with an apparent drop-off (the so-called "visual cliff"). When an infant, in the course of exploration, encounters the uncertainty situation (e.g., the apparent drop-off surface) he looks to mother's face. If she signals fear or anger, the infant ceases exploration or withdraws; if she signals pleasure or interest, the infant continues exploration.
>
> (Emde, 1990b, p.893)

The hypothesised process of goal-corrected empathic attunement is represented in the chart on the following page.

While affect attunement is expressed cross modally, empathic attunement is expressed verbally; it is an intuitive grasp of the underlying emotional state of the other that draws on empathic knowledge and is an acknowledgement of an emotional state, e.g. a therapist says to the client: "You are showing me your despair." There is acknowledgement of the correctness of the fit between the experience and the explanation by non-verbal and possibly verbal gestures of relief. The key indicator of correctness of fit is the non-verbal feedback from the client and this is best read by paying attention to the vitality affects of the careseeker.

Goal-corrected empathic attunement within the context of psychotherapy

Behaviour of careseeker	Caregiver's response	Implicit goal of caregiver's behaviour within a therapeutic context	Function in attachment terms of caregiver's behaviour	Vitality affects within a system of responsive interactions between careseeker and caregiver
expression of concern or distress	affect matching for intensity and vitality	settle initial anxiety: affect regulation	signals emotive message are understood and accepted	relief
displays concerns	empathic response	influence internal working models of relationship	signals the competence of the caregiver	relief
raises further concerns or shows further distress	attunement to the affect combined with empathic input	regulate arousal levels, signal intended continuing proximity and a benign cognitive appraisal	signals the range of material that it is safe to explore in this context	relief
exploration of concerns	attunement to affect, affect regulation and empathy	facilitate a sense of continuity with past experience	survival, integration and development	enlivenment and well being

In line with the chart above I suggest that it may be possible to identify a sequence of behaviours in therapeutic situations that can be tracked.

I set this out in a diagram to indicate the possible flow and direction of interaction, though many variations are possible. The diagram illustrates that the process of exploration of deepest concerns is fluid and dependent on checking the response of the caregiver to see whether it

The deepening spiral of goal-corrected empathic attunement.

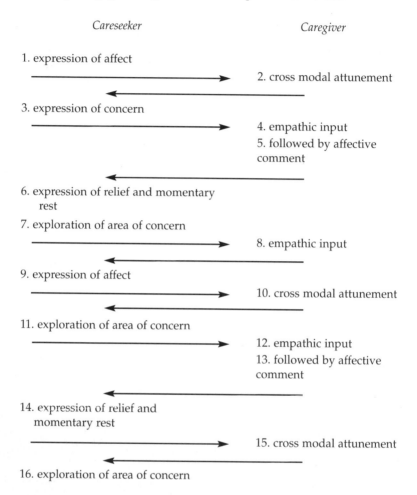

Careseeker   *Caregiver*

1. expression of affect

2. cross modal attunement

3. expression of concern

4. empathic input
5. followed by affective comment

6. expression of relief and momentary rest

7. exploration of area of concern

8. empathic input

9. expression of affect

10. cross modal attunement

11. exploration of area of concern

12. empathic input
13. followed by affective comment

14. expression of relief and momentary rest

15. cross modal attunement

16. exploration of area of concern

is safe enough to proceed. As will be noted in the diagram, sometimes empathic input from the therapist on its own will trigger affect in the careseeker (see 8 and 9). Slight hitches in the responsiveness of the caregiver will throw the careseeker back into careseeking behaviour and inhibit exploration. This process characterises psychotherapy as a careseeking/caregiving partnership in which each party has their own set goals. In short the interaction between therapist and client is part of a goal-corrected sequence governed by biologically based, instinctive goal-corrected systems.

Since formulating these ideas, and conducting the experiments to be described in the next three chapters, I have carried out detailed work on a collection of videos showing interaction between careseekers and caregivers and have identified a distinct number of patterns of interaction. I detail these in chapter eleven and the final chapter, chapter twelve.

Where have we come so far?

The concept of goal-corrected empathic attunement is based on the idea that in situations arousing attachment issues, careseeking will be activated and remain active until assuaged, at which point the exploratory biological instinctive system will engage.

In this chapter I have used the context of psychotherapy to explore the dynamics of careseeking and caregiving. I did this because in the main it is the medium we have selected to address the aetiological roots of failed and successful caregiving. However, careseeking is not only aroused within the psychotherapeutic context.

I started in chapter one with an account of my mother's consultation with a cardiologist and suggested that the consultation might have taken another form or at least that she would have come out from the consultation feeling differently about it if the cardiologist had been able to detect and regulate her affect in such a way that both remained in dialogue until the goals of the consultation had been met.

It is crucial in the process of medical consultations that the careseeker's exploratory faculties remain active so that they can discuss all aspects of the problem to their satisfaction. This is not going to happen if the instinctive careseeking system is aroused and its goals remain unmet. The impulse to give up one's own authority for what one knows and submit to the direction being offered by a medical consultant is strong. The vitality affects associated with submission will then manifest themselves and be responded to consciously or unconsciously, to the well-being or detriment of the careseeker. The sheer context of medical consultations invites careseeking. Caregivers of whatever profession or none, if concerned to meet the needs of those asking for their help, could benefit from having some awareness of their own caregiving instincts, what they respond to in careseeking, what they deflect careseekers away from (such as anxiety, distress, sadness) and what triggers their own instinctual systems for self-defence.

Careseeking can be aroused in a multitude of contexts but particularly in consultations with social workers, care staff, nurses and others in the 'caring professions'. The thesis being developed and presented here is based on the assumption that the processes explored in psychotherapy have relevance to other situations involving human interactions in times of crisis and distress.

For their part, psychotherapists have traditionally been aware of the crucial importance of the therapist's attitude, empathy, communication skills, attention to verbal and non-verbal clues, and attunement. It therefore made sense to begin an exploration of these concepts with research in this field.

In chapter two I drew attention to the contribution made by those who have researched the psychotherapeutic process. In particular I commented on their understanding of the importance of process for the development of a sense of self, and of the relationship between defensiveness and self-acceptance. These researchers also drew attention to the importance of affect matching and intensity and the role of empathic response. Carkhuff and Berenson particularly emphasised the importance of the quality and depth of empathy, not just at the start of therapy but over time as the therapeutic process developed between client and practitioner. We noted the research into Luborsky's concept of the 'Core Conflictual Theme' and its links with early experience of relationship. Finally we looked at research into the quality and nature of affective response from the therapist and its role in regulating arousal levels (Anstadt, 1997).

I concluded chapter two with the argument that psychotherapy was in need of a theory of interaction between careseekers and caregivers that would help us to understand the psychotherapeutic process between adults. In particular I felt that:

(i) research on interaction between infants and caregivers could throw light on the processes occurring in psychotherapy which have been identified over many years as being of critical importance;

(ii) psychotherapy can be understood as an attachment-eliciting activity which arouses, maintains and resolves the dynamics of attachment in the clients who come for help.

In chapter three I focused on the findings of developmental psychologists who 'discovered' that infants were not just 'gas bags, full of wind'; neither were they bundles of instincts born ready made with a theory of mind and able to attribute persecutory intent to other people.

In contrast, in support of the psychoanalyst Ronald Fairbairn, researchers found that from within a few hours of birth infants were ready to meet other people, interact with and enjoy them. We saw that the infant cannot do this on his or her own and that in order to achieve this goal he or she needs help from an attuned, sensitive and empathic caregiver who is willing to search out what the infant is communicating and then make sense of it.

I ended chapter three with the suggestion that attachment theory offers an explanation of the interactive roots of this phenomena and the biological basis for it.

In chapter four, I located the interactive patterns developed between infants and caregivers within the context of attachment theory as developed by John Bowlby and extended by Ainsworth and Heard and Lake. The fine nuances of intrusiveness and deliberate misattunement on the one hand, and affect regulation, sensitive attunement and empathy on the other, were found to be associated with secure, insecure and disorganised patterns of attachment.

In addition we saw from the work of the Grossmanns that sensitive attuned responsive interaction from a caregiver when the infant was exploring, maintained and enhanced exploration, while intrusive interaction from the caregiver when the infant was exploring stopped the infant in their tracks. Non-responsiveness from the caregiver when the infant was flagging simply left the infant to their own devices in a state of non exploration.

While it is enough (in fact essential) for infants to get an attuned response from their caregivers which is basically communicated at a non-verbal level, such is not the case for adults. Post infancy (in other words after the infant has acquired language and can communicate with others who are not their primary attachment figures) the sharing of vitality states in situations where the dynamics of attachment have been aroused leads the careseeker (toddler, adolescent or adult) to *expect empathy*. I formed this view on the basis of thinking that the experience of attunement in these circumstances can give rise to the feeling of being known – of one's emotional state being understood. In this case when the person does not get an empathic response he or she develops defensive strategies to cope with the emotional disturbance aroused – what Heard and Lake describe as the pain of failed careseeking. See Weil (1992) for a discussion of the connection between deprivation of empathy and severe emotional abuse.

At this point I began to put together ideas about what I considered essential for understanding the dynamics of careseeking and caregiving between adults when the dynamics of attachment are aroused.

Based on my reading of infant development and attachment processes, together with the empirical work about to be described in the next three chapters, it became clear to me that what facilitated exploration and the development of personal and social competence was non-defensive, supportive, companionable relating (as indicated by Heard and Lake, 1997). Such relating could engage with and regulate all shades and intensity of emotion (or lack of emotion); seek out, activate and validate effectance pleasure; and sustain an empathic stance over time. Affect arousal or regulation, identification, containment and empathic attunement are what are sought by the careseeker and offered by the caregiver. When it 'works' – is provided with sufficient skill – the careseeking system shuts down and the exploratory system goes into action. In this way the process of careseeking and caregiving is goal-corrected. Such a formulation is an expansion on the Ainsworth, Bowlby paradigm (which remains essentially within the parameters of careseeking, having the set goal of proximity and comfort) and draws heavily on the work of Heard and Lake and their formulation of several goal-corrected systems in dynamic equilibrium.

In situations which have triggered the dynamics of attachment, a careseeker who has experienced attunement from the caregiver and then does not receive an empathic response will, according to the theory, experience distress – in the form of anger, sadness or despair. It should be possible to track what happens between careseekers and caregivers when this happens. This is not *just* about tracking sequences of behaviour, facial expression, intention movements and the whole array of verbal and non-verbal responses; it is about noticing

(i)   which instinctual goal-correcting system is aroused in the careseeker and caregiver;

(ii) whether the *pattern of interaction* changes when there is or is not a lack of empathic response;

(iii) the accompanying affect in careseeker and caregiver alike.

Examples are provided in chapters eleven and twelve.

I have identified goal-corrected empathic attunement as a process within the instinctively based careseeking and caregiving systems which contributes to the delivery of effective care. Effective care is that which assuages the careseeker so that the careseeker has the subjective experience of accessing competence. When this happens the instinctive system for careseeking will shut down and the exploratory system within the individual will have more energy to engage with the problems of living. The concept of goal-correction means that the delivery of effective care is a dynamic, responsive interactive process – not something that can be fully anticipated in advance or fully planned for. The goals are satisfaction and relief, accompanied by a sense of autonomy and effective capacity to influence one's environment.

What is sought by the careseeker whose vitality levels might be very low, comfortable or very high is a relationship with someone which puts them in touch with how they might, with or without help, reach their goals for themselves; or if their goals are unrealisable and not possible, the interaction promotes that sense of well being that comes from being in touch with another person who can stay with and name what one is experiencing rather than denying it, changing it or fleeing from it.

The idea of goal-correction operating between two people shows how dynamic and creative the process of careseeking and caregiving is. Both parties are engaged in bringing about the desired result and using all their ingenuity to achieve it. The research quoted in chapter three shows just how interactive and responsive this process is. We saw that when an intrusive adult wanted contact with her infant, the infant who spurned such inauthentic contact dodged her attentions and tried to escape as best he could. This while held in her arms, the infant used what was available – the ability to move his head and *avoid eye contact*.

The concept of goal-correction takes us away from the notion of 'getting it right'. 'Getting it right' is clearly what it is all about, but this cannot be judged on the basis of verbal or non-verbal behaviours and affects considered in isolation from each other or from the behaviour and affects of the other party.

The concept of goal-correction directs us to think in terms of *the state of correction*, as it were, and how we know when that state is achieved. The beauty of attachment theory is the simplicity of the answer to this question. As said before, there is a behavioural and an experiential dimension to this. Some behaviours shut down and others emerge. The person who has the experience of something being triggered inside themselves knows that that trigger is no longer active and that they feel calmer; the experience is relief – physiological relief – of feeling settled.

There is one further dimension to add before leaving goal-corrected empathic attunement. This dimension is the place of eye contact in the communication, identification and regulation of affect. We saw in chapter three how the baby searches out eye contact minutes after birth. With video technology we can follow the expressions in the eyes of the careseeker and caregiver as they move in and out of contact with one another. We will look at examples of this in chapter eleven. The role of eye contact in terms of psychobiological regulation in relation to the different systems of careseeking, caregiving, sexuality, interest-sharing and self-defence would benefit from systematic study.

In summary, therefore, my thesis, is that when the dynamics of attachment are aroused, the caregiver needs to be alert to *the meaning of the behaviours being presented by the careseeker in attachment terms.* Attachment theory provides a framework *for monitoring the interaction process itself* between careseeker and caregiver. In addition, attachment theory suggests that when the goal of the system is met, this is experienced and known subjectively. The person themselves experiences whether the goals of the instinctive system for careseeking have been reached or not.

Such a view of the process of interaction between careseeker and caregiver was not available to me when I started out on this research, as explained in chapter one. The ideas were developed during the course of the research that I am about to describe in the next three chapters. I started out wanting to test my hypothesis that affect attunement by the therapist was associated with whether or not the client explored or was inhibited from exploring. The first step in this process was to see whether affect attunement could be identified. My next chapter describes my first experiment.

First experiment: the identification of affect attunement in adult psychotherapy

... the activity that is characteristically scientific begins with an explanatory conjecture which at once becomes the subject of an energetic critical analysis. It is an instance of a far more general stratagem that underlies every enlargement of general understanding and every new solution of the problem of finding our way about the world. The regulation and control of hypotheses is more usefully described as a *cybernetic* than as a logical process: the adjustment and reformation of hypotheses through an examination of their deductive consequences is simply another setting for the ubiquitous phenomenon of negative feedback.

(Medawer, 1962, p.154)

Introduction

As stated in chapter one the overall aims of my empirical research were:

1. To obtain a measurement of affect attunement.
2. To see whether students who were given training directed at encouraging them to attune to client affect would subsequently do better at attuning to affect than those students who were not.
3. To see whether the attachment status of the students affected their ability to attune to client affect.

As a first step I needed to see whether the concept of affect attunement which had been developed in the infant domain (Stern, 1985) fitted the adult domain, and in what ways it might need developing to meet the needs of the adult context. Having established a definition of the concept I needed to see whether it could be reliably rated. I then needed to see whether what I was rating had any validity within the area that I was studying – could I relate the measure to other related measures? Finally I needed to see whether I could train people so that they were better able to attune.

The research design

I conducted three experiments. For the first experiment I prepared six, 1.5-minute videoed extracts of clinical material and had them rated for affect attunement by senior clinicians and students. The basic aim was to see how far attunement, as I defined it, could be identified by both groups.

Building on experiment one, I now had a clear example of affect attunement and a clear example of non attunement. For experiment two I prepared three videoed extracts of clinical material and had them rated by two groups of students. Both groups were given definitions of affect attunement. In addition, one group of students was given indicators to help them judge the extract and the other group was not given indicators. The aim was to see whether the addition of indicators improved the students' ability to identify attunement.

The third experiment consisted of role plays designed to elicit the dynamics of attachment. I involved professional actors as the care-seekers (clients) and students as the caregivers (social workers/therapists). The role plays were videoed and the students rated by the actors on prepared scales. The students also rated their own performance.

The students were then divided into two groups. One group was given training, the other group was not. Two weeks later both groups then interviewed the actors again. The role plays were videoed as before and the students work was again rated by the actors and by themselves.

At the end of the second day of working with the actors all the students completed three self-report, attachment-style questionnaires. The aim was to see whether attunement could be identified and measured by an external observer; whether this measure and the students' and actors' self reports related to their attachment status, and whether training improved performance on all these measures.

First experiment

My first experiment, therefore, concerned the initial exploratory attempts to identify and define affect attunement in the adult context.

As a first step, I started with my colleagues in the field of psychotherapy and social work to see if they could agree with me and with each other about whether an interactive sequence between client and therapist was attuned or not. At the stage of devising my first experiment I was not as clear as I am now about the difference between affect attunement and empathy – I had blurred them in my mind to mean empathic attunement and the reader will see this when they read the design of the experiment. Nevertheless, it was a first step in clarifying the concept.

I set out to see whether:

(i) it was possible to identify affect attunement in adult psychotherapy;

(ii) one could get a clearer understanding of the processes involved in affect attunement in the adult context;

(iii) students were as good at identifying affect attunement as expert clinicians.

The study was based on excerpts from psychotherapy sessions which had been classified by practising therapists as attuned or non-attuned, and in each case a detailed account was obtained as to the reasons for the judgements which were made. These excerpts were then shown to a sample of social workers in training, to discover whether their assessments would correspond to those made by the expert panel. It was intended that detailed analysis of the responses by both therapists and students would show which particular features of the interaction were used to make judgements about the degree of attunement, including the degree to which observers used behaviour of both therapist and patient to arrive at their judgement.

In summary, the study was aimed at assessing; (a) the extent to which experts could agree on the attunement or non attunement in video-taped excerpts from therapy sessions; (b) the extent to which their judgements corresponded with those made by relatively inexperienced students; (c) what cues experts and students used to arrive at their judgements.

Materials and procedure

Six excerpts, each lasting one-and-a-half minutes, were selected from a corpus of video-taped psychotherapy sessions. Five of the excerpts were from sessions by two senior therapists, while the third was obtained from a BBC programme on counselling.

The excerpts were selected to reflect an initial judgement of attunement or non-attunement made by myself and a colleague, both of us with extensive clinical experience. The six excerpts were divided into two groups of three which, in our opinion, showed either attunement or non-attunement by the therapist. The initial judgement thus provided a baseline for the study, with excerpts 1, 4 and 6 (therapist A) representing attunement, and excerpts 2 (therapist C), 3 and 5 (therapist B) representing non-attunement.

Copies of the tape were sent to the nine experts, who were blind as to the attunement status of the excerpts. The instructions included a definition of attunement which stated that "attunement is a way of communicating to the other that one has recognised the affect they are experiencing. Attunement conveys to the other that one has a feeling sense inside of what it feels like to be them right now." They were asked to view each tape twice, stopping after each excerpt on the first viewing and simply rating it as to whether, in their view, the therapist was attuned or not. On the second viewing they were asked to rate each therapist again, but also to make notes giving the reasons for their judgement.

Based on the judgements made by the experts, a second tape was created for the students comprising just three excerpts: one which the experts had unanimously classified as non-attuned (excerpt 5); one which eight out of nine experts had judged to be attuned (excerpt 6); and one where the experts were divided in their judgement (excerpt 1). Excerpts 1 and 6 were recordings of the same therapist, and to control for this and for ordering effects, the excerpts were presented in counterbalanced sequence[7] to the groups of students using three versions of the tape.

The students were all asked to provide a written definition of an attuned therapist before being given the definition used for the experts. The students then viewed one of the three counterbalanced tapes in

---

7. I prepared three video tapes of the six excerpts. Each tape presented the excerpts in a different order. This minimises the effects of order on the results. As a favourable or negative attitude towards a therapist's work is likely to depend on which of her excerpts one saw first, it is also relevant in this regard.

groups of three or four. The tape was stopped for thirty seconds after each excerpt to allow students to record a score based on a 6-point scale. Scale labels classified points 1 and 2 as attuned, 3 and 4 as undecided, and 5 and 6 as not attuned. The students then viewed the tape for a second time, with a pause between each excerpt to allow the reasons for the judgement to be recorded.

Subjects

There were two groups of subjects. The first comprised nine senior psychotherapy clinicians: three consultant psychiatrists who held posts in psychotherapy; three social workers who held senior practitioner posts; and three research academics who had extensive clinical experience. The second sample comprised 31 students from a two-year post-graduate social work training programme, all of whom volunteered their participation. The students were divided approximately equally between the first and second year of training, and the sample included four men and 27 women with an overall mean age of 31.5 years (SD 6.3). Thirty-nine percent were aged between 26 and 30 years, and an equal percentage had between 4 and 6 years' social work experience prior to training. A further 13% had no experience, 29% had between 1 and 3 years and the rest (19.5%) had between seven and 15 years experience prior to training.

Results

Descriptive analysis of the data showed that the experts were unambiguous in judging excerpt 6 (therapist A) as attuned, and excerpts 3 and 5 (therapist B) as not attuned. The judgements of excerpts 1, 2 and 4 were more mixed, and overall there was relatively little change from the first to the second viewing. These results are summarised in Table 1.

The students' judgements of the attuned and non-attuned excerpts were in sharp contrast, with only 36% agreeing with the experts that excerpt 5 was non-attuned and only 19% agreeing that excerpt 6 was attuned. Indeed, over two-thirds (68%) were undecided as to whether excerpt 6 was attuned, whereas the experts had been unanimous in judging it to be so. These findings are summarised in Table 2.

Table 1: Ratings of excerpts given by the experts (N = 9)

		Non-Attuned		Attuned	
Therapist A	(excerpt 1)	5	(55.6%)	4	(44.4%)
	(excerpt 4)	3	(33.3%)	6	(66.7%)
	(excerpt 6)	0	(0%)	9	(100%)
Therapist B	(excerpt 3)	8	(88.9%)	1	(11.1%)
	(excerpt 5)	8	(88.9%)	1	(11.1%)
Therapist C	(excerpt 2)	3	(33.3%)	6	(66.7%)

Further inspection of the data showed that only three of the students made judgements of both attunement and non-attunement which corresponded with those made by the experts.

Table 2: Rating of the excerpts by experts and students

Students' judgement	Experts' judgement	
	Not Attuned	Attuned
Not Attuned	11(36%)	4 (13%)
Undecided	13 (42%)	21 (68%)
Attuned	7 (23%)	6 (19.3%)

Creating two groups of students whose judgements corresponded with the experts' judgements of attunement or non-attunement and comparing them with the unsuccessful students, by means of one-way analyses of variance for unequal samples, also yielded non-significant results. Further statistical analyses showed that there was also no relationship between the accuracy of the trainees' ratings and measures of age, sex, previous experience in social work or experience in counselling.

The reasons given by the experts for their judgements of the excerpts were examined by coding their responses, which yielded four primary characteristics in each of the categories of attuned and non-attuned therapists. These were:

Attuned therapist

Engrossed	Modulates response	Provides empathic input	Facilitates exploration

Non-attuned therapist

Distracted	Non-modulated response	An absence of empathic input	Stopping exploration

The first two categories seem primarily concerned with the management of feeling and the second two with the management of content. This classification of the responses of attuned and non-attuned therapists is outlined overpage.

Applying a similar analysis to the students whose judgements of attunement and non-attunement corresponded to those of the therapists gave a broadly similar classification. Sample responses were "Therapist gave full attention" for the engrossed category; "Much quicker response by client to therapist's comments, as if agreeing that therapist has described how they are feeling" for the facilitates exploration category; and "Therapist seemed unable to get a sense of client's feelings, except by asking questions directly of client" for the non-empathic input category.

The gender of patients and therapists was not systematically varied in the study – indeed, all three therapists were women, and with the exception of excerpt 5 the patients were also all female. However, excerpts 3 and 5, which had the same female therapist but different gender patients, were both judged by the experts to be unambiguously non-attuned. At least in the case of this particular therapist, there is no evidence that gender differences in the patients affected the experts' judgement of attunement.

An attuned therapist

Examples of an attuned therapist as given by the experts	Characteristics of an attuned therapist derived from data from the experts	Behaviour of therapist
"Attentive listener, still body posture etc."	Engrossed	Management of feeling
"The therapist seeks, either voluntarily or involuntarily, to match the feeling of the other through their tone of voice, facial expression, hand or body movements etc."	Modulates response	Management of feeling
"Appropriate comment. The therapist offers something in the form of an idea or a feeling in the same general area that the client is working in which the client seems able to take up, build on or pursue."	Provides empathic input	Management of content
"Client discusses/pursues what matters to them in response to something the therapist does."	Facilitates exploration	Management of content

A non-attuned therapist

Examples of a non-attuned therapist as given by the experts	Characteristics of a non-attuned therapist derived from data from the experts	Behaviour of therapist
"Therapist is nervous; not comfortable; self conscious; patient's response makes therapist agitated." "Both fidget, a lot of physical irritation; both looked bored."	Distracted	Management of feeling
"Although the therapist listens to what the patient is saying there is no response or feeling."	Non modulation of response	Management of feeling
"Uses question and answers"; "Therapist tries to cut short some of client's comments."	Non-empathic input	Management of content
"Stops exploration – uses voice tone and closing remarks such as 'that's all right then?' to shut down exploration of particular subject."	Stops exploration	Management of content

Discussion

I had expected that the students' judgements of attunement would correspond to some degree with those of the experts, though moderated perhaps by professional experience and other attributes such as personality. In fact, the judgements made by the two groups of subjects were very different, and the degree of disagreement between experts and students raised a number of interesting questions. It might be argued that the students' judgements were confounded by the introduction of an 'undecided' category into their rating scales, but even if this category is omitted from the analysis there is little consistency with the experts' ratings.

The coding of the therapists' behaviour as managing feeling or managing content helps to shed further light on the question. The characteristics of the therapists judged to be attuned by the experts convey development and progress, a regard for the importance of what the patient is saying and a willingness to interact and respond to it, whereas non-attunement suggests a lack of rhythmical interaction, boredom with what is being spoken about and a lack of synchrony between therapist and patient. The usefulness of the proposed classification is strengthened by the fact that similar categories were identified in the coding of those students whose judgements were similar to those made by the experts.

The students whose judgements did not agree with those of the experts fell into two groups: those who thought the experts' non-attuned therapist was attuned, and those who thought the experts' attuned therapist was not attuned. In both groups, the students paid insufficient attention to the sequence of interaction. For example, those who thought the non-attuned therapist was attuned were aware that the therapist asked questions but failed to notice that she did not pick up on the answers, changed the subject or looked as if she were bored with the answer. Students who thought the experts' attuned therapist was not attuned commented on the therapist's didactic approach but failed to notice that the client was not affected by it. Thus both types of failure to agree with the experts involved not looking at the sequence, but while in the one case the answer lay in observation of the therapist, in the other the answer lay in the interaction between therapist and patient.

In addition to the findings in relation to the experts and the students, the experiment suggested new ideas about the nature of the concept under investigation. I had started with the intention of finding out whether Stern's understanding of affect attunement was relevant to the interaction that occurred between two adults in a careseeking care-giving context. I wanted to see whether a therapist who mis-attuned to a client's affect would inhibit the exploratory process in much the same way as a parent who mis-attuned to their infant would stop the infant in their exploring. To illustrate the process that I am referring to in infancy I will present the observations of Stern (1985) and his team:

> In the videotape of an initial play period, a nine-month-old infant is seen crawling away from his mother and over to a new toy. While on his stomach, he grabs the toy and begins to bang and flail with it happily. His play is animated, as judged by his move-ments, breathing, and vocalisations. Mother then approaches him from behind, out of sight, and puts her hand on his bottom and gives an animated jiggle side to side. The speed and intensity of her jiggle appear to match well the intensity and rate of the infant's arm movements and vocalisations, qualifying this as an attunement. The infant's response to her attunement is – nothing! He simply continues to play without missing a beat.
>
> (Stern, 1985, p.150)

Stern then instructed the mother to carry on doing as she was doing but to 'misjudge' her baby's level of animation, to pretend that the baby was somewhat less excited than he appeared to be and to jiggle accordingly. "When the mother did jiggle somewhat more slowly and less intensely than she truly judged would make a good match, the baby quickly stopped playing and looked around at her, as if to say "What's going on?" This procedure was repeated with the same result ... When the mother was to pretend that her baby was at a higher level of joyful excitement and to jiggle accordingly ... the result was the same." (p.150).

It seems to me, from the result of the experiment being described in this chapter, that those who correctly judged the mis-attuned excerpt notice a process of affect attunement *which is then followed by a lack of affect regulation and empathy*. The careseeker is left in the state they arrived in. The attunement to affect is accurate but there is no attempt to modulate it and there it no empathic response. There is an example of this in chapter eleven.

The capacity to attune to affect as I said in chapter four is largely a pre-verbal and non-verbal facility. It happens largely out of con-sciousness and we seem to be born with it. We pick up and resonate to the other's emotional state. Affect regulation, on the other hand, seems to be associated with non-defensive caregiving. Affect de-regulation seems to be associated with insecure, dismissive or pre-occupied caregiving. Active abuse at the level of regulation and deregulation is something that we require further research on in terms of caregiver attachment status. Empathy is a metacognitive capacity which seems to involve the ability to (a) translate the infor-mation from affect attunement into an appreciation of the other's experience; (b) locate this information in the context of the other's life and times; and (c) put this understanding into words in a way that the client gets the feeling of having been understood.

Affect attunement or attunement to the affect of the other appears to be, as suggested by Stern (1985), a state of "being in the rhythm of the other" – the rhythm of their vitality affects, whether that is the affects associated with despair, joy, depression, sadness fear, anger or bore-dom. What this experiment brought home to me was that attunement on its own was not enough. Two quotations may help make my point.

> Therapist is nervous; not comfortable; self conscious; patient's response makes therapist agitated.
> Both fidget, a lot of physical irritation; both looked bored.

In these examples the therapist and patient may be seen as being 'in rhythm' with one another. However, this attunement on its own seems to maintain and possibly deepen the status quo.

There is another way in which being in rhythm seemed to be not helpful.

> Although the therapist listens to what the patient is saying there is no response or feeling evidence of attunement from the nods. She just seems to be making sure the patient is happy with the situation.
> Does not notice disjunction between verbal and non-verbal behaviour of client which may indicate he is not pursuing some-thing he may want to pursue.

In these examples what is criticised is not the lack of rhythm but rather a failure by the therapist to engage with contradictory signals. The reader will remember from chapter four the research evidence that showed that avoidant children were unable to 'read' emotional signals, and that Haft and Slade when looking at caregiver responses found that carers with dismissive AAI status found ambiguous situations provoked confusion and anxiety, e.g. when the babies signalled to the mothers that they needed to know what to do the mothers tended to become anxious at their own inability to understand their babies' persistent requests for clarification.

Along with mis-attunement to affect, e.g. "Therapist moves physically away from client; uses question and answers", this process was linked in the raters' minds with inhibiting the client's exploration of their concerns.

Stops exploration – uses voice tone and closing remarks such as 'that's all right then?' to shut down exploration of particular subject.
Therapist tries to cut short some of client's comments.

We can see, therefore, that the process of affect attunement as described by Stern is not on its own sufficient to capture the complexity of adult to adult interaction in psychotherapy. Substantial misattunement to affect may well inhibit exploration but attunement to affect on its own does not promote exploration. What is required in addition is the willingness to engage with the affect in a non-defensive exploratory way, amplifying where necessary, modulating and regulating in such a way that the person feels engaged with. What gets in the way of caregivers being able to respond in non-defensive ways when approached by careseekers is the subject of chapter twelve.

Summary

The agreement between the students' judgements and those of the experts were little better than should have occurred by chance, even amongst those students who had prior experience. One of the features of the judgements made by students which did not match those of the experts was their emphasis on the therapist's behaviour to the exclusion of the patient's response.

It seemed from the first experiment that students were influenced primarily by the behaviour of the therapist and were not paying attention to how the client was responding to the therapist and vice versa. The next step it seemed was to construct an experiment to see whether if students were pointed in the direction of interaction they would increase their chances of making a correct judgement. I also wanted to explore in more depth their perception of the interactive process between therapist and client. A second effect of the experiment is that I decided that the concept that I was investigating was more accurately described as empathic attunement.

In my next chapter I will introduce the reader to my second experiment.

CHAPTER SEVEN

Second experiment:
is empathic attunement interactive?

Introduction

As explained in the last chapter I wanted to test the hypothesis that in comparison with the students the experts had paid greater attention to the interaction between therapist and client. If so, this would provide a reason for seeing empathic attunement as goal-corrected and requiring close attention to how each responds to the other. One would also expect that if the students were given training in attending to interaction they would improve their level of agreement with the experts.

Hypothesis

My hypothesis was:

Students who are given instructions to pay attention to the interaction between therapist and client will produce more accurate ratings of empathic attunement than those who are not given such instructions.

Overview of experiment

The design of the experiment involved creating two matched groups. The groups were matched on three grounds:

   (i) Whether they had rated the material previously

   (ii) Gender

   (iii) Whether they were in year one or year two of training

Each group rated the same videoed clips of clinical practice. Both groups were given written definitions of affect attunement. One group, in addition to the definitions, was given written instructions on what to pay attention to while viewing the extracts. Each of the participants attended a de-briefing session where they were asked to respond to two questions. The de-briefing session was tape recorded.

Methodology: subjects

First and second year students on the two-year postgraduate master degree course in social work were recruited. In all, sixteen students agreed to be involved. Fourteen of these agreed to be involved in both parts of the project, the first part involving the identification of attunement in tapes of clinical practice (the subject of this chapter and which I am calling experiment 2), and the second part involving taking part in interviews on two separate days with professional actors (the subject of the next chapter, experiment 3).

Method of allocation to groups

Two groups were matched for previous exposure to the material, gender, and year of training, and allocated to one or other group on the toss of a coin.

The chart below illustrates the final allocation of students to each of the two groups.

Table 3: The experimental group and the control group

	Experimental Group	Control Group	Total
Previous exposure to test material	1	1	2
Male	2	3	5
Female	6	5	11
Year one	5	5	10
Year two	3	3	6

The extra man was allocated to the control group on the toss of a coin, and therefore the extra woman went to the Experimental Group.

Confidentiality

The project was passed by the ethics committee in the psychology department within the university. In addition each individual student signed a consent form which allowed them to withdraw from the project at any time they so chose. No student withdrew from the project. Two failed to complete as they were called for job interviews on the last day of the main experiment.

Materials and practical arrangements

I used the 1.5-minute extracts from the clinical material that I had used in the first experiment. I chose three out of the six original extracts on the basis that one clip was rated unambiguously as attuned by the experts; the other clip was rated not-attuned by 80% of the experts, and the third clip got a mixed rating – half thought it was attuned and the other half thought it was not-attuned. I myself considered that this clip demonstrated the process of 'tuning in'. In this experiment, therefore, clip one demonstrated tuning in; clip two demonstrated non-attuned interaction; clip three demonstrated attuned interaction.

Procedure

1. As in the first experiment, the excerpts were shown twice. On the second viewing the tape was stopped after each clip to allow sufficient time for the participants to make their ratings.
2. All participants attended a debriefing session after the rating session, where they were shown the extracts again and asked to give their reasons for their judgement. This session was tape-recorded and later transcribed.
3. All were asked to maintain confidentiality about the process until the work of all experiments was completed, which would take a further month.

Rating instruments

Two forms were used, one for the Experimental Group and one for the Control Group.

The form for the Control Group had the two working definitions of attunement that I had used in the experiment described in chapter two.

The definitions being used for the purpose of rating the excerpts are as follows:

1. Attunement is a way of communicating to the other that one has recognised the affect that they are experiencing

2. Attunement conveys to the other that one has a feeling sense inside of what it feels like to be them right now

The form for the Experimental Group, in addition to the above definitions, also had the following typed instructions:

In making your decision, it may be useful to keep in mind the following indicators:

(i) The therapist conveys a regard for the importance of what the client is saying along with a willingness to interact and respond to it

(ii) The therapist appears to be engrossed in what the other is saying, they modulate their response in relation to it, they provide input and they facilitate exploration

The mechanics of the debriefing

The students were seen on their own and told the discussion was going to be taped. The interviewer checked the form to make sure that the student agreed with what they had entered and that there was no mistake about the way they had entered their rating. They then watched each excerpt on a video monitor. As will be seen later on, some students wanted to change their rating following the second (actually third) viewing.

Each student was asked two questions:

(a) Why did you rate the therapist as attuned or not attuned?

(b) What did you see that made you decide the therapist was attuned or not attuned?

There were sixteen debriefings in all. All the sessions were audio taped and subsequently transcribed either by a professional typist or by myself. In all cases I listened to the tapes myself while reading the typescript in order to make notations relating to pitch, emphasis, timing and tone of voice, and to get a feel for the way the student was approaching the task. I also checked for accuracy of the transcript.

My experience of the debriefing sessions

I found doing the de-briefing sessions with the students immensely interesting. First of all, the physical set up of the small interviewing room, the monitor and the very focused task gave a sense of seriousness to the endeavour. The students were aware that I did not have the answers to what I was exploring, that I was genuinely trying to understand the process of affect attunement between therapist and client, and wanted their observations and views about the clips that we had just shown. Having the monitor within inches of the student and myself and viewing the excerpt through together provided a sense of intimacy and concentration.

Managing and collating the qualitative material

By definition I had four categories:

1) those who correctly identified the non-attuned excerpt;
2) those who incorrectly identified the non-attuned excerpt;
3) those who correctly identified the attuned excerpt;
4) those who incorrectly identified the attuned excerpt.

The three key questions I set out to answer from the transcriptions were:

1. Were the students paying attention to indicators from the therapist that they were tracking and responding to the communication of affect from the client?
2. Were the students paying attention to the affect signals (non-verbal) as well as the verbal signals being communicated to the client by the therapist, and were they tracking how the client responded?

3. Were the students paying attention to whether or not the client explored the situation of concern to them?

Statistical analysis

The chart below sets out the numbers of students who correctly identified the excerpts

Correct Identification of Attuned and Non-Attuned Excerpts by the Experimental Group and the Control Group

Student Identification

		Attuned	Not attuned	Total	No of students who correctly identified both excerpts	% of correct identifi-cations
Experimental Group	Attuned	6	2*	8	5 62.5%	75%
	Not attuned	2*	6	8		
Control Group	Attuned	4	4	8	2 25%	44%
	Not attuned	5	3	8		

The above chart indicates that the Experimental Group did better at correctly identifying both the attuned and non-attuned excerpts than the Control Group, scoring twelve 'hits' and four 'misses' as against seven 'hits' and nine 'misses'.

I gave each student a score based on whether they had 2, 1, or O 'hits'. I used the Mann Whitney test to examine the significance of the difference between them. Statistical analysis revealed that the two groups were statistically different; on a two-tailed test: $p = .041$, slightly greater if allowance is made for ties, and falling to $p<.01$ if the inattentive student is dropped. (One of the students in the experimental group had been observed on the day of the experiment not to have read the instructions regarding the importance of paying attention to the interaction.)

The experiment supported the hypothesis that students who were given instructions to pay attention to the interaction between the therapist and client would be significantly better at identifying empathic attunement and non-attunement than those who were judging the interaction using only loose definitions of the concept. This was a good result, confirming that my concept of empathic attunement was goal-corrected, i.e. responsive and interactive, and could only be judged correctly by focusing on the interaction between therapist and client.

I expected that the qualitative analysis should support this finding and in addition I hoped that the debriefing sessions would provide me with a more in-depth understanding of the students' perception of the interaction between the therapist and client.

Qualitative analysis

I was interested to see whether the students who made correct identifications of the episodes associated empathic attunement with a highly interactive and responsive process which facilitated the client's exploration.

To observe this process correctly requires that the student pay attention to the behaviour of the therapist and the client in terms of the verbal and non-verbal signals they are giving each other, how they each respond to these signals, and in particular whether the client explores or whether their exploration is stopped or inhibited.

What I found was that while both groups paid attention to verbal and non-verbal interaction, they clearly had quite different views of what they saw and heard and came to different interpretations and conclusions. The question therefore was, 'what distinguished one group from the other?' In other words, what enabled one group to interpret the verbal and non-verbal behaviours 'correctly' and the others to get these behaviours 'wrong'?

While both groups observed the process of interaction taking place between the therapist and client at verbal and non-verbal levels, the group who got the episode 'wrong' did not seem to pay attention to the goal of the interaction – to the outcome, i.e. whether the client succeeded in exploring their concerns or whether they were inhibited from so doing by the behaviour of the therapist. This was true for both episodes – the attuned and non-attuned. In both cases those who got the episode 'wrong' paid no attention to whether or not the client explored, or if they did, as in the case of one of the 13 students concerned, they overrode this observation based on their view of the therapist behaviour.

The 'attuned' episode that I used for this experiment consisted of a process of interaction between therapist and client that led to the client exploring their concerns. The 'non-attuned' episode used for the experiment contained a process of interaction which resulted in the client not exploring their concerns.

The following charts give details of the student's observation which illustrate these points. I will present the comments on the attuned excerpt first and then move on to the non-attuned excerpt.

Episode 1: Attunement

This episode takes place between a female therapist and a female client. The episode starts at the point where they have been exploring why the client responds to the therapist as if she (the client) had to conform in some way. The client says there is something that gets in the way between her and the therapist. The therapist suggests that there is particular kind of relationship with herself that probably started in her relationship with somebody else. The therapist then asks if this makes sense. The client responds and takes up the idea. There is a slight pause which is then followed by the therapist putting into words what she thinks the client is experiencing. After another slight pause, the therapist asks another question in a very open-ended way and in a tone that suggests she is in touch with something quite tender that is going on inside the client. There is a pause. The therapist is watching the client closely and murmurs something that indicates she is seeing something happening in the client's mind (maybe some thought or something). The therapist says "What?" The client picks this up and goes on to indicate that she is indeed in conflict – doesn't know which way to go:

It looks as though ... again ... I can't tell if I am being pulled to someplace else ...

The therapist intervenes and says "Go for it". The client carries on thus:

that's big. Someplace else that's big that denies me. A big part of me that denies me. Or a part of me that denies me in a big way. (pause) It is the part that makes it *inconceivable* to tell the truth (pause) to confront people that matter to me in a meaningful way. To tell them what's really going on with me.

Ten students correctly identified this excerpt as attuned, six students rated this excerpt as not attuned.

As noted above, I went through the transcripts to see whether the groups could be distinguished on whether they were each paying attention to both verbal and non-verbal behaviours. The chart below shows that both groups paid attention to both aspects of communication. It also shows the strikingly different ways in which the students interpreted what they saw and heard. Finally, the chart illustrates that one group paid attention to the goal of the interaction, i.e. exploration, and that the other group did not.

Chart 1

Attuned extract	Correct identification	Incorrect identification
Non-verbal behaviour	It was the body language of being forward and listening. She wasn't frightened of the client. She wasn't frightened of what the client might say – she seemed to be quite actively in the client's space – student J	She was leaning forwards, so again, quite invasive – student S
	But again there was that focus, she [the therapist] was constantly watching her eyes [the client's] and their heads were always straight-forward together ... she was leaning slightly forward which indicated to me that she was concentrating on the client. She allowed a lot of space for her to speak – student A	... the client didn't disagree she was nodding in agreement and ... the therapist was nodding as well while the client was talking – student U

As one can see from the chart, the students who make incorrect identifications pay attention to the interaction but form a judgement of the interaction based on their view of the behaviour of the therapist rather than on the outcome of the interaction for the client – whether the interaction facilitated or inhibited the goal of exploration.

Attuned extract	Correct identification	Incorrect identification
Verbal behaviour	She [the therapist] would interject but it seemed appropriate. It didn't seem to be to divert her from the way things were going ... or anything which would deflect her from exploring what she was feeling – student A	The woman was saying a lot of things and she sounded very confused and lost about being in a big space and the therapist really didn't say anything about it ... didn't make it easy I suppose – student D
	... and then there was a really nice pause when there was a period of time when the counsellor said 'Go for it' ... I felt at that stage the counsellor was sort of demonstrating some sort of listening and empathy – student P	There didn't seem to be that much empathy for what was going on from the counsellor – student R
	... she [the therapist] was still trying to clarify a lot – student B	she [the therapist] didn't communicate with the client in a way that showed understanding ... she had an interpretation she came up with when the client hadn't said anything – student U

The group who incorrectly identified the excerpt saw the therapist as intrusive and unempathic:

She was leaning forwards, so again, quite invasive – student S.

There didn't seem to be that much empathy for what was going on from the counsellor – student R

And they saw the client as compliant:

She [the therapist] had given her an interpretation and the client was trying to fit into it – student U.

Attuned Extract	Correct identification	Incorrect identification
Attention to exploration	The woman being interviewed sat back and said what she really felt and how she felt it was difficult to communicate with others. At that point their body language was symmetrical and they were both in the same position and so that was really striking – student L	She [the therapist] had given her an interpretation and the client was trying to fit into it – Student U
	The client expanded but also the therapist was offering an explanation … in quite a simplistic straightforward way … [and] the client nodded in agreement and the way she [the client] opened it up was a brave thing to say, admitting that she wasn't honest [with people] … she [the therapist] was coaxing by saying 'Go for it' and I thought that was nice and really very encouraging – student X [female]	
	I saw the client actually really look like she was reflecting on something, that there was something that was actually giving her a spot of bother to mull over and then the way the client went on from that … she got into a lot of material, that did seem quite important for her – student C	

In my view the students' lack of attention to the goal of the interaction meant that they failed to notice the detail of what the client was saying and the way that she said it:

> The woman being interviewed sat back and said what she really felt and how she felt it was difficult to communicate with others – student L

> it was a brave thing to say, admitting that she wasn't honest [with people] – student X

Apart from the fact that she went on to explore, the way that she explored had the air of being new or novel – a new understanding of her behaviour. In my view, in addition to being able to pick up that the client actually did go on to explore, there was another element which the students could have commented on but did not in fact do so. I refer to a sense of liveliness, a fluency of speech associated with the exploration. Building on the work of Stern (1985) with infants I would call this mode of expression in adult – i.e. the rhythm, pace, timing – *the vitality affects*. The reader will see how I use this idea in adult-to-adult interaction when I describe the patterns of successful and unsuccessful careseeking/caregiving in chapter eleven.

I think the vitality affects are possibly *the* cue to identifying the presence or absence of exploratory activity. I was not aware of this at the point of designing this research but it has become clearer to me as I have reflected on the results of these experiments and I will take this up later in the book. I will now turn to the 'non-attuned' excerpt and continue my analysis and exploration. As in the 'attuned' excerpt, the distinguishing factor between the students rested on whether they took account of the goal of the interaction, and whether they observed what happened in relation to that. In other words, whether they observed and commented on whether or not the client pursued their exploration.

Episode 2: Non-Attunement

This episode takes place between a female therapist and a male client. The episode starts with the client referring to a problem he has with his back, but he then immediately moves away from further discussion of it and introduces the fact that he is now doing more of what he wants, spending his time the way he wants to and as he has been advised (who has given this advice is not clear but one assumes he was given the advice by the therapist in a previous session). The therapist ignores the problem with his back and asks him questions about what he is doing with his time and whether he is enjoying himself.

He goes on to say that his wife is not too happy with him taking time for himself, but dismisses that as 'her problem'. He doesn't sound very convinced that he believes this. The therapist changes the subject and asks him if his wife has seen X (the implication is a medical consultant). The client answers the question about the appointment. He ends this discussion with the comment that even though he has tried to get her to chase up the appointment she hasn't done so and 'she won't change'. This is said in a tone which could be interpreted as a mixture of exasperation and despair. The therapist cuts across what he is saying and asks him how all this is for him. When he says he is 'all right' about it she says:

> T: But you are feeling all right? I mean that was the main thing I wanted to check out?
> C: Right. I am. Yeah. That feels alright for me now

Nine students correctly identified the therapist in this excerpt as not attuned. Seven students rated her as attuned.

The chart shows the way each group saw and interpreted the verbal and non-verbal interaction and whether or not they paid attention to exploration.

Chart 2

Non-attuned extract	Correct identification	Incorrect identification
Non-verbal behaviour	... and I think she looked really bored – student B	She showed an interest in him and was listening to him though she did fidget a lot – student K
	She was sitting quite back from him and she seemed to sort of smile at the inappropriate times or looked up at the ceiling. She didn't really look that interested in what he was saying – student D	The client seemed very relaxed ... there was a mirroring of the body language between both people – student P
	She didn't have much eye contact or watch actually face to face. She looked down a lot sort of thinking on her feet, not really listening to what he was saying – student A	The tone or the atmosphere was very relaxed and they seemed to be talking in the same tone of voice and she was very much sitting back and letting him have his way – student L

As one can see from the chart both groups observe and interpret non-verbal behaviour.

... and I think she looked really bored – student B
(Correct identification)

She showed an interest in him and was listening to him – student K
(Incorrect identification)

Clearly both groups of students are interpreting what they see: one is putting a negative gloss on what they are seeing and the other is putting a positive gloss on it.

Non-attuned extract	Correct identification	Incorrect identification
Verbal behaviour	When she asked him how he felt and how it made him feel, she sort of asked it then saying 'that's enough', she was putting her hand up as if to say 'that's enough'. It was inappropriate, if she wanted to explore with him what he was feeling before he got a chance to she was cutting him off – student A	She actually checked with him that the decisions he had made were the ones he felt happy with and that they were the decisions he wanted to make – student R
	... and there were real issues around his wife ... but she didn't pick up on them – student B	She gave him time to think and at the end when he said he was feeling better and she made it clear to him that this is what she wanted to hear and re-affirmed to him that that was a good feeling to have and that she was glad. – student S.
	First of all you heard about the pain in his back and she said, 'Oh well, that's a different problem' – student D	She was very much sitting back and letting him have his say but also asking questions and probing more but doing it in a way I really felt she really understood this person... – student L

When it gets to noticing the verbal behaviour, however, differences begin to show up between the two groups. This time it is not to do with having a different *interpretation* of what they hear, it is more to do with the fact that one group apparently does not hear the therapist cut the client off in mid flow:

> ... when she asked him how he felt and how it made him feel, she sort of asked it then saying 'that's enough', she was putting her hand up as if to say 'that's enough' – student A

Non-attuned extract	Correct identification	Incorrect identification
Attention to exploration	When she asked if he was feeling alright about it [his wife's attitude to him], he said he was alright. But then she said 'Right, fine' and cut him off and didn't carry on with the feelings; she just went, 'oh alright' – student D	
	I saw the counsellor actually not responding to some of the things that the client was saying. The client said there was, he actually said 'problem' with his wife, but the counsellor didn't respond. I saw her not responding in a way that got him to explore his problem.	

The group which rated the excerpt correctly are highly tuned in to whether or not the client explores, and to the behaviours of the therapist that inhibit him doing this. The other group makes no comment on this either way other than to imply that the therapist was supportive, non-intrusive and that this was a good thing to be or do:

She actually checked with him that the decisions he had made were the ones he felt happy with and that they were the decisions he wanted to make – student R

Discussion

From my examination of the transcripts of both groups of students I conclude the following:

1. Both groups pay attention to verbal and non-verbal interaction and in general seem to see and comment on the same behaviour.

2. Their interpretation of what they see differs radically from each other.

3. Group A seems to judge the interaction between therapist and client as empathically attuned based on the outcome for the client.

4. No member of Group B comments on the outcome for the client in terms of whether they explore or are inhibited from exploring. They seem to come to a premature conclusion about the episode based on their interpretation of the therapist's behaviour.

The results of the qualitative analysis therefore point to the importance of judging the interaction in terms of the exploratory outcome. One cannot judge the extract based on attention to verbal and non-verbal behaviours alone, however much attention one is paying to the process of feedback at these two levels. The feedback that is important in this exercise is whether the client explores or is stopped or inhibited from exploring.

It is interesting to speculate about why some students seemed able to 'see' this – see the importance of the exploratory process – and why others did not. When I examined the comments of the group who failed to identify the excerpts correctly, what stood out was that they had formed a view about the therapist. There were two therapists involved, but nevertheless the attitude formed seemed to centre on two dimensions of therapist behaviour: whether the therapist was seen as intrusive or respectful of privacy; and whether the therapist responded or failed to respond to expressions of distress.
Respect for privacy:

She actually checked with him that the decisions he had made were the ones he felt happy with and that they were the decisions he wanted to make – student R

Intrusiveness:

> ... she [the therapist] didn't communicate with the client in a way that showed understanding ... she had an interpretation she came up with when the client hadn't said anything – student U.

On the other hand, the students who got the excerpts 'right' had quite a different understanding of intrusiveness and distress. For them, the therapist failed to pick up distress in the male client when he spoke about his physical pain and his emotional pain in relation to his wife. They did not see the therapist's behaviour as conveying respect; for them it would have been more appropriate for her to show that she had heard what the client had said and was willing to engage with it:

> She was sitting quite back from him and she seemed to sort of smile at the inappropriate times or looked up at the ceiling. She didn't really look that interested in what he was saying – student D

> ... when she asked him how he felt and how it made him feel, she sort of asked it then saying 'that's enough', she was putting her hand up as if to say 'that's enough'. It was inappropriate, if she wanted to explore with him what he was feeling before he got a chance to she was cutting him off – student A

Again with the 'Attuned' excerpt, the group that failed to rate it correctly seemed to think that the therapist left the woman floundering when she should have moved in to help her:

> The woman was saying a lot of things and she sounded very confused and lost about being in a big space and the therapist really didn't say anything about it ... didn't make it easy I suppose – student D

This student seems to focus on whether the therapist responds to distress or not.

The group that misses what is going on fails to understand the meaning of the emotion being signalled by the client. This group seems to think that the client should be protected from whatever it is they are experiencing – whether that be distress about oneself (own health), someone close, or distress arising from some thought or memory triggered by the work with the therapist.

From an attachment perspective one could see this as a failure to distinguish between two types of careseeking. On the one hand there is careseeking which is a signal for care and protection, and on the other there is careseeking which is a signal for support for exploration having been temporarily thrown off balance, as it were. It is easy to see that if as a caregiver one muddled these two signals up and responded to careseeking as if a call for protection, when in fact it was a call for support to carry on exploring, one might well contribute to shutting down the exploratory process. This in turn could give rise to frustration, irritation or despair in the careseeker.

Adult caregivers who intrude in unwanted ways on infants' and young children's exploratory process create defensiveness and upset in the infants and children, as we saw in earlier chapters. It seems possible that the students who misjudged what they saw taking place between the therapists and the clients may well have been sensitised to these kinds of intrusions based on their past experience. They may well have unconsciously responded to perceived intrusiveness in the caregiver and not waited to judge the sequence as a whole from the point of view of the client that they were observing (see Bartholomew, 1990). This is speculative and would need to be tested. In the meantime it provides a possible reason for why one group failed to grasp what was taking place.

Summary

I designed this experiment in order to test the hypothesis that empathic attunement was connected with interaction and could only be judged by paying attention to the responsiveness of both parties to each other, but particularly the responsiveness of the therapist to the client.

The statistical analysis provided evidence that students who were given instructions to pay attention to interaction did significantly better at judging the episodes than those who were not given such instructions. This is an important finding. The qualitative analysis suggested that in addition to paying attention to the interaction, one needed to look at whether the goals of the interaction had been met as far as the client was concerned. In other words, one had to pay attention to whether the client explored or was prevented from so doing by the therapist. The therapist could prevent the client exploring in various ways, such as failing to pick up hesitation in the client, cutting across them with something else, or deliberately stopping them in their tracks.

Finally I speculated as to why some students miss the exploratory process in action as it takes pace in front of them. I suggested that for some students, the behaviour of the therapist may resonate with early experience of caregiving, which may well have interfered with their own exploratory process. My suggestion is that when they saw what they considered to be intrusive and non-supportive behaviour in the therapists they were observing, they came to a premature judgement of what the therapist was doing and lost sight of the exploratory process for the client.

As a result of this analysis I put forward the idea of at least two different types of careseeking: one that is a request for care and protection, and the other that is a request for support to carry on exploring. I suggested that it was important that caregivers should be able to distinguish between these two forms. The issue that is being presented to a caregiver is embedded in the vitality affect accompanying the communication; e.g. when the male client above mentions he is not sure his wife likes his new-found concern with his own interests, the tone in his voice is flat – there is little if any vitality evident in his presentation of himself. The students who were aware that the therapist was not responding seemed to pick this up, but did not comment directly on affect; instead they used the words 'not interested' or 'bored', which captures vitality affects but somehow misses the significance of what is being observed. I return to this in chapter eleven.

In conclusion I would suggest that correct identification of empathic attunement requires attention to the process of interaction taking place between therapist and client at verbal and non-verbal levels, in particular tracking whether the goal of the interaction has been achieved – whether the exploratory system is activated or whether the client goes into self-defence – and the clearest way to judge this is by tracking the vitality affects.

The concept of goal-corrected empathic attunement is located within an understanding of the dynamics of attachment, which suggests that when caregiving is effective exploration will be activated, and that when caregiving is ineffective exploration will be inhibited.

In the next experiment I set out to see whether:

(i) empathic attunement could be reliably rated;

(ii) whether training would improve 'caregivers' performance;

(iii) whether caregiver attachment style was associated with empathic attunement.

Chapter eight sets out the design of this experiment.

Third experiment: an experiment designed to test whether secure attachment style correlates with empathic attunement and whether empathic attunement can be improved with training

Introduction

In the last chapter I presented the results of an experiment designed to see whether empathic attunement was an interactive process and did this by establishing whether students could improve their capacity to rate empathic attunement if given instructions to pay attention to interaction and responsiveness. I found that this was the case but that in addition the students who made correct judgements about the clinical excerpts had a different idea about how therapists should respond to client affect, and also about the exploratory process itself. Associated with these distinctive attitudes was the fact that the group which misjudged the excerpts perceived the therapist as intrusive. Given that the Grossmanns (1988, 1991, and discussed fully in chapter four) amongst others identified that secure caregivers responded more appropriately and actively in free-play situations with their toddlers than did their insecure counterparts (the insecure group intruded on their offspring in a way that stopped or inhibited play, or else failed to engage when the infant was flagging so that the infant lost interest and became distressed), I decided to see whether empathic attunement, which is an interactive process and seems to involve relating to and engaging with the vitality affects of the careseeker, correlated with secure attachment style of the therapist.

I also wanted to see whether empathic attunement was something that could be taught or whether it was simply something that was instinctive and innate. My sense was that, given that the process I was interested in was *empathic attunement* not just affect attunement, it was likely to be more permeable to training than if it were an instinctive process that happened completely out of consciousness. In order to test whether this was so I had first to develop a measure of empathic attunement. Overall I wanted to achieve:

a) a reliable way of testing empathic attunement in situations arousing the dynamics of attachment;

b) a measure of attachment style;

c) a training programme designed to improve empathic attunement.

In this chapter I will address the design of the study and the rationale behind the design, the training programme, and the adult attachment, style questionnaires that the students completed.

Overview

This experiment involved:

(i) creating two groups, one group received training, the other did not;

(ii) measuring individuals from both groups for attachment style;

(iii) measuring empathic attunement for each individual at two points in time;

(v) providing training input between time one and time two;

This enabled the development of:

a) an account of the relationship between attachment style and empathic attunement;

b) a testing of the objective measure of empathic attunement against the two subjective measures;

c) a test of the effect of training.

Table 4: The design and rationale for the study

Time 1	Training		Time 2
Interaction experiment	Training in interaction	Theoretical training	Interaction experiment & attachment scales
12 June	19 June	24 June	26 June

For reasons of time, ethics and experimental control, I decided to design the study with the participation of students and actors rather than clients and therapists. A method had to be devised which would produce comparable material which could provide ratings from a variety of perceptions and experiences, and be economical to operate. There is no doubt in my mind that this work needs to be tested in the real world of practice and I will return to this at the end of the book.

I had a small budget generated from my own consultancy work. I had access to trainee students on a postgraduate social work course. I had access to the audio visual department in the university, and had a close and long standing relationship with the technicians and cameramen who were used to either filming students on the skills training course that I was responsible for designing and operating, or filming my own work with couples and families in clinics in the city. I had access to my colleagues offices – they were willing to let me use them for two days in the middle of the marking period in the summer term. I had many years' experience and skill in designing and working with role plays, and understood the power of role play, the effect of role play on the participants, the requirements to debrief, and both the strengths and limitations of the medium.

Reasons for employing professional actors

I decided to engage professional actors for two days work.

I wished to carry out a tightly controlled experiment in which as far as possible all the participants were exposed to similar experiences and in which experimental variables were introduced in a controlled way. This would allow me to compare results.

Hiring actors would have the following advantages:

(i) it would allow me to provide consistent experiences for the students so that they could be rated against each other;

(ii) actors would have the training to survive re-enacting the same role play all day and have the training to get out of role at end of the day;

(iii) actors would take the task seriously as a job to be done and accord it the gravity it required – this would allow me to get as near the real thing of live practice as possible;

(iv) using actors meant I could control for gender by asking for two male and two female actors;

(v) the actors had no involvement in the overall professional assessment process that the students were going through to qualify as social workers. I needed objective ratings of the students' performance but it was important in terms of their participation in this experiment that they could feel absolutely clear that their professional qualification was not put in jeopardy by the results.

Hiring the actors

This turned out to be surprisingly easy. It simply required a phone call to an agency that dealt with such things; I explained what I wanted and why, and the manager struck an agreement with me over rates of pay, dates and times.

Reasons for deciding the number of actors and students to be involved

I had £2000, 3 cameramen, four video cameras and recorders, two days and four rooms. I wanted to work with the classic responses to threat of loss, or actual loss, which are fear, anger sadness and despair. Given the time, space and money available and the particular emotions that I wanted to work with, I decided to employ 4 actors and advertise for 14 students. This would allow me to construct four scenarios around the themes of fear, anger, sadness and despair and allocate one theme each to the four actors for day 1 and the same again for day 2. I worked out a time schedule that started with a briefing meeting with the actors and cameramen at 9 a.m. followed by a briefing meeting with the students at 9.30 and a start time of 10 a.m. I worked out a schedule of interviews lasting 10 minutes each with a ten-minute break in between to give the students time to be briefed for the next interview, and the actors time to adjust, prepare for the next interview and to rate the interview that had just happened; this gave enough time to fit 8 interviews into the morning and six interviews into the afternoon. As a result of these calculations it was clear that I could cope with four actors, each being interviewed by 14 students. Each interview would be videoed live (in three cases by a cameraman present in the room), with sufficient time for the actors to rate the students and the students to rate themselves and also for the students to prepare themselves for each interview in turn.

Constructing the scenarios

I constructed the scenarios around the theme of loss. The theory I am using for understanding careseeking/caregiving relationships is attachment theory, so therefore loss is an appropriate theme. It also raises strong emotions. It should, therefore, allow me to test the students' ability to attune to affect, test the effect of training and test the effect of individual attachment status.

I constructed four scenarios around the following themes:

   a) threatened loss of relationship through organic brain dysfunction;

   b) loss of relationship through desertion;

   c) loss of relationship through medical negligence;

   d) loss of life through terminal illness.

The briefs are attached as appendix 1.

In the interest of creating a sense of authenticity and deepening the level of involvement for the participants, I decided to keep the scenarios the same over the two weeks but to move them on in time. This meant, for example, that on day one, actor one would convey feelings of sadness in response to hearing her mother had just been diagnosed as having Alzheimer's; on day two, she would be discussing her feelings of anger with the services her mother was receiving from the local authority. Organising the role plays in this fashion meant that the actors and students had a) actually met in real life before (on day 1), and b) had actually met to discuss this same issue once before at a previous point in time.

*Creating a control group and an experimental group
for the purposes of training*

Fourteen students elected to take part in this experiment. I needed to split this group into two so that I could have a trained and untrained group. As already mentioned this group had a complex composition, consisting as it did of students who had taken part the previous year in the identification exercise, and students who had either received or not received instructions in relation to identifying attuned and non-attuned audio-visual clips from psychotherapy sessions. I organised the total set of students into two matched pairs so that one set could be given real training and the other dummy training.

The process of creating matched pairs

I created two matched pairs by taking account of the following four factors: number of correct identifications of clinical material during experiment two; whether or not they had been given indicators in that experiment; whether they had been involved in rating the material the previous year; and whether they were in their first or final year of training. Allocation was achieved through tossing a coin. If it came down 'heads' the first member of the pair went into group one and her partner went into group two. If it came down 'tails' the opposite occurred.

*Creating a measure of caregiving: the careseeker's
and the caregiver's perspective*

Having devised the experiment I wished to get a subjective evaluation of the interviews from the perspective of both the actor and the student – the careseeker and the caregiver.

The measure for both the actor (careseeker) and the student (caregiver) each consisted of 6, six-point scales (see appendices 2 and 3). The careseekers measure asked for a rating from one to six on such aspects as feeling understood, being able to say what one wanted, feeling the caregiver was interested and attentive, whether they offered a new perspective or said anything helpful. The caregivers' measures asked for ratings of similar factors: did they think they conveyed that they understood what the client was feeling or meaning; did they think they were attentive and interested, enabled the client to say what they wanted, offered anything new or said anything helpful? The scale was from 'very much' to 'not at all'.

Briefing for students

The following is the brief used with the students:

> We have commissioned four actors to role play four different situations which all of you will encounter during the course of the day. You will see from your time sheet the times that you are interviewing and the room you will be using. We will give you a background brief of the situation before each interview.
>
> Your brief is to set the interview for 10 minutes and then to find out what the client is feeling about things at the moment, responding as appropriate in ways that might be helpful.
>
> 1. There will be 5 minutes 'travel time' between role plays. During this time we will give you the brief the actors are working to. Read it to orient yourself to the context, e.g. Relate Counselling Service, Social Services, whatever.
> 2. The role plays will take place in the offices along the staff corridor.
> 3. After each role play, my colleague or I will give you the actor's notes for the next interview – please find us, we will be on the corridor.
> 4. At the **end** of the sequence of four role plays, please pick up four forms from my colleague or myself. These forms relate to your own appraisal of the role-play sessions. We want you to fill in these for each role play you have done and return them to us before leaving the building today.
>
> Again please do not discuss with each other or with other students what you are doing, whether they are taking part in the research or not.
>
> If you do not understand anything, seek out my colleague or myself.

Briefing for the actors

I met with the actors and cameramen together, 15 minutes before the students were timed to arrive, and explained the structure and purpose of the day. I gave a brief account of empathic attunement and its role in exploration. I explained the link as I saw it between empathic attunement and attachment, and explained the scenarios chosen for the day and the fact that each one depicted a particular emotional response to abandonment or threat of abandonment. I gave out the measurement scales and asked if they would fill them in after each interview. I also explained that the experiment was separate from the students' training and that the actors' evaluation would not be used in any way that would affect the students' qualification.

Briefing for cameramen

The cameramen were present during the briefing of the actors so that they would know as much as possible about the design and purpose of the day. In addition they were asked to set up the cameras so that I would get a view of both the student and actor, as I wanted to be able to study the verbal and non-verbal interaction between them. I also asked them to label the video cassettes with the name of student, date and time of interview. Due to demands on technical staff I was only able to have three cameramen on day one. This meant that one of the actors controlled the camera in his room. I will discuss the implication of this later in the book. The reasons behind having the cameramen present were that the actor and student could be free to concentrate on what they were doing and not have to think about time or output in terms of video and sound quality. There are of course drawbacks to having the cameramen actually in the room, but these are not serious problems for the students involved in this project in that, through other parts of their training, they had already become used to having their interviewing filmed, often by these same camaramen. Having the cameraman keep time was an enormous advantage to the project; the interviews were short, and very intense and the fact that the actors and students could become wholly engrossed in what they were doing came through in the quality of the tapes, and was distinctly different for the last few minutes of each session for the actor who was keeping time and doubling as cameraman.

Observations of the day

I have been describing the thinking behind the organisation and structure of the day. Equally important, of course, and to some extent unanticipated, was what *actually happened* on the day itself.

I had asked the same colleague who had helped me with the administration of the identification experiment to help with the organisation and administration of both interviewing days.

In addition to the four rooms commandeered for the interviews, we also had a large room available to us as our headquarters, as it were. In this room, I briefed the actors, students and cameramen. In addition this room became base for all the students throughout the day and for my colleague and myself.

At 9.30 a.m. the actors and cameramen had left to prepare themselves and the rooms. At the same time the first four students appeared who were scheduled to begin interviewing at 10 a.m. I gave them written material to help orient them to their work (see appendix 4)

At 10 a.m. they left the room to do the interviews and the project was underway. My colleague and I waited. I had never used professional actors before and at this point had simply to wait and see what was going to happen. At 10.10 the four students reappeared. They were absolutely quiet, one looked ashen, they all had the appearance of having gone through a powerful experience. Naturally, I could not say anything to them at this point and certainly not for at least a month until the whole experiment was over. I was very worried about what on earth I had exposed them to. As important as my emotional and intellectual responses to the students' presentation was the *behaviour* of my colleague and myself in relation to them. We had a job to do which was to give them the brief for the next interview and remind them that they had their next interview at 10.20. This we did. But we also had the impulse, which we acted on, to offer to get coffee, biscuits, chocolate, milk, water, whatever, and one of us dashed downstairs to the canteen to get supplies.

The four students duly went off for their next interview at 10.20; hardly a word had been spoken between them or between them and us other than us offering food and drink during the 10 minute interval. At 10.30 they emerged again. Again they were solemn, silent, white-faced; this time one or two talked briefly and the effect on my colleague and me was as before. We offered drink, food, anything. We gave them their brief for their next interview and they went off at 10.40, reappearing at 10.50. By this stage I was actually seriously worried about what was going on behind the interviewing doors. I had worked with students for nearly 25 years in one form or another and I had never seen them so subdued and serious.

At this stage we were three quarters of the way through. The new cohort of four students who would begin their set of interviews at 11.20 had arrived and needed briefing. By 11.10 our first group had finished their fourth interview and I was relieved to hear one say and the others agree, "My god, that was good". That was all that was said and they obeyed the brief not to discuss the process while it was still underway. My colleague and I took turns between briefing the new group of four and distributing rating forms to the four just finished so they could rate their performance over the four interviews. We proceeded like this for the remainder of the day. By lunch time my colleague and I were conceptualising our briefing room as a secure base. The students came there to be briefed, they left from there to do their interviews, they returned to food and drinks from us, got their next brief and set forth to do their next interview. It took on a rhythm of its own; we were in no doubt that having the same room available and the fact that we were there throughout the day was enormously important to the smooth running of the enterprise, and to the students' morale and sense that what they were doing was important.

With hindsight, I would certainly structure such an experiment along the very same lines and insist, as this time, that they did not discuss with each other what was going on. An unexpected outcome of this instruction was that it meant that they did not discharge their energy, they kept focused on the task and they contained the experience. It also created the conditions for my concern. I was not used to seeing students contain their experience – hence the source of some of my panic as described earlier. It was also true, as I saw later on when I watched the video recordings of the interviews, that the actors had gone straight into role and created very convincing scenarios.

At the end of that first day, I had a video record of 56 interviews, each lasting ten minutes; ratings on all fourteen students from four actors; and the students' ratings of their own performance.[8]

---

8 I used a video camera which had both people in view in three-quarter profile. It would have been better for the purposes of the research if I had used the system devised used by Beebe and Lachman (1988) to film mothers and babies. This gave access to the actual image that was available to the participants. It would have allowed a view of the eye contact between the two parties which was not available on the system I used.

Training

I devised a training programme for each group prior to the next session with the actors which was scheduled for two weeks hence. As mentioned earlier I had split them into two groups with a view to giving one group training in relation to interaction, which I hoped would improve their performance at time two, and the other group a training at the level of theory, which I thought unlikely to impact significantly on their performance. I am not going to describe the training programme in any great detail in order to save space for later in the book to provide examples of effective and ineffective caregiving. Suffice to say that the training for the experimental group was tailored to each individual's interactive style and based on an analysis of their first interview. (For a full account of the training programme see McCluskey 2001.) The training for the control group was based on reading, seminar and video related to the work of Alice Miller and John Bowlby's 1988 paper on memory and dissociation, entitled 'On knowing what you are not supposed to know and feeling what you are not supposed to feel'.

Discussion

I was satisfied with both programmes of training from the point of view of design, execution and relationship with the students. I was not convinced that I had achieved a wholly neutral training effect on the seven students being given dummy training. However, in terms of the goals of this project, what was important was that I see whether training directed explicitly rather than implicitly at interaction made a difference.

I think it is probably more accurate to conceptualise what I did as providing two types of training; one at the level of theory and one at the level of interaction. I expected that those given training in interaction and responsiveness would do better on day two, but I would expect both trainings to have a positive impact.

In addition I would expect all the students to do better on day two than they did on day one, simply because they would feel more at ease with the structure and be familiar with the people they were about to interview. They would have less novelty to cope with on day two, therefore I would expect them all to be more available emotionally to be attuned to the clients simply based on the impact of familiarity. I will now turn briefly to a description of day two.

Experiment time two

There were two main issues to be dealt with on day two. The scene had to be set for the interviews with the actors, students and cameramen and I had to introduce to the students the idea of completing attachment questionnaires, and ensure to my best ability that this happened. I will deal with the design first and then address the attachment questionnaires.

Structure and administration

a) One of our interview rooms was different: this we had no control over, as I was being given the rooms freely on the goodwill of my colleagues and their ability to make them available on the day required.

b) We had four cameramen. I was very pleased about this as it meant that all the actors could concentrate on the job in hand and not have to concern themselves with time boundaries. It is difficult to keep track of time when absorbed in emotional work, as the images and memories evoked often take one to the past and away from the reality of the present.

Briefing

The briefing procedure was similar to day one. The cameramen simply needed a word about room changes. The actors were given their new role plays (see appendix 6) and I explained the reasons for keeping the scenarios the same but moving them on in time. The brief for the students was the same as on day one. In addition, those who had received training in interaction were reminded to be conscious of the goal they had set for themselves.

Attachment questionnaires

As mentioned at the beginning of this chapter, I wanted to test whether the adult attachment style of the caregiver correlated significantly with their attunement to affect signals from the careseeker in situations arousing the dynamics of attachment. This was a primary purpose for this experiment. Mary Ainsworth's work in relation to her Ganda project (1967) and subsequently her Baltimore study (1978) had shown that mothers who were more tuned in to the nuances of their infant's behaviour could describe their behaviour spontaneously, with great detail, and those who responded and interacted with them (as seen from the home observations) were much more likely to have children who were classified as securely attached (using the Ainsworth Strange Situation) at one year of age than those who seemed unaware of their children's responses and interactions.

This association between attunement and responsiveness to affect and attachment status I thought important to pursue. What Ainsworth noticed was that the caregiver's responsiveness to the infant was a key factor in determining her infant's sense of security. In my study I am examining the capacity of would-be professional caregivers to attune to the affect of their clients, and to respond and interact in ways that enable the instinctive biological goal-corrected careseeking system to shut down and the exploratory system to function. Haft and Slade (1989) had also found a correlation between maternal security and capacity to attune to a range of affect in infants. I was therefore testing the hypothesis that:

(i)   secure individuals will be effective caregivers;

(ii) effective caregivers will attune to a range of emotional complexity in careseekers and seek out its meaning in situations arousing the dynamics of attachment;

(iii) insecure caregivers will fail to respond to a range of affect signalling from the careseeker indicating that they are distressed.

I therefore needed some measure of the students' adult attachment style against which I could test this hypothesis.

There were two choices in relation to this, only one of which was realistic: I either got an assessment of the attachment status of the students using the Adult Attachment Interview designed by George and Main (1985), or I got a measure of their attachment style using self-report measures in the public domain (Brennan *et al.*, 1998). The first solution, which is by far the more rigorous and actually gets at the defensive structures of individuals in relation to attachment issues, was not available to me. In order to administer and code such an interview one has to undergo two weeks of training, followed by extensive reliability training on several transcripts of interviews. In addition even if one had such training, the time required to do the coding afterwards is enormous. For this reason there has been interest in the field in developing self-report measures of attachment style. It was these I turned to and I chose three – all of which were based on the theoretical ideas underpinning attachment. The three I chose were: Feeney Noller and Hanrahan (1991), Assessing Adult Attachment; M. West, A. Sheldon, , & Reiffer (1987), The Reciprocal Attachment Questionnaire, University of Calgary, Faculty of Medicine; and Brennan, K. & Shaver, P. R. (1995), Dimensions of Adult Attachment, Affect Regulation, and Romantic Relationship Functioning.

Summary

This chapter has described the data collected in order to establish:

   (i) an independent measure of empathic attunement;

  (ii) the correlation between attachment style of the caregiver and empathic attunement;

 (iii) the correlation between caregiver and careseeker measures of empathic attunement;

  (iv) the impact of training on empathic attunement.

At the end of this experiment I had three measures:

   (i) caregivers' measure of empathic attunement;

  (ii) careseekers' measure of empathic attunement;

 (iii) a measure of attachment style of each of the 14 caregivers.

I did not have an independent measure of empathic attunement. This proved quite difficult to establish. In my next two chapters I describe the process leading to a successful method of measurement. This process was essential in helping to discover that empathic attunement could not be judged on the basis of behaviours alone. My next chapter describes the shift from an examination of behaviour to an examination of interaction, rather like the intellectual journey of my predecessors described in chapter two but building on what they discovered and getting a deeper understanding of the complex processes involved in careseeking and caregiving.

CHAPTER NINE

The process of obtaining a reliable measure for goal-corrected empathic attunement

Introduction

In the last chapter I described an experiment constructed to elicit the dynamics of attachment. I wished to test the hypothesis based on the work of Haft and Slade (1989) that caregivers who were securely attached would be better able to attune to a range of emotion. I had suggested that attunement was necessary for effective caregiving, therefore I was hoping to achieve a positive correlation between a score for attunement and a secure attachment style. I also wished to see whether students could be trained to attune to their clients' affect and respond with empathy.

Before I could do any of these tests I needed to achieve an independent, reliable score of empathic attunement for each of the twelve students. This chapter sets out the work involved in obtaining such a measure. After almost a year's work and two failed attempts we eventually achieved a correlation of 0.8 between two independent raters based on the average score of seven 1.5 minute segments of interaction from each of 12 videoed interviews.

The work of obtaining a reliable score involved developing a much more complex understanding of attunement, one which involved empathy, goal-correction and attachment theory. I will present the process of obtaining reliable ratings as it happened over three phases.

Phase one: method

I asked a colleague in the social policy department to act as an assessor for the student-actor video tapes.

Creating a measuring instrument

There were three stages to the process of creating a measuring instrument. The first stage was devising a form that I could use to get a measure of the performance of those students whom I had selected for training. The second stage involved incorporating more detail about the process of empathic attunement gleaned from the training exercise as a whole. The third stage involved incorporating observations from clinical material. I will describe each of these in turn.

Devising a form for rating purposes

As described in the last chapter I devised a measuring instrument that I could use to rate those students who were selected for training. This work produced a six-scale measure. Each of the scales were scored from one to six, ranging from 1 = 'very much' to 6 ='not at all'.

The six scales were:

1. Does the student look and sound present?
2. Does the student bring their imagination to the problem?
3. Does the student respond in an appropriate and relevant way?
4. Is there a creative exchange of ideas or feelings going on between student and client?
5. Does the student enable the client to explore?
6. Is the atmosphere strained or sticky?

Incorporating other material
from the experience of rating the tapes

I had made a number of notes in the margin of each form that I had used to rate the seven students who took part in the training programme. I had used these on the training day as specific markers and indicators of each student's style that either needed modifying or sustaining and improving. They were therefore integral to my new understanding of what would facilitate or inhibit the exploratory process. I therefore made a list of the type of behaviours, responses and interactions that I had noted. These were:

- wooden
- unresponsive
- energy focused
- positive approach
- brings imagination to it
- not putting in enough
- sticky
- dry atmosphere
- dragging
- client having to do too much
- searching out the client's eyes
- asks a question
- jumps around
- gives information
- going a bit too fast for client
- shares personal information
- looks, sounds present
- explores the fact there is a feeling there
- client feels able to talk
- client quickens their response
- interprets
- talks too much
- affirms feeling
- fixed physical posture
- not saying enough
- delayed response
- railroading over client's emotion
- getting own points across
- not noticing client's response to input
- elicits feeling but does not know what to do with it

I asked two colleagues to join me in grouping the above items. This gave me the following groupings of the material: (i) items relating to the verbal input of the worker; (ii) items relating to the non-verbal input of the worker; (iii) items relating to the understanding of the worker; (iv) the flow of interaction.

This led me to modify the original rating form. I increased the scales from 6 to 13 in order to capture different aspects of the verbal and non-verbal interaction. These were:

1. Does the therapist look and sound present?
2. Does the therapist look frightened, nervous, anxious, defensive or distracted?
3. Does the therapist help the client discuss and develop the thoughts they have about their problem?
4. Does the therapist help the client discuss and develop the feelings they have about their problem?
5. Does the therapist misunderstand what has just been said?
6. Does the therapist ask a question focusing on an irrelevant detail or change direction when the client has said something very painful?
7. Does the therapist inhibit further exploration by either timing, tone or content, e.g. jumps in too quickly, body language, moves away/back into the seat, develops a fixed posture, etc.?
8. Does the therapist talk too much?
9. Does the therapist say too little?
10. Does the therapist help the client explore?
11. Is the flow of input from the therapist appropriately paced for the client?
12. Does the therapist match the emotional intensity of the client?
13. Does the therapist intrude into the space around the client in a way that makes the client look uncomfortable?

The scales were marked out on a range of 1–4, where 1 = 'very much' and 4 = 'not at all'.

Obtaining the clinical material

I wrote to colleagues from the field of family therapy for help with access to pre-existing videos of interviews. However, I came up against procedures, policies and contracts with clients that were not conducive to lending out this material for research purposes. I decided to advertise for assistance and placed an advertisement in *Psychotherapist* (the newsletter of the United Kingdom Council for Psychotherapy) asking for help with a project I was running on Attunement in Psychotherapy.

I got a range of responses; some were from psychoanalytic practitioners in London, and others more local and from different sections of the psychotherapy fraternity. This public appeal for help, combined with personal contacts, produced enough material for me to move forward. In all I got fifteen samples of clinical work from humanist therapists, gestalt therapists, NHS medical psychotherapy consultants, psychoanalysts in private practice, psychodynamic social workers working in departments of child and family psychiatry, and family therapists. This literally provided me with a view of the settings, as well as different therapeutic modalities. Some therapists worked in very informal surroundings sitting on cushions on the floor with their clients. Some others were sitting face-to-face on hard chairs; others sat in armchairs at a slight right angle from each other and so on. Nobody used a couch for this exercise. One of the people who took part was an analyst. They had got permission from a patient who was in five-times-a-week therapy to let us video a full week's worth of sessions.

Getting the video material involved sending a technician from our audio visual department to set up cameras in the therapists' consulting rooms. I wanted the material to be such that I could have a view of both parties. The technician was not present during filming and the therapists operated the equipment themselves. In all cases care was taken to get the full and informed consent of the clients/patients involved.

Working on the clinical material

This work provided me with material that I could use to sharpen and refine the measuring instrument. My colleague and I used it as follows:

> We started by looking at the videos and discussed the behaviours and interactions between therapist and client that we were agreed facilitated exploration. We then checked our observations against the scales that I had put together to see whether we thought that using the scales would have picked up what we wanted.

> To ensure that our scales were relevant to the student population that we needed to assess, we then used these scales to rate two interviews undertaken by the students who had not completed the project for reasons referred to earlier. We then discussed our procedure and identified areas of agreement and disagreement between us, modifying slightly the phrasing of the different scales in the process

The following list gives an indication of the kinds of behaviours we identified at this time (prior to the development of the concept of goal-corrected empathic attunement) as being associated with facilitating or inhibiting exploration.

Facilitating exploration

- leaning forward into the client's space
- coming in relatively quickly after the client has spoken
- actively exploring feeling with the client
- naming the feeling
- getting the client to explore their thoughts
- bringing energy to the encounter
- searching out the client's eyes
- mentioning the feelings present in the client and bringing them into the relationship between the two of them so that they are present and available for discussion.
- modulating tone of voice to display a range of affective response to the client
- sitting in a way that comes across as in balance or balanced, in other words a posture that conveys one is not going to be literally thrown off balance.
- picking up on complex or contradictory feelings and names them
- opening up the conflict
- promoting fluid atmosphere
- putting stress on own body – reaching out to the client.
- keeping one's eyes on the client – almost like a predator – when providing input, ideas, reflections etc.
- talking in a way which allows the client to see where you are going before you get there and then stopping ... to let them take over and finish it in their own way
- coming in on the tail of the other person, tracking what they are saying and adding a little, not too much, difference
- taking charge appropriately to contain the feelings being expressed so that they can be managed between the therapist and the client
- matching the client's emotion with one's own tone of voice or body movements.

Inhibiting exploration

- being silent too long
- energy in voice does not match client – either too strong or too weak
- feet stretched forward, leaning back in chair and resting head on hand
- not getting sufficiently emotionally involved
- looking too detached
- not responding enough
- eating or drinking in the presence of the client
- recapping at the expense of adding anything new
- rounding it off and closing down the conversation by a clever remark, a synopsis, tone of voice, etc.
- reassurance as the main mode of response
- not getting in there and lining up with the client's emotion.
- being too laid back and apparently unaffected.
- coming in too quickly to name the feeling
- asking questions that take the client away from where he is in his thoughts or feelings
- getting the client to think about future scenarios when he is not ready
- attaching meaning to what the client is saying that the client disagrees with
- asking hypothetical questions
- looking frightened
- being physically agitated
- switching to talking about services and practical details when the client has been pursuing more personal matters.
- coming across as out of one's depth
- asking too many questions
- not coming in quickly enough to name the feeling.
- not being focused
- not getting hold of what the problem is
- keeping the conversation cerebral and way from emotions

Of course, all the above is context specific and can only be judged in the context of the interaction between client and therapist. One can see that there is a bewildering array of behaviour to take into account and that the task that I had set myself was complex.

Even though it should have been clear to me that working out specific indicators of empathic attunement from such material was bound to fail (given the subjective nature of many of the judgements and the interactive nature of the concept), I was still at the stage of thinking that the behaviours which facilitated exploration could be sufficiently clarified to get a significant correlation between independent raters.

Modifying the rating instrument

A close examination of the 13 scales that my colleague and I were using revealed that three scales referred to focused attention (scales 1, 2, 5); three scales referred to moderated responses (7, 8, 9); one scale to input (11); four scales to exploration (3, 4, 6, 10); and two scales referred to attunement (12, 13). I decided to increase the number of scales to fifteen in order both to increase the dimensions that we could rate based on our observations, and to have an even number of scales for each category (scales 1, 2 and 3 represent focused attention; scales 6, 7, and 11 represent modulates response; scales 9, 14 and 15 represent input; scales 8, 9, and 12 represent exploration; scales 4, 5 and 13 represent attunement). At this point it seemed better to err on the side of including too much rather than narrowing the focus of what we were looking at.

Creating a second measuring instrument

In addition to these 15 scales I created a second measuring instrument which had five scales corresponding to the five categories that I was measuring: Focused Attention, Modulates Response, Input, Exploration and Attunement

I started by working out definitions for each of the categories. The following is an example of initial work on the concept of attunement (before the concept of goal-corrected empathic attunement was developed).

Definition of attunement

Attunement is more than mere mimicry of another's state; it has as its reference the inner state of the other, their somatic experience of that state, and their cognitive and affective processes. The process of attending to the inner state of the other in this way demands intense concentration on verbal and non-verbal signals, including breathing, colour, tiny muscle movements in the face or hands, and other signs that indicate where the other person might be in themselves.

What happens between the two is like a dance or some creative moving together, with one person adding words, ideas, sense, meaning, while the other is building, joining, adding, creating, so that between them there is a sense of play, of something new being formed, some new understanding, something that could not have happened without this sense of sympathy between them, as if they could search out what the other was thinking even before the other had formed the thought, so that sometimes there could be an overlap of speech which did not interrupt, distract or take away from the ideas being followed through. While there may be an occasional mis-timing, there is no overall impingement.

Indicators

A quickness of speech between the two, like a spilling over each other with words. An increase in energy level in the voice, a sense of liveliness.

Having mapped out a similar range of material for the other categories, I then reduced my definitions to two lines each for the five categories. The brief definitions were:

(1) Focused attention:
   Does the student look as if they are attending to the client with their full concentration?

(2) Modulates Response:
   Does the student moderate their tone of voice timing, pacing etc. in relation to what the client is saying?

(3) Provides input:
   Does the student provide something extra for the client other than simply repeating what they say themselves.?

(4) Facilitates exploration:
   Does the student respond to the client in such a way that the client carries on exploring and developing what is of concern to them?

(5) Attunement:
Refers to rhythm and harmony between student and client so that each is responding to the other in such a way that the experience for the client intellectually and emotionally is deepened.

Overall the second measuring instrument comprised:

a) brief definitions of each of the five categories (as given above);

b) a 6 point scale to rate each category;

c) space for the rater to note indicators and counter indicators for the category in question.

I now had two measuring instruments to use to rate the videos. The first instrument had 15 scales and the second instrument had five scales – one for each category.

Rating procedure

I chose 12 tapes from day one – one for each student. The independent rater and myself rated these tapes using the two measuring instruments described. We ended with two scores for each student – one for each of the instruments.

The following is an example of the scoring sheet

		Measuring Instrument 1																*Measuring Instrument 2*				
		F A	F A	F A	M	M	M	1	1	1	E X	E X	E X	A	A	A		F A	M	1	E X	A
U	R1	4	4	6	3	3	2	3	4	4	3	5	6	5	5	5		4	5	4	5	5
U	R2	4	4	5	3	5	2	3	5	5	4	5	6	4	5	4		3	4	5	4	5

In relation to the scoring sheet above :

U   refers to the code allocated to a particular student

R1   refers to the independent rater

R2   refers to self

FA   refers to focused attention
      (3 scales)   – [cumulative score for R1:14]
M   refers to moderated response
      (3 scales)   – [cumulative score for R1:8]
I   refers to input (3 scales)   – [cumulative score for R1:11]
EX   refers to explore (3 scales)   – [cumulative score for R1:14]
A   refers to attunement (3 scales) – [cumulative score for R1:15]
FA   refers to the overall category of focused
      attention using definitions alone – [score for R1:4]
M   similar for modulates response – [score for R1:5]
I   similar for input   – [score for R1:4]
EX   similar for exploration   – [score for R1:5]
A   same for attunement   – [score for R1:5]

We used two instruments for the following reasons:

(i)   we thought that by using the individual scales relating to
      the five dimensions we would be less likely to miss material
      which we had identified as important;

(ii) we thought that being alert to the detail of the interaction
      would help us make a more informed judgement when we
      came to using the second instrument which relied on
      definitions of the behaviour and not discrete aspects of it.

However, we hoped that there would be a correspondence between the
two instruments, i.e. that the score we gave on instrument 1 for focused
attention (the sum of the three scales relating to focused attention,
reverse scoring where necessary) would be similar to the score we gave
for focused attention on instrument 2.

Examinations of the ratings made by my colleague suggested that
there was little value in using the scores based on the more specific
scales. The correlation between these scores and the relevant overall
rating varied from 1 to .82. This suggested that whatever they were
measuring it amounted to much the same thing in each case.

A rather more worrying feature of the overall ratings was that there
was a very high degree of correlation between them. The correlations
varied from .95 ($p < 0.001$) to .55 ($p = 0.07$). This suggested that in the
raters' minds at least the different ratings were tapping the same (or at
least highly related) rather than different aspects of performance.

I examined the correlation between my ratings and those made by my
colleague. All were positive but none were significant. They varied in
size from 0.27 to 0.50. I then calculated a score based on adding up the

overall ratings. The correlation between the sum of my ratings and the sum of hers was .54 (p = 0.07) – encouraging but not conclusive evidence of reliability. These findings suggested that we were seeking to rate an aspect of interaction that did not divide easily into separate parts. The correlation between the 'parts' into which we had tried to cut it was exceedingly high. The correlation between the two of us was higher on a global measure than on our more specific ones. As we shall see we later decided to use just one score rather than the five outlined above.

Issues arising from the first attempt at getting a reliable rating

When we discussed our reasons for scoring the way that we did it seemed that we were understanding the concepts differently. This could possibly be accounted for on the basis that one of us has a clinical background and the other does not. For example, my colleague gave the students high marks for input if the student brought in something new or gave the client something to think about. She did not adjust her score in relation to how the client responded to the input. She was therefore not working within an interactive frame.

I decided to invite a colleague who had therapeutic experience to work in the project. I still wished to retain my colleague from social policy for two reasons: (i) I was too intimately involved with the research design to be involved in the final rating process myself; and (ii) it seemed to me that if I were going to establish a reliable measurement of empathic attunement then it should be possible for non-clinicians as well as clinicians to use it .

Involving a second independent rater

The second independent rater was also trained on two tapes. I introduced her to the 15 scales, the aggregate scales, and the definitions, and went through the training video tapes identifying the behaviours and the sequences that we were after. She and I then rated two tapes using the 15 scales (as warm up) and the 5 aggregate scales. To get a score for empathic attunement we used the sum of the scores for each of the five dimensions. We then compared our results. We followed this with a detailed and intensive debriefing. The second rater then rated the original 12 tapes. (Though she rated 12 tapes one of these was the wrong tape; it took a while to figure out the mistake. We therefore had 11 tapes that all three of us had scored as is evident in Table 5.)

Table 5: Empathic attunement score correlation between two Independent raters and self *

	Independent rater	Independent rater 2	self
Independent rater 1	1.000 n = 12 P = .	r = 0.1938 n = 11 p = 0.568	r = 0.39 n = 11 p = 0.209
Independent rater 2			r = 0.6294 n = 11 p = 0.038

* the empathic attunement score was established by adding the scores achieved by each student using instrument 2.

As predicted (based on the assumption that having a clinical background was helpful in rating the tapes) there was a much better correlation between myself and the second independent rater. The correlation between the two independent raters, while positive, was poor, and so further work needed to be done to see why this was the case.

Phase two: method

Over the next few months myself and the two independent raters met at regular intervals with the following agenda:

1. To look in detail at the tapes where there was the biggest discrepancy between us.
2. To get markers for the five aspects (categories) that we were rating – focused attention, modulate response, input, attunement and exploration.
3. To get an example of 'good practice' and 'bad practice' for each category of behaviour.

Over a period of six months we met every three weeks for three hours and went through the interviews where there was the highest level of disagreement between us. We observed and tracked sequences of interaction. We stopped the video at points of interest and replayed sequences until we were clear we each understood what we were looking for and how we would rate it. We taped our discussions. I transcribed them, we used the transcripts to keep track of our discussions and read them before the start of the next session so that we were not going over the same ground.

Our debriefing and ongoing training took the following form:

1. We checked our understanding of the five categories by going through tapes in detail and identifying examples of 'focused attention', modulates response', 'input' and 'attunement', and therapist behaviours which facilitated and inhibited exploration.

2. Having discussed in detail the behaviours that we had seen and how we thought they fitted the different categories, we would then assign a rating to the student for each of the categories and compare our scores.

3. We made minute observations of the process of interaction between the actor and the student, noting eye contact, tone of voice, gestures, mirroring behaviour. We noted when there was a flow of head movements from the actor which seemed to have the purpose of scanning the face of the student as they brought in emotionally laden material (this behaviour I considered to be akin to social referencing).

4. We noticed the response of the actor to the way in which the student responded to his material and replayed these sequences over and over again, stopping sometimes frame by frame to examine the way they were tracking and responding to each other.

When we were satisfied that we were clearer about what we were rating, we rated another set of 12 unseen video tapes and correlated our results; to our astonishment our correlation had gone down. I present the results in table 6.

I was now negatively correlated with the first independent rater. The correlation between myself and the second rater had gone down. What had improved was the correlation between the two independent raters.

In order to try to make sense of what was going on, I looked at the raw scores.

Table 6: Empathic attunement between independent rater and self [*]

	Rater 1	Rater 2	Self
Rater 1		r = .5201 12 p = .101	−.3001 12 p = 1370
Rater 2			.2474 12 p = .463

[*] the empathic attunement score was established by adding the scores achieved by each student on instrument 2. The correlation between rater 1 and rater 2 is .52, p = .101; the correlation between myself and rater 1 is negative, −.30; and the correlation between myself and rater 2 was .25, p = .463.

What is clear from the raw data is that the correlation between myself and rater 1 is influenced by our ratings of student C and student N. These are the students where there are major differences. For similar reasons the correlation between myself and Rater 2 is influenced in addition by the scores of students F and M. Table 7 provides the raw data on the scores.

Table 7: Scores of all three raters for each of the 12 students

Student	Independent Rater 1	Independent Rater 2	Self
L	20	22	17
U	23	21	21
M	17	12	18
F	24	23	16
D	10	20	18
C	5	13	22
I	16	24	22
X	21	13	10
H	24	26	25
N	7	14	24
G	15	22	17
A	23	22	23

Rater one thought C and N were very good, I rated both students as poor. Rater two marked them in the middle. If one looks at all the scores for rater 2 one sees that these two students were amongst the most highly rated by her. There was only one student who scored better, that was student M. Therefore, even though the discrepancy between myself and rater 2 was not numerically as big as that between rater 1 and self, raters 1 and 2 were obviously in agreement that these students were doing comparatively well.

In relation to students M and F, the independent raters were in very close agreement about F, I was the odd one out, and with M it was rater 2 who had a different view.

Learning from our mistakes or repeating our mistakes

We returned to undertaking a detailed look at those tapes on which we were furthest out. We selected students N, C, D and X to go through in detail to see why we scored them so differently. Again this entailed detailed analysis of tone of voice of student or actor, whether we heard the tone, how we thought the one party responded to it, whether we thought this was input or modulated response or attunement, and so on. Finally we realised that we were becoming obsessed by the categories and not really addressing a problem that we actually knew was lurking in the background: *this was the way in which our own personality structure and defences were influencing our response to the interaction that we were observing.*

It was becoming clear to us that there was a possibility that because of these differences we may have been assessing different levels of attunement:

1. attunement to the defence;
2. attunement to the feeling against which a defence is constructed.

An example of number 1 above, 'attunement to the defence', would be when someone presents as if everything is fine when it clearly is not – in this case the therapist relates to the surface feeling and ignores what is underneath. The therapist might do this for any number of reasons, such as a sense timing, and also because they themselves find it difficult to access or attune to the particular feeling being defended against. In this case the response is likely to be out of consciousness.

An example of number 2, 'attunement to the feeling against which a defence is constructed', would be when one picks up the despair behind the witty remark.

This and other factors made us think that we needed to review our rating procedure and make radical changes to it. Another five months went by with extensive viewing of the contentious tapes, rating them, and discussing our judgements and transcriptions before we took the third and final step in the rating process.

Analysis of our attempts so far

There were many factors that might account for the continuing discrepancy between us. We concentrated on four.

1. Training
2. Time
3. Interaction
4. Concept

1 Training

We had trained on students C, F, M and N (albeit in relation to different actors) because we had been 'out' on these students in our previous rating. We had memories of these students associated with examples of what we had classified as either good or bad practice, and were therefore open to having a prejudiced view of them. This could have influenced our present judgement.

Also, we felt that we had got very vivid images from our training sessions of what we were looking for that fitted the categories we were using; for example, we had used the image of an alert animal when defining 'focused attention'. These and other images may have influenced how we went about viewing the tapes. It may have introduced a certain rigidity of expectation that could have got in the way of seeing what was there to be seen.

2 Time

We were scoring on the basis of watching a ten-minute video. We were all aware from our previous training and de-briefing sessions that one's view of the student and the interaction between the student and client changed from moment to moment during the session, and that one's score depended on which sequence of the interaction one had in mind when rating. One's final score was based on a composite impression. We knew this was a very crude and imprecise measure.

3 Interaction – the pattern of global and specific measures

Rater 2 said she was aware of having a lot more information to look at this time, having become much more tuned in to the interactive process between the student and actor during the debriefing sessions following the last bout of rating. This left her feeling she had twice as many judgements to make.

I felt that I was much more focused on a pattern of interaction between student and actor based on the client's communication of distress. *I felt I was rating a process* and was not giving my full attention to the individual categories and thinking out what score I should give them based on definitions alone.

Before each rating session all three of us had read through the transcripts of our training sessions, which had detailed descriptions of the various categories. We all found that this was a lot of information to hold in our heads (comparable to the difficulty of rating a ten-minute tape) and wondered if we remembered particular bits from the transcripts more than other bits. In addition it was clear that we were all doing different things with this information. I was scoring a process and then backtracking and filling in the indicators; rater 2 was spending a great deal of time very carefully attending to the indicators; and rater 1 was doing similarly to rater 2, if less intensely. (Myself and rater 1 took 30–40 minutes to rate each tape while rater 2 took over an hour.)

4 Concept

What had become almost completely lost in the process of rating was the concept under consideration. At this point I took a much more active part in the team and reasserted my view of the concept of goal-corrected empathic attunement as described in chapter five. This concept is based on an understanding that careseeking and caregiving form an instinctively based goal-corrected complementary partnership. The complex pattern of careseeking engaged in by insecure careseekers is likely to be difficult to track.

Concentrating on behaviours alone (as we had been doing), either of the therapist or the client, was unlikely to get at the nature of the process set in motion when the dynamics of careseeking and caregiving are aroused. The theory suggested that ineffective caregiving gave rise to defence and self care. It was the process of goal-corrected empathic attunement that we needed to track within the theoretical framework of the dynamics of attachment.

At this point in the process of re-focusing us on the task of achieving a reliable rating, I constructed the model which I referred to as the spiral of goal-corrected empathic attunement, and which I presented in chapter five, p 108. This would help us track the process under observation.

The spiral of goal-corrected empathic attunement depicts the following process:

> expression of distress in the careseeker (actor)
>
> met by attunement to affect from the caregiver in such a way that the vitality affects of the actor is regulated so that it comes within manageable and optimal limits for exploration (student)
>
> expression of relief from the careseeker
> (may be momentary – may be so brief as not to be visible)
>
> followed by expression of concerns from the careseeker
>
> met by attunement to affect and empathic response from the caregiver
>
> expression of relief from the careseeker (again may be momentary – may not be visible)
>
> exploration of concerns from the careseeker
>
> resonance with and attunement to underlying affect by the caregiver followed by empathic comment from caregiver
>
> followed by input from caregiver
>
> visible expression of relief from careseeker

(See chapter five for more variations on this pattern.)

The following analysis of interaction between a careseeker and a caregiver taken from the videos of student/actor interaction is an example of the processes that we were attempting to rate. I give two examples – one where there is goal-corrected empathic attunement and the other where there is not. The brief for the interview being observed was as follows:

Sadness

> You are 36, living in the north of England where you have a job that is very important to you. Your family are in Kent where you were brought up. You don't have a partner and despite the geographical distance had a very close relationship with your parents. You thought for years that you would move back down south at some stage, but kept putting it off. Your father died five

years ago, leaving your mother alone. She encouraged you to pursue your career rather than to move down to live with her. You know your mother has been having some memory problems, but you have put this down to recent stresses she has had with her house. However, her GP has contacted you to say that he thinks your mother has Alzheimer's disease. You are very upset and have contacted social services.

Example 1: Goal-corrected empathic attunement within the context of psychotherapy

Behaviour of careseeker	Caregiver's response	Implicit goal of caregiver's behaviour within a therapeutic context	Function in attachment terms of caregiver's behaviour	Vitality affects within a system of responsive interactions between careseeker and caregiver
expression of concern or distress	affect matching for intensity and vitality	settle initial anxiety, affect regulation	signals emotive messages are understood and accepted	relief
displays concerns	empathic response	influence internal working models of relationship	signals the competence of the caregiver	relief
raises further concerns or shows further distress	attunement to the affect combined with empathic input	regulate arousal levels, signal intended continuing proximity and a benign cognitive appraisal	signals the range of material that it is safe to explore in this context	relief
exploration of concerns	attunement to affect, affect regulation and empathy	facilitate a sense of continuity with past experience	survival, integration and development	enlivenment and well being

Example 2: Poor goal-corrected empathic attunement

Careseeker	"My mum is a strong capable awesome woman, so this is ... I know it must be shocking for everyone ... but it feels, it just feels wrong, and I feel he must have got the files muddled up or something (looks at ceiling), because this can't be happening to my mum (runs her hands through her hair)".	*expression of affect*
Caregiver	(Very calm still posture elbows on arms of chair, hands on thighs, voice has a clear questioning tone). "Have you actually seen your mum recently to see for yourself?"	*avoidance of affect*
Careseeker	"No. I do speak to my mother very often on the phone (hand on neck looking very stressed) and I have ... "	*momentarily disorganised, reasserts care-seeking non-verbally*
Caregiver	"How do you find her?" (clips the end of careseeker's sentence)	*avoidance of client's here and now affect*
Careseeker	"Yeah." (clearly not understanding)	*momentarily disorganised*
Caregiver	"How do you find her, do you find her any different?"	*avoidance of client's here and now affect*
Careseeker	"I do find her". Pause. (Nods head up and down as she says this. She looks very preoccupied, brings hand up to face and starts to twirl a piece of hair on her temple.) "Although it wasn't until the Dr. told me that I put all the pieces together and thought she is distracted, yes, she is sounding much older all of a sudden and she is talking about things that don't have an immediate relevance to what we are talking about. But I don't want to leave her there all by herself. My instinct is to love her ... " (puts a lot of emphasis on the word instinct, puts energy on voice as she says it and locks both hands together points to her chest with her thumb and opens hands forward as she says 'love her').	*momentarily disorganised, reasserts care-seeking*

Caregiver	(Cuts in again) "That is understandable. Have you discussed this with your mother at all?"	*avoidance of attachment behaviour*
Careseeker	(Careseeker at this point is looking at caregiver, her mouth is slightly open as she is in fact in the middle of talking, but her mouth stays open as if in freeze in response to caregiver's question.)	*momentarily disorganised*
Careseeker	"No" (purses mouth, looks down). "No, I ..."	*possibly the reassertion of careseeking*
Caregiver	"Does she know that your Dr. has told you?"	*avoidance of affect*
Careseeker	"Oh yes, she does, but she isn't really willing ... she may be to him, but to me she isn't ... " (Careseeker is clearly looking distressed – sad tone of voice and a bit preoccupied.)	*careseeking*
Caregiver	(Again cuts in before careseeker has clearly indicated she has finished speaking.) "Have you discussed it at all? (Upbeat tone, coming across as slightly inquisitorial.)	*avoidance*

Phase three: method

Having arrived at the above conceptualisation of the process under consideration we made the following changes to our rating method.

(i) We changed the unit of time on the video that we chose to rate from the full unit of 10 minutes to 1.5-minute segments. This was to deal with the issues outlined just now, namely length of concentration and difficulty in knowing whether we were more influenced by one section of the interaction than another.

(ii) We stopped using the 2 measuring instruments as we felt:

(a) They distracted us from observing the interaction by focusing us more on behaviour;

(b) They vectored our energy and attention to our cognitive processes of thinking and conceptualising and away from our apprehensive sense of what was taking place between the two people that we were observing.

(iii) To be congruent with the above change in direction we decided to reintroduce the definitions that I had originally used with the senior clinicians and with the students in the experiment described in chapters four and five.

(iv) Before each rating session we read through the definitions of affect attunement and reminded ourselves of the sequence of goal-corrected empathic attunement as described on page 230.

(v) It was agreed that the rating by the two assessors would be done in the same room on the same segment of tape at the same time so that there would be no ambiguity about which section of the tape or what length of tape was being rated;

(vi) The rating was to be done on a scale of 25 divided into three segments 1–8 represented attuned; 9–17: represented tuning in; and 18–25 represented non-attuned.

(vii) Finally, as mentioned at the conclusion of the last section, it seemed highly probably that our own defensive structures were influencing the way that we were rating the interaction between student and actor, and we developed a way of dealing with that problem.

Techniques for managing defensive processes

Given that it was impossible to really know for certain how and in what way our defensive structures were interfering with the rating process, I decided as a first step to introduce a method from systems centred theory (SCT) and practice, devised by Yvonne Agazarian (Agazarian, 1997; Agazarian and Gantt, 2000) and in which I am a licensed practitioner, to deal with the most obvious problem of moving out of a social or academic role and into the role of a rater of psychodynamic process. The technique used to move from one role to another in SCT is known as the 'Distraction Exercise' (Agazarian and Gantt, 2000, pp.199–200 and 244–246).

The goal of the *Distraction Exercise* is to cross whatever role boundary it is so that one has one's full energy available for the task.

Our experience of operating this system was that the feelings we worked on that were causing distraction (for example, meeting a colleague in the photocopying room just before meeting with the research team and being reminded of essays still awaiting marking) were similar to the feelings being stirred up by the task (for example, feelings about not being competent for the task, or letting the research team down in some way). The distraction exercise proved a powerful method for recognising these feelings and checking them out with members of the research team. Not being distracted by these thoughts and feelings and seeing them as shared by other members of the team made it possible to have one's full energy available to concentrate more fully on the information on the videos.

So in summary the new method consisted of:

1. dividing the tape to be rated into 1.5-minute segments;
2. reading the definition of affect attunement used in the first phase of the research;[9]
3. reminding ourselves of the processes involved in goal-corrected empathic attunement;
4. performing the distraction exercise;
5. rating the segments using a 25-point scale divided into three parts.

We tested the method on the set of tapes belonging to the two students who had not completed the project. Each tape was divided into 1.5-minute segments. Each of these segments was scored independently by the two raters. The four interviews provided between them 21 segments of tape. The test achieved the correlations shown in table 8.

Table 8: Correlation between the two independent raters on 21 segments of tape taken from four interviews

	Rater 1	Rater 2
Rater 1	1.000	.7439
	21	21
	p = .	p = .000

9. The definitions were: attunement is a way of communicating to the other that one has recognised the affect that they are experiencing; attunement conveys to the other that one has a feeling sense inside of what it feels like to be them right now

The correlation between the raters was highly significant r = .74. Much encouraged by this result we carried on discussing the observations being taken into account for the ratings made and proceeded to rate another 12 tapes using the same procedure. This time we arranged the score for the segments by giving each tape a single score. Table 9 sets out the result.

Table 9: Correlation between the two independent raters on the average of 1.5-minute segments of tape from twelve interviews

	Rater 1	Rater 2
Rater 1	1.000	.8901
	12	12
	p = .	p = .000

Again we achieved a highly significant result based on the average score of the segmented interview.

As a final test we chose 12 tapes that we were absolutely sure had not been involved in previous rating attempts and divided them into 1.5-minute segments. We used the method as described above and correlated the results. A correlation of 0.798 was achieved between the two independent raters, at which point we were satisfied with the result. See table 10.

Table 10: Correlation between the two independent raters on twelve tapes*

	Rater 1	Rater 2
Rater 1	1.000	.7981
	12	12
	p = .	p = .002

* These 12 tapes were divided into roughly 7 segments each of 1.5 minutes in length. Each of these segments was given a score. An average was computed for the seven segments. The average score for each of the 12 tapes was the subject of the correlation.

It then remained to get a score for all the 96 interviews. It was decided that one of the independent raters would take on the job of rating all 96 videos and that the second rater would rate one video in every batch of ten in order to compare the results and discuss any differences. This would ensure that the first rater was rating in line with the standard developed rather than creating a standard of her own.

The work was done over a period of six weeks and went on in batches of 6 videos a session. I met with the main rater before she rated each batch and we went through the definition of attunement, reminded ourselves of the process of goal-corrected empathic attunement, and of what she was looking for in terms of sequence of interaction and the signals that the goal of careseeking had been met. I then did the distraction exercise with her and left.

By the end of this procedure I had an empathic attunement score for all 96 interviews.

Summary

This chapter has described the process involved in getting a reliable measure of goal-corrected empathic attunement. It was eventually achieved by clarifying the nature of what was being observed. The concept referred to *a process that was triggered under certain conditions and came to an end under other conditions,* at which point other behaviours would then come into play. What was required was the *observation of both the activation and deactivation of a process.*

In addition, we recognised the impossibility of trying to rate all 10 minutes of an interview, so we divided the interview into segments, thus ensuring that the raters were at least not rating an unmanageable number of interactions. We abandoned all previous rating measures, returned to using definitions of key elements of the process under observation (the subjective experience of goal-correction – successful empathic attunement), instigated a single 25 scale marked off in three segments – attuned, tuning in, not attuned – and attended to defensive processes in the raters through using a technique from Systems Centered Therapy (Agazarian, 1997) called 'the distraction exercise'.

This new method was tested on several tapes, ending with a final rating of 12 completely new tapes on which a correlation of .8 was achieved between two independent raters. At the conclusion of this work I had an empathic attunement score for each of the 96 interviews.

In my next chapter I present the results of all the experiments.

CHAPTER TEN

Results of the Third Experiment

Introduction

I set out in the third experiment to explain:

(i) whether careseekers (actors) and caregivers (students) shared a similar evaluation of their experience of caregiving, and whether these experiences were related to the independent measure;

(ii) whether the attachment status of the students was related to (a) their ability to attune to client affect and be empathic and (b) to the way actor and students evaluated their experience;

(iii) whether students who were given training directed at encouraging them to attune to client affect and be empathic would subsequently do better at empathic attunement than those students who were not given this training.

The reasons for this exploration should be apparent from earlier chapters. Basically I expected that the measures I used would prove valid in the sense that they would relate to each other and distinguish between students. I also expected that students who had a secure attachment style would 'do better' on all these measures. Finally I expected (or to be more accurate hoped) that the performance of the students could be improved by training.

I now present what I actually found, starting with a presentation and analysis of the results of the subjective and independent measures. I will then present the results of the attachment questionnaire and conclude with the results of the training programme.

Measures

Subjective measures of empathic attunement:
caregivers' (students') score

The measures consisted of six questions, each presented on a scale marked 1–6 in decreasing order of agreement. So, point 1 on the scale indicated high levels of agreement with the question (very much) and point 6 indicated low levels of agreement with the question (not at all).

The questions used were:

1. Do you think you conveyed to the client that you could see what they were feeling?
2. Do you think you conveyed to the client that you understood what they were saying?
3. Were you attentive and interested in the client?
4. Did you think you enabled them to say what they wanted?
5. Did you feel you enabled them to see things in a new way?
6. Do you think you said anything helpful?

These questions were chosen based on the research carried out in the pilot study (experiment one) and described in chapter six. In that study I discovered that the experts associated empathic attunement with: focused attention; modulating response; input and facilitating exploration. My analysis of the experts' answers suggested that the therapist had to attend to the feelings that the client was expressing and conveying, and to the content of what they were saying. They had to respond in such a way that they facilitated rather than inhibited the client's natural capacity to explore the meaning of their predicament and their feelings about it.

At the end of the experiment I received completed forms from all the students giving me answers on all six scales for each of the eight interviews. I wanted to see whether the questions I had put together for this measure were in fact measuring aspects of the same thing. For example, if a student scored well on attention to feeling, did they also score well on enabling the client to say what they wanted? This would provide support for my analysis of the data from the first experiment, and suggest that the elements of the therapists' response that were important, i.e. affect attunement and empathy, went together in a meaningful way. A measure of their 'internal consistency' is provided by Cronbach's alpha. As can be seen from table 11 this was very high.

Table 11: Internal consistency of the scales involved in caregivers' measure of caregiving

No. of cases	96.0
No. of items	6
Alpha =	.8723

Table 12: Frequency of distribution: caregivers' (students') score

Score	Number	%
6–10	4	5
11–15	23	23
16–20	34	35.4
21–25	19	20
26–30	16	17
Total	96	100%

The range goes from a score of six to a score of 30. Clearly there is a considerable variation in the way the students rate their performance.

Subjective measures of empathic attunement:
careseekers' (actors') score

This measure also consisted of six questions presented on a scale marked 1–6 in decreasing order of agreement, as described above, with a mark of 1 indicating high levels of agreement with the question (very much) and a mark of 6 indicating low levels of agreement with the question (not at all).

The questions used were:

1. Did the student convey to you that they could see how you felt?
2. Did the student convey to you that they understood what you were saying?
3. Did you feel that the student was interested in you and attentive?

Chart 3: Students' score/frequency of distribution

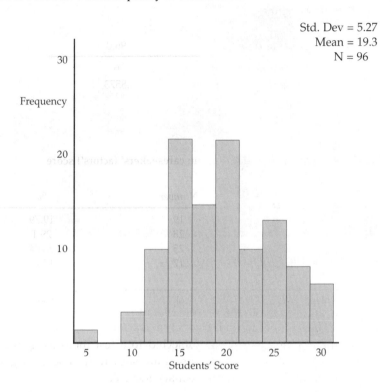

Std. Dev = 5.27
Mean = 19.3
N = 96

Frequency

Students' Score

4. Were you able to say what you wanted?

5. Did the student enable you to see things in a new way?

6. Did the student say anything helpful?

Again, these questions were based on the results of the pilot study but were also designed to mirror the questions being put to the students. They were designed to get the actor's view of the interaction, the response they felt they were getting from the student; whether they felt they were being understood at the level of their feelings and their concerns; whether they felt they were encouraged or inhibited in pursuing what they wanted to explore; whether they were able to use the student's input; and finally how they evaluated that input. The questions were designed to get at the nature of the contact between actor and student and to assess whether the student was interactive, responsive, and tuned in to the actor's emotions and concerns.

Table 13: Internal consistency of the scales involved in careseekers' measure of caregiving

No. of cases	96.0
No. of items	6
Alpha =	.8573

Table 14: Frequency of distribution: careseekers' (actors') score

Score	*Number*	*%*
6–10	19	19.79
11–15	28	29.1
16–20	25	26.04
21–25	17	17.70
26–30	7	7.29
Total	96	100%

These questions were then subjected to a test measuring internal consistency and the results obtained are shown in table 13. I got an extremely high level of internal consistency: .86

The next question I addressed was whether the actors rated the students as similar to or different from each other. Table 14 depicts the spread of scores given by the actors.

The scores range from 6 to 30. Six was the best score that any student could get, 36 was the worst. The actors were clearly using the full range of the scales to score the sessions.

Chart 4 shows that the actors discriminate between the students in quite substantial ways along a fairly normal distribution curve.

Independent measure of
goal-corrected empathic attunement

I now looked at the scores given to the students by the independent rater in order to see whether there was a normal distribution.

One can see from chart 5 that there appear to be two distributions: one group of interviews gets ratings in the lower end of the scores, i.e. between 6–12, and the other group bunches at the higher end, 16–19.

Chart 4: Actors' score/frequency of distributuion

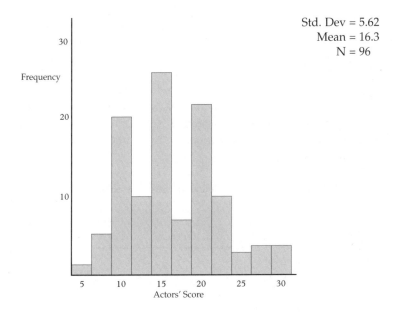

Std. Dev = 5.62
Mean = 16.3
N = 96

Chart 5: Independent measure of GCEA/frequency of distribution

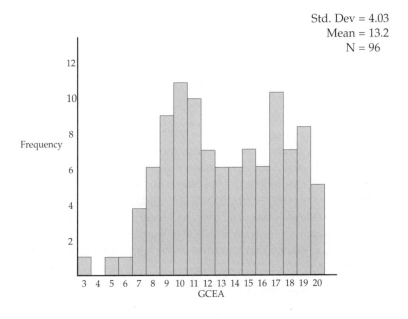

Std. Dev = 4.03
Mean = 13.2
N = 96

Correlations between the measures

A test for goal-corrected empathic attunement has not yet been devised. It was therefore not possible to test the validity of these measures using an independent and already validated criterion. I therefore needed to see the extent to which the three measures of careseeker/caregiver interaction correlated with each other. If I got a significant correlation the chances were that I was measuring something real, something which all three parties to the observation (actor, student and observer) could agree about. Table 15 gives the correlation achieved.

Table 15: Correlation between measures of careseeker/caregiver interaction

		Independent Rater	Student (Caregiver)	Actor (Careseeker)
Independent (Rater)	Pearson Correlation	1.000	.295[†]	.246[*]
	Sig. (2-tailed)	–	.004	.016
	No.	96	96	96
Student (Stutot)	Pearson Correlation		1.000	.510[‡]
	Sig. (2-tailed)		–	.000
	No.		96	96

[†] Correlation is significant at the 0.01 level (2-tailed)
[*] Correlation is significant at the 0.05 level (2-tailed)
[‡] Correlation is significant at the 0.001 level (2-tailed)

As can be seen there is a highly significant correlation between the actor (careseeker) and the student (caregiver) in terms of their experience of the interaction between them. The correlation of .295 between the independent rater and the student is also significant at the .01 level (2-tailed). The correlation between the independent rater and the actor is not as high at .246 but is significant at the .005 level (2-tailed), which means that it is unlikely to happen by chance more than 5 in a hundred times.

Chart 6: Student score by actor score

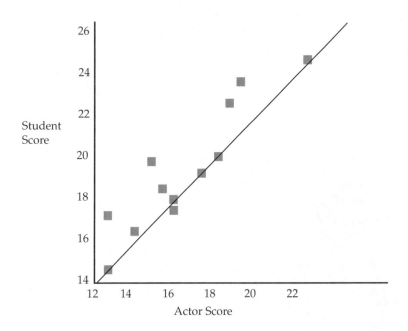

Analysis of variance

I next set out to examine whether some students were better than others, as measured by themselves, the actors and the independent rater. I took the students' score and subjected it to an analysis of variance to see whether the students differed significantly from each other, whether all students on average did better with some actors than others, and whether some students performed better with some actors while other students 'preferred' other actors. I present the results in table 16, where it can be seen from table 16 there were three main results.

1. There was a highly significant difference in how the students rated themselves (student effect, $p < .00$) – i.e some rated themselves consistently higher than others.

2. Students on average did, as they saw it, better with some actors than with others (actor effect, $p < .00$)

3. The 'interaction' was not significant – particular students did not, as they saw it, do better with particular actors ($p < .8$).

Table 16: Analysis of variance student score

Source	Sum of Squares	df	Mean Square	F	Signif-icance
Corrected Model	1720.33	47	36.603	1.912	.014
Intercept	35882.667	1	35882.667	1874.176	.000
Student	881.333	11	80.121	4.185	.000
Actor	416.750	3	138.917	7.256	.000
Student/Actor	422.250	33	12.795	.668	.887
Error	919.000	48	19.146		
Total	385222.000	96			
Corrected Total	2639.33347	95			

I then looked at the actors' score with similar questions. I present the results in Table 17.

Table 17: Analysis of variance actor score (total score)

Source	Sum of Squares	df	Mean Square	F	Signifi-cance
Corrected Model	2147.906	47	45.700	2.564	.001
Intercept	25447.591	1	25447.594	1427.802	.000
Student	698.531	11	63.503	3.563	.001
Actor	421.865	3	140.622	7.890	.000
Student/Actor	1027.510	33	31.137	1.747	.038
Error	855.500	48	17.823		
Total	28451.000	96			
Corrected Total	3003.406	95			

It can be seen that:

(i) there was a highly significant difference by student (.001) in how the actors saw the different students, i.e. some students were consistently seen as doing better than others ($p < .001$);

(ii) some actors were consistently more generous with their ratings than others ($p < .001$), i.e. individual actors rated some students significantly better than others;

(iii) there is some evidence that some actors 'favour' some students while other actors 'favour' different students ($p < .038$).

Table 18: Analysis of variance: independent measure

Source	Sum of Squares	df	Mean Square	F	Signifi- cance
Corrected Model	1046.36	47	22.263	2.142	.005
Intercept	16637.163	1	16637.163	1600.722	.000
Student	438.904	11	39.900	3.839	.001
Actor	50.000	3	16.667	1.604	.201
Student/Actor	557.452	33	16.892	1.625	.061
Error	498.890	48	10.394		
Total	18182.409	96			
Corrected Total	1545.246	95			

I then looked at the independent measure of the students' performance. The results for that are presented in table 18. On this measure:

1. some students do consistently better than others (p < .001);
2. on average students do not do better with some actors (p < .2);
3. there is some evidence that some students do better with some actors and others with other actors (interaction) – p = .061.

Summary

(i) There is a high level of internal consistency between the individual scales which comprise the subjective measures.

(ii) There is a highly significant correlation between the subjective measures.

(iii) There is a significant correlation between the independent measure and the subjective measures.

(iv) All three measures distinguish between students in the sense that some students do consistently better than others.

I will discuss these results more fully later in this chapter.

Goal-corrected empathic attunement and attachment style

I had predicted that the attachment style of the caregiver was associated with a capacity to attune empathically to the presentation of distress in another person. In order to test this it is necessary to have measures of a) attunement and b) attachment status. The measures of attunement were those already described. This left the problem of assessing attachment.

The most credible method of assessing adult attachment status is probably the Adult Attachment Interview (George *et al.*, 1985). However, this was not used for three reasons: a) it would yield a more detailed knowledge of the individual's history than was appropriate for a tutor; b) I was not qualified to carry out the test, and even if I could find someone who was (which is very difficult to do as so few people are trained) it is time consuming and expensive.

Instead of the Adult Attachment Interview it was decided to use three 'paper and pencil' self-completion questionnaires. These were: Feeney, Noller and Hanrahan's 'Assessing Adult Attachment: Developments in the conceptualisation of security and insecurity' (Feeney *et al.*, 1994); West and Sheldon's 'The Assessment of Dimensions Relevant to Adult Reciprocal attachment' (West and Sheldon-Keller, 1992); and Brennan and Shaver's 'Dimensions of Adult Attachment, Affect Regulation, and Romantic Relationship Functioning' (Brennan and Shaver, 1995). For a full discussion about the reasoning behind this choice see McCluskey (2001).

There is a large and growing literature on the actual value of self-report questionnaires and what precisely it is that they are measuring (e.g. Fraley and Waller, 1998). One of the main criticisms is that they fail to address the underlying personality structure, the basic defensive organisation which is largely concealed to consciousness. The Adult Attachment Interview is seen as the gold standard in this area. Attempts have been made to reconcile the findings of the AAI and self-report measures (Bartholomew & Horowitz, 1991; Bartholomew & Shaver, 1998). There does seem to be some association. However, the whole concept of security, and what we mean by it, needs to be examined more thoroughly. What we mean by attachment security continues to be explored in the context of imtimate adult relationships (see Clulow, 2001). Given the work of the Grossmanns it is clearly the case that we feel secure or insecure in different contexts. We need measures that address this fact and we need to get more precise at what triggers insecurity and what promotes security in relationship. This is a project I am currently pursuing with Dorothy Heard.

Table 19: Correlation between measures of compulsive caregiving and insecure attachment with the careseekers', caregivers' and the independent scores for empathic attunement

		Insecure Attachment	*Compulsive Caregiving*
Careseeker score	Pearson Correlation	−.001	−.521
	Sig. (2-tailed)	.997	.081
	No.	12	12
Caregiver score	Pearson Correlation	−.041	−.603
	Sig. (2-tailed)	.899	.038
	No.	12	12
Independent score	Pearson Correlation	.552	−.265
	Sig. (2–tailed)	.063	.406
	No.	12	12

To return to the work of the experiments currently being described, I chose to use three self-report questionnaires. These three questionnaires (see appendices 24, 25 and 26 for the actual scales used, coding etc.) yielded 20 sub-scales. To simplify the analysis and reduce the chance of spurious correlations, it was decided to combine them into a smaller number. Ideally this would have been done by administering the questionnaires to a large sample of adults and then carrying out some form of factor analysis. Again this was not possible. The best that could be done was to reduce the number of scales by analysing the data from the 12 students in the study.

The procedure used to reduce the scales was rough and ready. A correlation matrix showed that most of the sub-scales were correlated with each other. The scale with the highest average correlation with the others was 'angry withdrawal'. Six of these correlations were significant' with values ranging from .79 to .57; nine were not significant, although sizeable (.5 to .29); and five were low (.1 to 0). It was decided to form a general measure of 'disturbed attachment' by simply adding the fifteen scales (reversing the score where necessary) which showed significant or sizeable correlations with 'angry withdrawal'. I termed this 'Insecure Attachment'.

Chart 7: Goal-corrected attunement score by attachment score (mean)

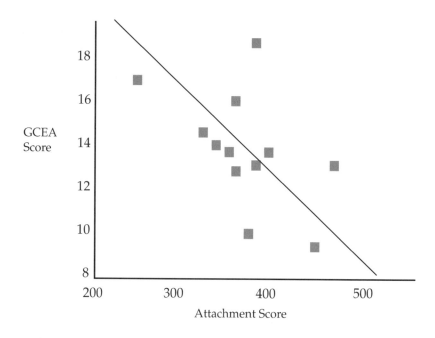

Further examination of the correlation matrix showed that three of the scales were not correlated with 'angry withdrawal' but were highly correlated with each other. These were 'Need for Approval', 'Compulsive Caregiving' and 'Self Reliance'. Compulsive Caregiving had a correlation of .79 with Need for Approval, and a –.71 with Self Reliance. The correlation between Need for Approval and Self Reliance was –.71. These three scores were therefore combined after reversing the score for 'Self Reliance' to yield a kind of 'Other Directedness' score. I termed this 'Compulsive Caregiving'. Individuals who scored high on this measure would perhaps deal with their reluctance to look after themselves and their need for approval by looking after others.

We correlated these two scores, Insecure Attachment and Compulsive Caregiving, with the three measures of attunement. Table 19 gives the result.

Examination of the correlations and graphs suggested that there was a significant correlation between the 'Insecure attachment' score and the independent measure of empathic attunement, p = .063. In other

Chart 8: Mean goal-corrected attunment score by predicted GCEA score

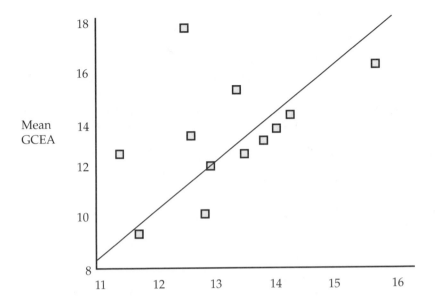

Unstandardized Predicted Value

words, those students who got a rating of insecure attachment style did worse on the score for goal-corrected empathic attunement. As the theory predicted this we can halve the correlation achieved, thus bringing the correlation to around .03. There was a significant correlation between the score for 'Compulsive Caregiving' and the Actors' (careseekers') score, p = .038.

Further analysis tended to confirm these results and used the analysis package MIWin. This was written for educational research where it is often important to relate data at different levels – for example, to see how much of a pupil's performance can be explained through their individual characteristics, how much depends on their class teacher, and how much on the school. In this example, school, teacher and pupil represent different levels, but for the research on empathic attunement only two levels need be considered – the student and the episode. The question was whether the attachment status of the student related to the three measures of the episodes they had with the actors. I am grateful to professor Ian Sinclair, University of York, for carrying out this analysis for me.

On this analysis 'Compulsive Caregiving' was significantly related to the actors' assessment of the interaction (chi-square = 4.16, df = 1, p < .05) and the students' assessment (chi-square = 7.02, df = 1, p = < .01). In both cases the direction was the same – the more 'other directed' the student the better the interaction was assessed as being.

The 'Insecure Attachment' score was not related to either of these two scores. It was, however, related to the independent score (chi-square = 4.23, df = 1, p < .05). The higher the disturbed attachment score the worse the interaction was assessed as being.

This analysis is encouraging in the sense that it produces the results expected. From a statistical point of view the results are more dubious. Essentially they comprise an analysis based on 12 individuals. This is a small number on which to carry out the kind of analysis done here. The correlations assume a normal distribution; non-parametric correlations on the same data are not significant. Multi-level analysis of the kind done here also usually involves a much greater number of individuals. The results must therefore be seen as interesting and encouraging rather than definitive.

Results of training: Experimental group

I will now turn to see whether the training programme that I devised for the Experimental Group students made a difference to how they performed on day two.

Table 20 gives the averages for day one and day two for those students who received training. One can see from this table, the actors that the students and the objective rater agreed that there was an improvement in the students' performance on day two: the average score from all three sources dropped (i.e. it 'improved').

I then set out to examine each of the three scores in detail: the students' score, the actors' score and the independent score. Table 21 sets out the results of an analysis of variance based on the students' score for those students who had been trained. The table shows that there was a significant difference between students in how they scored themselves (.001); that time along with training did not make a significant difference to how they scored themselves (.138). However, there was a significant 'interaction effect' between time and student: some students improved significantly more (according to themselves) than others (.007).

Table 20: Trained students' average scores: day one and day two

		Actors' Score	Students' Score	Indepedent Score
Day 1	Mean	18.7917	20.6667	14.2790
	No.	24	24	24
	Std. Deviation	4.5010	4.2902	3.5378
Day 2	Mean	15.2917	18.9583	12.1181
	No.	24	24	24
	Std. Deviation	5.7971	6.0755	3.9896
Total	Mean	17.0417	19.8125	13.1986
	No.	48	48	48
	Std. Deviation	5.4302	5.2740	3.8867

Table 21: Student, time and student score: an analysis of variance

Source	Sum of Squares	df	Mean Square	F	Significance
Corrected Model	760.062	11	69.097	4.545	.000
Intercept	18841.687	1	18841.687	1239.471	.000
Student	437.428	5	87.488	5.755	.001
Time	35.021	1	35.021	2.304	.138
Student/Time	287.604	5	57.521	3.784	.007
Error	547.250	36	15.201		
Total	20149.000	48			
Corrected Total	1307.312	47			

Table 22: Student, time and actor score: an analysis of variance

Source	Sum of Squares	df	Mean Square	F	Signifi-cance
Corrected Model	668.417	11	0.765	3.049	.006
Intercept	13941.083	1	13940.083	699.433	.000
Student	388.167	5	77.633	3.895	.006
Time	147.000	1	147.000	7.376	.010
Student/Time	133.250	5	26.650	1.337	.271
Error	717.500	36	19.931		
Total	15326.000	48			
Corrected Total	1385.917	47			

Table 23: Student, time and independent score: an analysis of variance

Source	Sum of Squares	df	Mean Square	F	Signifi-cance
Corrected Model	154.573	11	14.052	.911	.540
intercept	8361.725	1	8361.725	541.968	.000
Student	82.035	5	16.407	1.063	.397
Time	56.035	1	56.035	3.632	.065
Student/Time	16.503	5	3.301	.214	.954
Error	555.424	36	15.428		
Total	9071.722	48			
Corrected Total	709.997	47			

I then looked at the actors' score and did a similar analysis. Table 22 sets out the results. One can see that the actors saw a significant difference between the students (.006). They also saw them doing better after training on day two (.010). However, their ratings did not suggest that some students had improved significantly more than others.

Turning to the independent score, table 23 shows the results. Within the trained group, the independent score did not differentiate significantly between the students. There was some evidence of improvement with training over time (.065). There was no 'interaction effect'. Though the effect of training comes out at only .065 – a result indicating that this was likely to happen by chance no more often than seven in a hundred times – I had predicted that change would make a difference, thus allowing us to think of this score in more robust terms – in the region of a significance level of .03.

To test whether the differences being seen for the trained group are not just the effect of getting used to the scenarios and the actors, I did the same analysis for the untrained group.

Results of training: Control group

Table 24: Average scores for untrained students on day one and day two: self-assessment. Actors' scores and empathic attunement scores

		Actor Score	*Student Score*	*Independent Score*
Day 1	Mean	17.1250	19.5000	13.1133
	No.	24	24	24
	Std. Deviation	5.1017	4.7913	5.0181
Day 2	Mean	13.9167	18.2083	13.1475
	No.	24	24	24
	Std. Deviation	6.0427	5.7557	3.3359
Total	Mean	15.5208	18.8542	13.1304
	No.	48	48	48
	Std. Deviation	5.7649	5.2794	4.2153

No. = number of interviews each day. Total refers to the number of interviews over both days.

One can see that from the students' and the actors' points of view the students got better by day two. The averages went down from 17.13 to 14, and from 19.5 to 18.2 respectively. Not so with the independent score. With that score the students did slightly worse on day two; the average went up just a fraction, from 13.11 to 13.15.

Table 25 sets out the analysis of variance based on the students' score. One can see that there is a significant difference between the students in how they rate themselves (007); on average they do not see themselves as doing significantly better on day two, nor, in contrast to

Table 25: Student, time and score: an analysis of variance

Source	Sum of Squares	df	Mean Square	F	Significance
Corrected Model	508.729	11	46.248	2.078	.049
Intercept	17063.021	1	17063.021	766.638	.000
Student	421.854	5	84.371	3.791	.007
Time	20.021	1	20.021	.900	.349
Student/Time	66.854	5	13.371	.601	.700
Error	801.250	36	22.257		
Total	18373.000	48			
Corrected Total	1309.979	47			

the situation in the trained group, do some students see themselves as improving significantly more than others.

Table 26 sets out the analysis of variance based on the actors' score. The actors do not differentiate significantly between students (.169). They do see them doing better on day two (.052). They do not see some students improving significantly more than others.

Table 26: Student, time and actor score: an analysis of variance

Source	Sum of Squares	df	Mean Square	F	Significance
Corrected Model	457.729	11	41.612	1.357	.235
Intercept	11563.021	1	11563.021	376.970	.000
Student	254.854	5	50.971	1.662	.169
Time	123.521	1	123.521	4.027	.052
Student/Time	79.354	5	15.871	.517	.761
Error	1104.250	36	30.674		
Total	13125.000	48			
Corrected Total	1561.979	47			

Improvement score

I next turned to the group as a whole. Tables 27 and 28 set out the average scores given by the independent rater at time 1 and time 2 to each of the twelve students.

Table 27: Students' average score at time 1: independent rater

Student	Mean	No.	Std. deviation
1	14.395	4	2.65
2	13.85	4	3.40
3	13.45	4	2.41
4	13.43	4	6.34
5	16.22	4	4.26
6	14.31	4	2.43
7	8.41	4	4.02
8	15.70	4	5.07
9	12.93	4	5.04
10	9.78	4	3.42
11	16.92	4	4.01
12	14.92	4	4.55
Total	13.6	48	4.33

Table 28: Caregivers' (students') average score at time 2: independent rater

Student	Mean	No.	Std. deviation
1	10.22	4	.97
2	12.22	4	4.32
3	11.51	4	2.03
4	11.38	4	4.54
5	15.90	4	4.92
6	11.46	4	5.26
7	10.29	4	2.44
8	14.35	4	2.07
9	13.70	4	2.78
10	10.26	4	1.18
11	17.45	4	.92
12	12.81	4	3.98
Total	12.63	48	3.67

Table 29: Improvement score for experimental and control groups

Student	Improvement
1	4.18
2	1.63
3	1.94
4	2.06
5	.32
6	2.84
7	−1.87
8	1.35
9	−.77
10	−.49
11	−.53
12	2.11
Total	12

Mann-Whitney U:5, p = .037 (2-tailed).

Table 30: Improvement score for careseeker (actor) and caregiver (student)

Student (Care-Giver)	Care-Giver Improvement Score	Care-Seeker Improvement Score
1	−4.00	1.25
2	6.75	6.00
3	6.50	6.75
4	1.50	7.00
5	−5.50	2.00
6	5.00	−2.00
7	.00	4.00
8	4.00	5.00
9	2.50	2.75
10	2.75	4.50
11	−3.25	−2.25
12	1.75	5.25
Total	12	12

Table 31: Student, time and independent score: an analysis of variance

Source	Sum of Squares	df	Mean Square	F	Signifi-cance
Corrected Model	378.571	11	34.416	2.714	.012
Intercept	8275.550	1	8275.550	652.523	.000
Student	356.758	5	71.352	5.626	.001
Time	1.404E–02	1	1.404E–02	.001	.974
Student–Time	21.799	5	4.360	.344	.883
Error	456.566	36	12.682		
Total	9110.687	48			
Corrected Total	835.137	47			

Independent score at time 2

To see the improvement at time two I subtracted the scores for time 2 from time one and subjected the results to the Mann Whitney Test. Table 29 sets out the improvement score. The first six students are the ones who received training.

As can be seen, the students who had been trained improved on average significantly more than the students who had not.

Table 30 sets out the improvement score by actor and student. I subjected the results of the actors' score and the students' score to the same procedure and got no significant result.

One can see that the independent measure differentiated significantly between students (.001), did not see an effect for time (.974) and did not see some students doing significantly better on day two than others (.883).

Discussion of results

I have three sets of results.

1. Measures of interaction between careseekers and caregivers.

2. Relationship between measures and attachment score.

3. Evidence that training can improve goal-corrected empathic attunement.

In short I have developed two measures of careseeker/caregiver interaction that are internally consistent and reliable. I have also set out the basis of a training programme for improving caregiver performance. I have developed a unique way of testing student performance based on short role-play scenarios using video and professional actors. Finally I have used the experiment to develop a theory of effective caregiving within the conceptual framework of attachment theory. I will discuss these results in order.

Measures

I have three measures of interaction: two subjective and one objective.

Subjective measures

The subjective measures have an internal consistency of .87 (caregivers) and .86 (careseekers). This is an impressive result, one that I hoped for, but much better than I expected. I had constructed a model of effective caregiving that I thought consisted of particular behaviours, attributes and responses. I devised these measures with these attributes in mind. This result suggests that the caregiving properties that I suggested should go together – do go together.

In addition, the two measures correlate in a highly significant way (p = < .001) with each other suggesting that both parties to the interaction evaluate it or experience it in similar ways. It also looks from this study as if I have found a way, through the use of these measures, of differentiating between caregivers (students). There was a highly significant difference between students based on their own score (.000) and on the actors' score (.001). This means that these measures actually get at which students are 'better' than others in their own and others' terms.

These measures therefore yield two sets of information both of which could be useful in selection, training and ongoing development of practitioner performance. Given these results, I consider that it would be worth the time and effort to replicate these measures in other contexts using a larger sample of subjects and locating the study in the real world of practice.

Independent (objective) measure

In addition to the very high correlation between the careseekers and the caregivers, there was a significant correlation between the careseekers' score and the independent score of .246 (p = .016) and a significant cor-relation between the caregivers' score and the independent score of .295 (p = .004). This suggests that the independent rater was measuring something similar to that of the caregiver and the careseeker. Like the latter measures it distinguished significantly between students.

The process that the independent rater was assessing was in fact a more complex process than was being assessed by the actors and the students. While the careseekers and the caregivers were each rating their experience of the interaction between them, the independent rater was rating the process of interaction as it went on between them. The *process of interaction* or *the pattern of interaction* is quite different to interaction as experienced. Patterns of interaction develop in relation to careseeking and caregiving and go back to the earliest experiences of relationship for all of us, as described in chapter three – they go back to our pre-verbal selves. The behavioural pattern of responses triggered by defensive caregiving or defensive careseeking will not necessarily be available to consciousness and accessible for the purposes of evaluating the session, as required by the measuring instruments used by the careseekers and the caregivers (which are self-report measures).

The fact that there is a significant correlation between these three measures suggests to me that the *experience* of interaction and the *process of interaction* may be related. It suggests to me that I should continue investigating the dynamics of careseeking and caregiving along the lines suggested in this book, and that I should continue refining the measures that I have developed. I return to this point in the next chapter, where I examine the connection between the vitality affects of the careseeker and the caregiver and the pattern of interaction developing between them.

Attachment style and independent measure of goal-corrected empathic attunement

There was a significant correlation between secure attachment style and the independent measure. I had hoped to find such an association. Despite the statistical caveat, the fact that I have found one provides support for the theoretical concept of goal-corrected empathic attunement. The theory of goal-corrected empathic attunement (GCEA) suggested that the instinctively based careseeking system will shut down (goal-corrected) when careseeking has been assuaged by the caregiver. I suggested that affect attunement and empathy were necessary components of effective caregiving and that without them careseeking will remain active in whatever form. When careseeking is assuaged, the natural and ever-present exploratory system goes into action and remains active until it is once again over-ridden by the careseeking system. I suggested that effective caregiving in the adult-to-adult context was associated with secure attachment.

In this study, caregivers with a secure attachment style got a significantly better independent score for effective caregiving than those who had a less secure attachment style. They did so in relation to working with four different emotions: anger, sadness, fear and despair. The reader will remember that a study by Haft and Slade (1989) in the parent/infant domain suggested that parents with a more secure attachment style attuned effectively to a range of emotions, while those who were less secure did less well with some emotions. (There is an expanding interest in looking at the effect of client and therapist attachment styles on the outcome of therapeutic intervention, see Hardy *et al.*, 1999, and Rubino *et al.*, 2000.)

The failure of the actors' and students' scores to correlate with the measure of secure attachment is disappointing. The fact that they did correlate with my measure of 'compulsive caregiving' is puzzling. Possible reasons are that these students can be experienced as other directed and effective in the short term but may need help to sustain empathy over the long haul. Sustained empathy is what is required for therapeutic change. It is the capacity for sustained empathy that we need to get clearer about, and the theory of interaction being presented in this book may provide a foundation from which to explore what facilitates and inhibits the capacity to sustain an empathic attitude to self and others.

Training

I have some evidence to suggest that even a short training programme designed to modify and improve responses to emotional reactions to loss made a difference to students' performance. The difference related to the objective rating of performance, not to those made by the student and actor. It was not accounted for by the raters' knowledge of who was trained and who was not, since the ratings were 'blind'.

The training programme was based on self reflection and audio-visual feedback of own work, a force-field analysis of driving and restraining forces in relation to self-selected behaviour targeted for change with very specific input from a facilitator who has also watched at length the video feedback of the previous session. It is very encouraging to find evidence that such a short and focused input makes a difference in the way the student subsequently responded to the presentation of acute emotional distress (the training programme is set out more fully in McCluskey 2001). In terms of the future, if I were to build on this research I would focus even more strongly on the concept of goal-corrected empathic attunement and the affective experience associated with goal-correction. This had not clarified in my mind as I put this training programme in place, and I would welcome the opportunity and the challenge of exploring how to build this into the design of such a training programme in future.

Given that the intervention was short and part of a controlled experiment, it is worth building on these results, developing the training programme and testing it in the real world of practice.

A first step in improving the training programme, apart from making it longer and more intensive, would be to include, as part of the video-feedback work, sessions where I worked with the students or trainees to identify the interaction which suggested that there was distress in the careseeking/caregiving partnership. Work which I have carried out following the experiments described here, and which I will go on to describe in the next chapter, has provided me with a detailed description of a limited number of careseeker/caregiver interactive patterns, some of which are effective and others which are not. Using this data it should be possible in the future to devise much more effective training programmes. I would envisage working collaboratively with students and colleagues, using the patterns as a guide but encouraging them to examine their own work, paying particular attention to their own vitality affects and those of the person they are working with.

Finally I would hope to be able to work out with the trainee what was going on in the interaction which disabled them and got them 'locked in' to a dissatisfying careseeking/caregiving pattern. I would also like to develop some strategy with trainees for noticing when this happens, and for devising ways to get round it in order to open up the flow of communication again or to seek help in regaining their empathic capacity from a competent supervisor.

Conclusion

As far as I know, no one has previously developed any measure or measures of social work student performance in a test situation which:

(a) distinguishes between students;

(b) correlates with a personality measure in a sensible way;

(c) can be improved by training.

For all the limitations and caveats, I feel I have done this. In my next chapter I will proceed to a detailed analysis of patterns of interaction associated with effective and ineffective caregiving responses, using film of recent therapeutic interactions.

CHAPTER ELEVEN

Patterns of functional and dysfunctional careseeking-caregiving partnerships

Introduction

The results of the empirical research suggested that goal-corrected empathic attunement was an interactive process, and could only be judged by paying attention to the interaction and particularly the vitality affects and emotive messages taking place between the two people concerned. Achieving an independent measure of GCEA proved to be dependent on moving away from considering individual behaviours to observing the process of interaction. I also obtained a highly significant correlation between the ratings of the careseekers and the caregivers in terms of the experience of their interaction. This suggested something quite new, that successful careseeking and successful caregiving could be known subjectively in terms of the affect associated with meeting instinctive goals.

While I had obtained a significant correlation between the objective assessment of the interaction and the subjective ratings, I was interested in the fact that the level of agreement was not as great as the subjective measures and returned to the raw data to see if I could make sense of this. I identified the interviews that got 'good' scores from the actor and student but which got 'poor' scores from the objective assessor. I then examined the video material in detail. What I discovered was that in many situations the objective assessor, using as they were the device of rating on the basis of 1.5 minute segments, often missed the complete sequence of interaction and missed out on crucial feedback from one person to the other. What this meant was that the independent assessor often missed a crucial 'repair' in the interaction and only got the disruption.

What I found was that some of these tapes, particularly ones achieving a poor rating from the objective assessor were a delicate sequence of fast moving interactions where the caregiver quite frequently, 'dropped', 'missed', interrupted or otherwise got it wrong with the careseeker, but then almost before they had completed their action, they would notice the non-verbal response from the careseeker and adjust what they were doing to the evident relief of the other and to their mutual delight and pleasure (not always expressed but clearly visible in the smooth resumption by the careseeker of the direction they were heading in and the renewed focus of the caregiver). These interactions were highly fluid, but seen and judged at the 'wrong' moment could convey the impression of ineffective purposeful misattunement. They epitomised for me the concept that I was developing: goal-corrected empathic attunement, and I began to describe this process as one of continual rupture and repair of the interactive process.

The fact that the independent rater was judging the interaction at predetermined intervals and therefore missed quite a lot of the subtlety of the interaction went some way to helping me understand why there was on occasion such discrepancy between the subjective and independent rating. In addition to examining this particular batch of tapes, I also looked closely at the tapes that were judged by both actor and student as very poor. Through this work I began to discriminate patterns of interaction that seemed to be associated with successful (e.g. GCEA) and unsuccessful caregiving. I identified two basic patterns related to unsuccessful caregiving.

The first pattern consisted of the caregiver making hardly any response to the careseeker. They seemed to become frozen. As the distress in the careseeker became more and more evident (as they for example went deeper into despair) the caregiver seemed to become more deeply locked in to a place of no response.

The second pattern was different. In this pattern the caregiver did respond, but they avoided the affect of the careseeker and kept relating at a cognitive level, with *apparent* empathy. Again the distress in the caregiver was obvious. One could visibly see them withdraw inside themselves. As one turned one's attention to the affect of the caregiver (as seen through focussing on the vitality affects on the video image) one could see signs of bewilderment and their distress, as they continued to try and contact the clearly by then withdrawn careseeker. It seemed to me important that I continue to try and clarify the patterns that I was observing in what appeared to be successful and unsuccessful interactions.

Since conducting the empirical work I have worked extensively with clinicians and organisational consultants with the goal of improving our mutual understanding and capacity to identify and regulate affect in careseeking/caregiving interactions and identify the processes involved in successful and unsuccessful caregiving. As a consequence of this work I have become clearer about two aspects of this project; first, that the theory on the dynamics of attachment put forward by Heard and Lake provide a theoretical framework for making sense of the processes one can observe taking place in the interaction between careseekers and caregivers when they are both meeting and failing to meet their respective goals and second, that there are distinct patterns of interaction associated with successful and unsuccessful caregiving. In this chapter I will present a detailed analysis of my findings to date and a chart of the patterns of interaction that I have detected through an analysis of a 150 videos.

Extended attachment theory and goal-corrected instinctive systems

Attachment theory is based on an understanding of instinctive biological systems that function to protect, growth, survival and development and are kept within tolerable levels through appropriate interaction with the environment. Extended attachment theory postulates the existence of five distinct biologically based instinctive systems. Each system has a function, for example, the function of careseeking is to get protection, or encouragement to carry on exploring, (the goal is to reach a caregiver who can provide that). The function of the caregiving system is to respond in a way that settles the careseeker or supports their development (the goal is effective caregiving). The function of the sexual system is to engage in mutual pleasure with someone with whom there is an affectionate bond or for one's own pleasure in defensive ways (the goal is orgasm). The function of the interest-sharing system is to share enjoyment with other like minded people in a context where one's level of skill competence and self esteem can develop (the goal is personal and social competence and the pleasure associated); the function of the system for self-defence is to respond when one of the other systems is activated but not reaching its goal (the goal is maintenance of maximum well-being). In this way one can see that the different systems have separate functions and different goals.

The beauty of the theory proposed by Heard and Lake is that they provide an explanation for what one observes when looking at interaction between a careseeker and caregiver which is clearly not going very well and where the careseeker is getting more and not less distressed. If one thinks of one instinctive system (such as careseeking) being infiltrated by another instinctive system (such as self-defence) that has been activated by feedback to the system as a whole (i.e. that the careseeking system is not reaching its goal), then one has a hypothesis about the dynamics of the interaction which one can begin to test. We have all been distressed watching ineffective careseeking/ caregiving interactions and have probably been on the giving and receiving end of them many times. When careseekers and caregivers fail to reach their goals, it may be that what one is observing is disorganisation of the careseeking system which is distressing to watch.

According to extended attachment theory, any of the systems can be infiltrated by the other systems when not reaching their goals. In this way one can therefore conceive of the careseeking system being infiltrated by defensive caregiving, by sexuality and by interest sharing. Care-giving can also be infiltrated by careseeking, interest sharing, sexuality and self- defence.

As mentioned above since completing the experimentally designed research I have been keen to identify as clearly as possible patterns of interaction associated with successful and failed careseeking and caregiving. I have worked with experienced therapists of many different theoretical orientations (both group psychotherapists and individual psychotherapists), and organisational consultants, in the UK, Sweden and America, in all over 250 people have taken part in workshops designed to identify the process of affect attunement and regulation in dyadic and group interactions. During the course of this work, several people agreed to be video taped as they engaged in both brief and extended consultations.

Using two digital cameras and a mirror strategically placed to create a split screen effect I have acquired a further set of good quality video images of interaction. Using video editing software (Final Cut Express for Macintosh and Adobe Premier 6 for Windows) I been able to analyse the verbal and non-verbal interaction frame by frame (the programme allows one to examine 25 frame a second, this allows one to track minute movements as the dyad interact and to capture the precise sound accompanying the interaction.

Data

The data that I have had available to me consists of three types:

1 *Experimentally controlled.* Videos generated for the original research under experimental conditions. Actors and trainees worked together for 10 minutes. (n=108)

2 *Simulated for educational and training purposes.* Videos generated during training workshops. All involved were experienced clinicians (psychiatrists, psychotherapists, clinical psychologists, social workers, nurses, other therapists and organisational consultants. Interviews lasted for approximately 20 minutes, and were videod using a split screen device. The volunteer careseekers all explored something of emotional importance to them. (n=20)

3 *Live practice between therapist and patients/clients.* Videos generated by senior clinicians of many different theoretical orientations working with their patients in their own offices. These sessions lasted for the usual period of one hour or fifty minutes. One psychoanalytic therapist and their patient allowed me access to one week's therapy sessions consisting of five consecutive sessions of 50 minutes each. (n=22)

The analysis of this recent material, the 108 videos created for the research project just described, and the 22 videos created at the beginning of that research with the cooperation of experienced clinicians and their patients in the privacy of their consulting rooms has confirmed me in the view that there are clear patterns of interaction associated with effective and ineffective caregiving.

In determining whether a pattern of interaction is present one is looking to see whether the caregiver responds to the careseeker in a predictable manner throughout the consultation. If one can detect this happening over the course of an interview then one can say one is observing a distinctive pattern of interaction.

Careseekers present differently to caregivers depending on the state they are in at any given moment. The skill of the caregiver is being able to be flexible enough to respond in such a way that the careseeker reaches their goals. Clearly this does not always happen. My empirical research allowed me to control for the effect of presentation of the careseeker on the response of the caregiver. What I found was that some-caregivers performed very poorly according to their own, and other's, standards (objective and subjective) while doing extremely well with different careseekers and with the same careseeker when that careseeker was in *a different state*.

What this tells us is that a dynamic gets triggered between the careseeker and caregiver that is fuelled by verbal and non verbal messages and that in situations that turn out badly an interactive patterns can become established quite quickly that is difficult to break. In situations that turn out well it seems from my analysis of the data that the caregiver needs to be active, focussed, flexible, non defensive, attuned to feedback and in exploratory cognitive mode. The function of these emotive messages between careseekers and caregivers and how they work will be much more fully explored in a separate book (Heard, Lake and McCluskey, in press).

Having successfully identified and reliable rated the pattern associated with effective caregiving responses (goal-corrected empathic attunement), it has taken me a long time to clarify the different patterns of interaction associated with unsuccessful caregiving. I have been aware for some time that the vitality affect of the careseeker was a key component in influencing the subsequent interaction – not with all caregivers, but with some. I was also aware that the way careseekers presented verbally, whether they were clear and succinct or whether they were ambiguous, rambling or unfocused, also affected the interaction with the caregiver. Lastly, I was aware that when the verbal and nonverbal behaviour contradicted each other, that that also affected the pattern of interaction.

However, as said many times in the book, what happens in the interaction is not just a product of one person. It was notable that some caregivers adopted different postures, and responded differently to similar opening verbal and non-verbal messages (the experimental design described earlier in the book lent itself to observing such phenomena in detail). Their posture could signal a dominant stance (chin tilted upwards) or a slightly submissive stance (chin titled downwards) or open and level (chin level, body slightly leaning towards the careseeker or just loosely centred. In addition how the caregiver responded verbally quickly indicated whether they were going to focus on avoiding the affect of the careseeker, pursue it regardless of feedback, or not respond at all.

What has been helpful to me in trying to distinguish the patterns has been to think first in terms of the *mode of expression* of the careseeker, second to consider their *initial vitality states* and third, the *state the careseeker is in at the end of the consultation* as judged by their vitality affects, verbal and other nonverbal messages. I found Grice's (1975, 1989) and Hesse's

(1996) elaboration thereof, four maxims for distinguishing rational, coherent and cooperative speech (i.e. quantity, quality, relation and manner) very useful in classifying the mode of expression. It helped me to discriminate between speech, which was coherent, succinct, relevant, sufficiently informative and orientating and delivered in a cooperative manner from that which clearly broke all these rules of expression.

I judged the 'state' the careseeker was in primarily through a detailed examination of the audio and video tracks of the video recording. I noted the pitch, tone and pace of the voice, the facial expression, whether the person made or avoided eye contact, had a centred, slumped (collapsed) or rigid posture and then made rough classifications into low medium, high and regulated vitality affects. Using these categories (voice, face, eye, and posture) the profiles of the different vitality states looked as follows:

Low vitality states:

The voice tone is low pitched, the pace of speaking is slow, the facial expression is relatively immobile, there is avoidance of eye contact when speaking, posture is generally slumped, and in general the person seems withdrawn into themselves. The whole face looks rather immobile, though there is some expression around the eyes.

Medium vitality levels:

The person expresses themselves similarly to the above but there is more eye contact when speaking, the posture is less withdrawn and slumped and the speech would is not as low or slow. There could be a suggestion or hint of a slight rocking motion. The upper part of the face around the eyes seems more expressive in contrast to the muscles in the jaw and around the mouth which appear tense.

High vitality levels:

The person's speech is fast and rapid, there is a lot of intense eye contact, a lot of movement in the body and a tendency to lean into the 'space' between the careseeker and the caregiver. The facial expression looks strained and tense. The general impression is of intensity.

Regulated vitality levels:

The person tends to look 'present' behind their eyes and to look lively and responsive. They make eye contact with the careseeker and tend to have a loosely centred posture. Their facial expression is fluid and mobile and their voice tone has a grounded and resonant tone.

Interactions patterns and the emotive messages that accompany them

The following series of picture have been chosen to depict vitality levels as communicated between a careseeker and a caregiver. All the people involved in the project and whose photographs I use to illustrate the phenomena under discussion have given me their permission to use the material in this book and for research and training purposes. I am very grateful to them indeed as I do not think what I am trying to convey could come across as clearly without the visual evidence.

What they see on each other's face.

The regulation or lack of regulation of careseeker vitality states through effective or ineffective misattunement or non-attunement by the caregiver

Caregiver amplifies the affect of the careseeker
(Effective purposeful misattunement – tunes up the affect)

Caregiver is to the right of the picture (Picture 1). Note she is expressing more sadness than the careseeker . Careseeker is receptive to the affect mirroring – note the expression in her eyes. Note the caregiver is leaning slightly towards the careseeker, indicating that she is willing to engage with her affect.

Picture 1

Picture 2

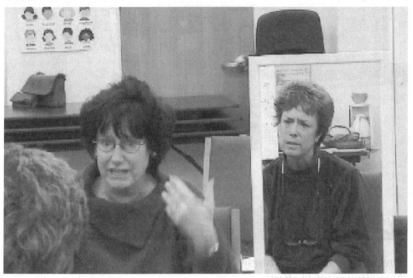

Careseeker approaches with heightened affect:
Caregiver comes forward to meet it with less intensity
(Effective purposeful misattunement – tunes down the affect)

The caregiver is to the right of the picture (Picture 2). Note they are both leaning in towards each other. Note the look of fear in the eyes of the careseeker. Note the serious but steady look in the eyes of the caregiver. This is vitality matching and regulation. Purposeful misattunement by the caregiver to the affect of careseeker with the purpose of lowering the intensity so that the careseeker can access interpersonal competence

High vitality levels in the careseeker
Caregiver has their own fear system activated in the interaction and so fails
to regulate the affect of the careseeker or attune to their goals
(Lack of affect regulation)

The caregiver is to the left of the picture (Picture 3). Note the intensity of affect in the eyes and posture of the careseeker. She has raised her hand to her neck to indicate the subject of her distress (she is telling of having noted a suspicious growth on the neck of her son). Note the slumped posture of the care-gi ver. There is a serious look in his eyes and he is clearly listening but he is not responding – he is not *showing* that he understands how distressed she is – there is no affect matching and the careseeker sees no impact of what she is saying on his face

Picture 3

Caregiver distances from careseeker affect, careseeker withdraws (Non-attunement to affect)

Careseeker is to the left of the picture (Picture 4). He is looking down, quite withdrawn. Note the way his hand is holding his arm and his posture is slightly slumped (self comforting behaviour). Meanwhile, the caregiver is clearly straining to understand and connect with what he saying. In fact she is focusing on the details of his story – trying to get them 'right' rather than following his affect and seeking out his goals and concerns.

Picture 4

In the above images, one can see the vitality of each person as they bring themselves to the encounter and what is happening to their vitality levels as they meet. Our focus is on whether the person (careseeker) is available to being met and whether they are or not. As one moment in the interaction one misses the previous encounter and subsequent interaction. Nevertheless, I think one can say that in the first two images there is the possibility of meeting in the sense that the caregiver is present and attending to the careseeker's affect, in the second, the careseeker while present physically is emotionally absent. In the first two images, while there is tension, stress and sadness there is an absence of distress associated with the encounter itself. In the last two images, the woman seems desperately to be seeking a response, to make an impression on the caregiver, in the latter, the careseeker's has withdrawn their eyes from the caregiver and gives the impression of being on his own.

In the first picture what one notices is that there is an imbalance between the two people in relation to the expression of affect. The caregiver is expressing more sadness. This is misattunement to affect, it is not an exact match, it captures the underlying affect and amplifies it. The purpose of the caregiver's response is to signal they understand the feeling being expressed, that it is alright and understandable and that it is alright with them if the careseeker enters more deeply into their affective experience. One also notices that the caregiver is looking at the careseeker and responding to them and not to something that is triggered within themselves. One judges the accuracy of this observation by what happens next. If the caregiver really is responding to the careseeker then one should notice fast, shifting expressions of emotion on her face that in slow motion (through video analysis) one can see are highly attuned and reflective of the careseeker's expressions. Further down in this chapter I show a sequence of interaction between these two people where one can see this happening.

In the second picture, again one has the highly attentive focus of the caregiver on the careseeker's face. There is however no sense that the careseeker is straining or putting themselves under pressure, they are just available. The careseeker clearly wants to convey 'something big' a big experience and to impress the caregiver with it. Her expression seems to convey 'are you getting this? What is important in the context of over arousal of affect is that the caregiver neither matches or amplifies it, but responds verbally in such a way that the careseeker knows they have 'got it'. The affect needs to be accepted, understood and not overwhelm or be seen (on the face) to be overwhelming. This is effective purposeful misattunement. The caregiver catches the affect but tunes it down by their own emotive messages to the careseeker. Again, to judge the accuracy of this observation one needs to watch what happens next between these two. If the caregiver is available to the careseeker one will notice that she remains leaning slightly towards the careseeker, that her head remains level and that there is cross modal matching of careseeker intensity of affect through for example her speech (speed, tone and resonance). In this way the caregiver will 'hold' and contain the flow of emotion and regulate the careseeker so that they do not get lost (become disorganised) or emotionally overwhelmed in the telling of their story.

With a careseeker in this 'state' one needs to regulate affect and orientate to context. One is working to create and maintain boundaries so that it is safe for the careseeker to actually access their deepest emotions, rather than encouraging them to express feelings that to a large extent are generated by defences against the original experience.

In the third picture, the careseeker is seeking to impress the caregiver that she experienced real fear when she discovered her son had a malignant tumour, (she herself had a similar tumour at about his age which turned out to be benign). There is a failure to respond by the caregiver. The caregiver is attuning to the fear but withdrawing into themselves with it, thereby distancing from the careseeker. The result is to leave the careseeker alone with their distress. To judge if this is true one would expect the pattern of no response and heightened distress to continue. This is what happened until the careseeker began to take care of the caregiver and attend to his feelings. Note the pictures of this sequence further down in the chapter.

In the fourth picture, one can see the caregiver straining to understand. This is very different from the first two pictures where the caregiver is simply present and available without fear or fear. The affect on the careseeker's face is very sad. He looks defeated. He has withdrawn into himself. In the sequence of pictures that I show further down, he attempts yet again to get his affect and his intentions across to the caregiver and when this doesn't happen yet again, he looks frustrated and a bit agitated. Meanwhile, as in this picture, one can see the strain and distress on the caregiver's face, they know they are 'not getting it'. This is non attunement to affect. The caregiver is paying far too much attention to getting the 'story; right and is not sufficiently centred in themselves to simply receive the communication.

Sequences of interaction depicting affect regulation through purposeful misattunement to affect

The following six pictures have been taken from a brief encounter to show the process of affect regulation in the context of the careseeker presenting with high vitality levels and a certain amount of fear. The careseeker is to the left of the picture (in the mirror)

Goal-corrected empathic attunement

Picture 5

CS 'I have this terror'.
Notice the expression in her eyes

I judge her demeanour to be intense and so would classify her as having high vitality levels. She has an almost startled look on her face and her posture is stressed, her back is pushed forward and up. Note the expression in her eye is more inwardly than outwardly directed. She is responding to affect generated by her thoughts or physical sensations not what she is experiencing in the interaction with the person of the caregiver.

In contrast observe the posture and expression of the caregiver. The posture is loosely centred and relaxed. The caregiver looks totally present and focussed on the careseeker. She does not have an inwardly directed expression in her eye, rather she seems to be 'tracking' what is happening in the careseeker. Her vitally levels appear regulated. I would judge her to be available, undefended, and free from fear. If the exploratory component of her instinctive caregiving system is activated one would expect that we will be able to see her continue to track and relate to what the careseeker is bringing and attend to her goals for the meeting.

Picture 6

CG 'Do you think you can tell the future?'
CS 'No. I don't' – note the relief expressed in her eye.

The caregiver is on the right. One can see from the expression on her face that she is totally present and related to the careseeker. They are each responding to the other. Note that the expression on the caregiver's face is not as dramatic as that of the careseeker. It is more 'toned down'. This is what I see as *purposeful misattunement*. The caregiver is actually picking up the affect of the careseeker but is reflecting it back in a moderated form, with the goal of reducing the affect so that the caregiver can access her cognitive capacities. This is *affect regulation*.

This careseeker got into what one might describe as a high vitality state within moments of the session starting (see picture 5). The caregiver takes her affect seriously (note expression) but at a much lower level of vitality. The caregiver might have arrived in a low, depressed despairing state – then the caregiver might well have responded with a slightly higher level of vitality – not too high (that might be experienced as out of touch and teasing in some way – that would be – *ineffective purposeful misattunement*). *Effective purposeful misattunement* should be close enough to join the other person where they were in themselves but different enough to convey a sense of presence, availability and competence to contain, regulate and promote exploration.

Picture 7

The careseeker and the caregiver are responding to one another.

Note the expression on both faces. The caregiver is putting something into the interaction, the careseeker is taking it in. In fact they were mutually engaged in finding a word to fit the experience of the careseeker. However the vitality affects of the careseeker are still high. Note the tense posture – she is sitting up as it were in a slightly rigid way. There is strain on the back. The caregiver is still loosely centred – one does not get an impression of postural strain.

Picture 8

Care-seeking turns to exploration

When careseeking is assuaged and exploration kicks in the vitality affects are of liveliness (Heard and Lake, 1997). When one sees the expression above, there is no doubt about the relief and pleasure in both parties. This is what people look like when instinctive goals have been met – careseeking and caregiving. There is as we know only temporary respite, the process of interacting is a constantly shifting one and within moments if the caregiver has been successful, the careseeker will either revisit what was causing them concern or bring in similar or deeper concerns. In fact within seconds, this is precisely what happened.

Picture 9

Revisiting the terror after the relief

Again note the way the careseeker has adopted a strained posture as well as the open eyed look associated with terror. What she is saying and how she is looking is totally congruent. However, look at the face of the caregiver. She is not reflecting terror back to the careseeker. She is looking quite relaxed as if she is accepting the feeling but not absorbed in it or overwhelmed by it. She is involved, through her non-verbal signals, in affect regulation. She is regulating the careseeker's affect. The message being conveyed is 'I am present (note she is leaning slightly towards the caregiver, not away from her, she is not looking up as if she were searching for some ideas, her chin is slightly down and she is looking directly at the careseeker) and waiting to become involved again, which she does and then one gets the next image.

Picture 10

Vitality affects associated with successful careseeking and caregiving

This was a successful consultation, both the instinctive systems for careseeking and caregiving were activated and met their respective goals, giving rise to pleasure and relief.

Affect identification, regulation and containment

I will now show a different dyad. Because of the sensitive nature of the information within this consultation, I have chosen to show just one image. Unfortunately one misses the interaction and the evidence for the subtitle above. I still think that showing even one picture is important to convey the way in which affect is conveyed muted, absorbed and regulated. The picture is taken from the video and is from the first few moments of the encounter as the careseeker explains what it is they wish to talk about. The careseeker is on the right. She wishes to discuss a marital problem but first wants the careseeker to know that as a child she had a very terrifying mother who never attuned to her. The picture shows the careseeker revisiting inside herself what that terror felt like. She wants the caregiver to have some understanding of her experience as a child and that she brings some of this experience and expectations into her most intimate adult relationship which she is about to discuss.

Picture 11

The careseeker is on the left of the picture, the caregiver is shown in the mirror.

Again note that the caregiver is clearly present and attending. She is not reflecting the same level of affect intensity as the careseeker, she is absorbing it but is not overwhelmed by it. This is a very important exchange just like we saw happening between the other couple. The message from the careseeker is that they are not frightened by what they are hearing. That signals to the careseeker that the caregiver can be relied on not to up the ante or heighten the affect as it were. In our terms they are *regulating the careseeker's affect,* by not mimicking it they are accepting it and *tuning it down.* Note the posture of the careseeker in this picture is very similar to the posture of the caregiver in the other series of picture (pictures 5-10). This posture I associate with *regulated vitality levels.*

In the above picture, note the careseeker is also exhibiting high vitality levels; their posture is tense and their affect is intense. They are intent on conveying their experience to the caregiver. In an interaction like this it is very important that the careseeker takes note of what is being said and that they show on their face that they see how serious the communication is. This is what regulates the affect. If the caregiver does not show that they know what is being communicated, the careseeker becomes even more distressed, will carry on trying to get their message across or will give up. It is a curious thing that the everyday language we use for this is to 'try to *impress* on someone'. In my view we do actually want to see the *imprint* of what we are communicating on the face of someone else. When we see that, we know they have got the message.

Non-attunement to affect giving rise to self-defence in the careseeking-caregiving partnership

The next series of three images show a sequence of interaction associated with failed careseeking and failed caregiving. Both parties are in distress.

Picture 12 shows the careseeker withdrawing and giving up.

One can see that in spite of the caregiver making an intense effort to 'get it right and to understand', she has failed to connect with the careseeker and he has withdrawn from her at this point. He is not looking at her, even though she is clearly focussed on him, or to be more precise what he has said, not on his affect. One can see from studying the vitality affects on both their faces that the careseeker's affect is more sad and withdrawn and is less intense than the caregivers. The caregiver has more vitality, they are mis-matched. This is not an *amplification of affect*. It is a *non-attunement to affect*. (I will show an example of amplification in the last set of pictures).

Picture 12

The careseeker is on the left.

Picture 13

The careseeker is on the left.

Note also that the careseeker's posture is slightly slumped (collapsed, remember the study by Tronick referred to earlier), in contrast the posture of the caregiver is slightly rigid as if she is under some stress. Both the instinctive goal-corrected systems of careseeking and caregiving are active but unassuaged and one can see the distress of the lack of connection between them on both their faces.

Picture 13 shows the caregiver trying to get his message across after several failed attempts when he clearly thinks the caregiver is not getting it. In fact the caregiver's mistake was to keep interrupting him and asking him questions about the content of what he was saying. She would have done better, as it were to have engaged with his feeling and supported his explorations in that direction.

One can see that there is a certain intensity in the careseeker's expression. He is trying to get something important across. From the caregiver's expression, she also is clearly concentrating and trying to 'get it'. One can see there is a failure of affect regulation. The caregiver is neither reflecting not regulating his affect; what she is conveying is that she is not quite sure where he is.

We get confirmation of the distress in the careseeking caregiving partnership from a picture taken just a few seconds from the end of the session (picture 14). One can see that they are both a bit irritated. He seems to have withdrawn further. She looks 'stumped' as to how to make contact with him.

Picture 14

Instinctive fear system overriding the arousal of exploratory caregiving

I will now move on to show a further example of a careseeker and care-giver 'missing' each other. This careseeker (on the right of the picture) started the session wanting to discuss a recent very frightening event that had happened in her family. Within seconds of her describing what had happened the caregiver had gone very quite and for the whole of the session hardly engaged with her and failed to engage emotionally. He said afterwards that he felt 'dumped on with a load of very heavy stuff which he hadn't expected to come up in a training context'. I think context does make a difference to how one responds. Working on real issues in front of an audience even when freely brought by the other person, can present a dilemma for how to respond, interfering with one's 'natural' response. Issues about pri-vacy, confidentiality, containment, boundaries and so on can surface in such a way that one fails to respond in the way one might do in the pri-vacy of a properly negotiated therapeutic contract. However, with the consent of the persons involved I have included this example here because I have seen it over and over again, in therapeutic and non therapeutic contexts.

As a caregiver, sometimes, one has only to hesitate even momentarily, from engaging authentically, for the interaction to become set in a pat-tern. The careseeker will pick up the hesitation immediately and will either renew pressure to connect or withdraw. The renewed pressure (given the ambiguity of meaning because it is non-verbal) might deepen the doubt in the caregiver, deepen the fear as to how to respond. What happened in this situation, I think, is that the caregiver's fear system did get activated quite quickly and over-rode his caregiving system.

Talking it over with the caregiver since the event, he thinks this is quite possibly what happened, it makes sense to him. However from a psychodynamic point of view he would understand the process that took place between him and the careseeker in terms of him picking up the careseeker's fear and that he was trying to reflect on how to respond adequately. This is as maybe. In interactive terms what is experienced by the careseeker is a lack of response and what is experienced by the caregiver is a feeling of being overwhelmed of not knowing quite how to make an adequate response.

To me this is immobilisation at the level of infiltration of one system by another. Whether it is one's own fear system that has become aroused or one has picked up the fear in the other. It makes more sense to think of one's own system being activated, whatever the trigger, it could well have been triggered by attunement to the affect in the careseeker. I have a shorthand way of thinking about this pattern of interaction, I refer to it as *affect attunement that disables empathy* (where the affect being attuned to is fear).

Picture 15

Lack of affect regulation by the caregiver.

The caregiver is on the left of the picture (in the mirror). This is taken over two thirds of the way into the session. The caregiver has hardly been responding at all. One can see from his expression that he is struggling as to what to say. His vitality levels are low. His posture is slightly slumped. In contrast, the careseeker's vitality levels are intense. At this point she is making a further appeal to the caregiver for a response that would show he is taking in what she is saying. The caregiver's point of view she is bringing in even further frightening material which is making it even more difficult for the caregiver to know how to respond.

It is obvious from the picture that the careseeker is in distress. This is distress in the context of the encounter with the caregiver. Not just in relation to what she is talking about but in relation to the caregiver and his lack of response. The distress in the caregiver is more difficult to *see* (it is more hidden). It is there in the focus in his eyes. He is looking intently at the careseeker and he is almost immobile.

Shortly after this episode, the careseeker shifted from careseeking to looking after the caregiver and said to him it must be difficult for him to listen to what she was saying.

Picture 16 shows the momentary relief (and embarrassment) on the caregiver's face as the careseeker attends to his feelings.

Picture 16

Picture 16 The careseeker (on the right) begins to look after the feelings of the caregiver. 'I am thinking here you are a young man, about the same age as my son (she was talking about her son who was seriously ill). I understand that what is happening here for the careseeker is that her careseeking system is not being assuaged and is being infiltrated (in order to self regulate) by her caregiving system. In other words her caregiving system is being used defensively to self regulate. As said earlier I understand that what is happening to the caregiver is that his caregiving system is being disabled by the arousal of his instinctive fear system and he has gone into flight.

Picture 17 shows the careseeker almost giving up and at this point the caregiver open his mouth to say something.

Picture 17

Picture 17. Note the acute sadness in the eyes of the careseeker and the way in which she has withdrawn eye contact from the caregiver. He is clearly moved to want to come in and say something, though one can see from the way he is angling his head that he is tentative and not sure he is on track. My understanding is that given he has been in flight from the affect, he is having to try and contact the careseeker's affect through his imagination not directly through an emotional attunement with her which he is able to think about and make available to her.

Goal-corrected empathic attunement: amplification
of affect and affect regulation

My final pictures show the caregiver amplifying the affect of the careseeker. This is in the service of affect regulation. The caregiver is tuning up the affect so that the careseeker can see it on her face and in a way make it easier (more acceptable?) to access it herself. When people are deeply cut off from their own affect, and do not feel their feelings (as so well described by Susan Vas Dias, 2000) then one is talking about much more serious defences than the social defence of embarrassment or shyness or whatever. In the cases that Vas Dias describes, the onus on the caregiver for heightened attunement and affect regulation of this sort is intense. This is not so here, but it is a minor version of detachment from affective experience.

In picture 18 the careseeker is to the left of the picture. The session has just started and she has just said how sad she is that she will never know her daughter (who is profoundly disabled). Note that the face of the caregiver (in the mirror) is showing more sadness.

The next few clips are from the session as it progresses, one can see how 'in tune' the caregiver was with the careseeker and the one brief moment of relief and exploration for the careseeker. What is striking is how receptive and responsive they are to each other. The caregiver is clearly not defended. She is concentrating on the careseeker all the time and is in exploratory mode. Unlike some of the other examples we have been looking at, in this context and in this instance the caregiver's instinctive caregiving system is not infiltrated by the instinctive system for self-defence.

Picture 19. Talking about the fact that the careseeker would rather have time for herself than to spend it with her daughter. Note how physically 'in tune' they are with the conflict – it is expressing itself more fully on caregiver's face

Picture 18

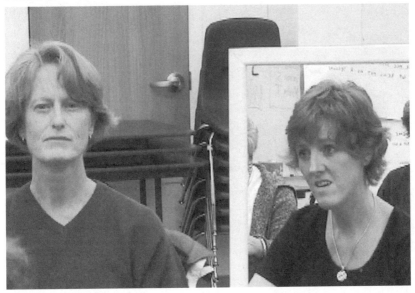

CS 'There is a feeling that I will never know her'. (Her daughter)

Picture 19

Picture 20 In tune with the conflict

Talking about the fact that the careseeker would rather have time for herself than to spend it with her daughter. Note how physically 'in tune' they are with the conflict – it is expressing itself more fully on caregiver's face

Picture 21 (Note the responsiveness in careseeker's eyes)

Caregiver: 'Remember how we can go to guilt when we have a thought about reality, when we have a 'should' about it'.
Careseeker: Yeah

Picture 22

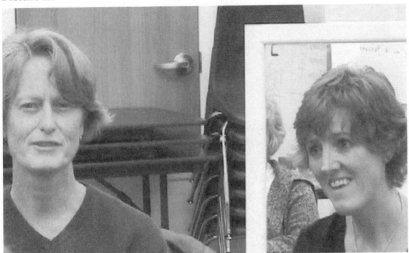

Caregiver: 'So you have a pull inside of you to do things for yourself or to do things for your daughter, it is a conflict most parents have...'
Note careseeker taking this in. And note the tenderness in caregiver

Picture 23

Caregiver: 'How does it feel to know that?
Careseeker: 'It felt good to have it normalised because it does not feel normal'

Picture 24

The reader can see for themselves how engaged these two are in spite of the subject matter being sad. The caregiver is not drawing back from the sadness but coming forward to meet it and explore it. This dyad show in images what I mean by goal-corrected empathic attunement.

Comment

One can think of careseeker–caregiver interactions in terms of connecting or failing to connect with another person through attunement, purposeful misattunement or non attunement to their vitality affects.

1   Connection with the other person through attunement to their goals, vitality matching, effective purposeful misattunement in the service of affect regulation and empathic containment and orientation

2   Failure to connect through non-attunement by the caregiver to the affect of the careseeker: careseeker withdraws into self-care

3   Failure to connect due to a state of disorganisation in the caregiver

4   Failure to connect through non-attunement. Careseeker dismisses caregiver: caregiver withdraws

What really stands out from the above analysis, is the importance of the caregiver responding to the affect of the careseeker, if that doesn't happen, there is a noticeable withdrawal from the caregiver by the careseeker. The vitality affects tell us something about the mood the person is in and they must be engaged with and regulated in such a way that the person becomes available. As a caregiver one cannot make contact with someone whose vitality affects are either very low or very high. Attunement, misattunement and non-attunement to vitality affects are probably the key caregiving behaviours that distinguish the foundations for successful or unsuccessful caregiving.

Through analysing adult to adult interaction in careseeking caregiving situations I am beginning to see that one gets patterns that seem to correlate with the major discriminations in the attachment literature: secure, avoidant, ambivalent, disorganised. Like in the infant situation without engagement with and accurate identification of affect and affect regulation, the careseeking system within the careseeker will be infiltrated with the system for self-defence and the behaviours associated with maximum self regulation. What is dramatic about the photographs is the contrast between those caregivers who are alert and affectively responsive to the careseeker and those who are not. What is also visibly clear is that goal-corrected empathic attuned interaction is accompanied by fluid face movements and that defensive interaction is accompanied by tension, which shows in the face and posture.

Careseeking: typical styles of communication

(i) Wants to discuss feelings, conflicts and concerns

(ii) Is reluctant to discuss feelings, conflicts and concerns

(iii) Brings in issues they are concerned about but tangle the caregiver when they try to help

(iv) Brings in issues they are concerned about but dismiss the caregiver when they try to help

(v) Is overwhelmed incoherent and disorganised in their presentation of feelings conflicts and concerns

Caregivers: typical responses to careseeking

One can broadly classify into five categories the way that caregivers respond to careseeker affect:

(i) Attuned to careseeker affect, regulate it (through purposeful effective misattunement) and attends to careseeking goals

(ii) Avoidance of careseeker affect and attempts to deflect careseeker from exploring it (through purposeful ineffective misattunement)

(iii) Avoids engaging with affect, becomes disorganised, then focuses on affect, regulates it and attends to careseeker's goals (non-attunement, attunement, effective purposeful misattunement)

(iv) Avoids engaging with careseeker affect and becomes immobilised

(v) Misattunes to affect, becomes disorganised

Using the procedure described earlier, I made a detailed analysis of the video data and identified nine distinct patterns of interaction between careseekers and caregivers. I have put together the following chart to illustrate my understanding of interactive patterns between careseekers and caregivers.

The chart provides details about:

(i) Initial presentation of careseeker (the state the careseeker is in in relation to vitality affects);

(ii) Pattern of interaction between careseeker and caregiver;

(iii) Process of engagement by caregiver with careseeker affect;

(iv) Attachment dynamics in the careseeking system;

(v) Attachment dynamics in the caregiving system;

(vi) Classification of caregiving responses.

Patterns of interaction associated with effective and ineffective caregiving

Initial presentation of careseeker in relation to wanting help	Pattern of interaction between careseeker and caregiver	Process of engagement by caregiver with careseeker affect	Attachment dynamics in the careseeking system	Attachment dynamics in the caregiving system	Classification of caregiving responses
(Style A) Wants to discuss feelings, issues and concerns and presents with low, medium or high vitality	(Pattern 1) Careseeker produces source of worry; caregiver responds to the affect and the thoughts and orients to context; careseeker carries on presenting issues; caregiver responds to affect and concerns; careseeker and caregiver are mutually responsive	Effective, purposeful misattunement by the caregiver to careseeker affect: comes forward to meet the careseeker and either amplifies their affect or tunes it down. Provides containment, orientation to context, focus and empathy	Careseeking is assuaged, the exploratory system becomes active, relief and hope are experienced	The caregiving system remains active and in exploratory mode	Attuned to goals of careseeker using the process of goal-corrected empathic attunement **Effective purposeful misattunement to affect which regulates, contains and attends to careseeker's goals**
(Style A) Wants to discuss feelings, issues and concerns and presents with low, medium or high vitality	(Pattern 2) Careseeker introduces issue: caregiver interrupts with questions; careseeker carries on with concerns: caregiver interrupts and diverts: careseeker returns to concerns; caregiver interrupts and diverts; careseeker withdraws and gives up	Ineffective purposeful misattunement to the affect of the careseeker. This generally involves the caregiver engaging with details in the careseeker's story and avoiding engaging with the feelings that they are presenting; careseeker stops exploring and becomes distressed or disorganised	Careseeking system is eventually overridden by the system for self defence (e.g. self-comforting, or defensive caregiving)	The caregiving system remains active and unassuaged	Avoidance of engagement with affect and capacity for affect regulation disabled. Mis-attunes to affective feedback **Ineffective purposeful misattunement to careseeker affect in an attempt to deflect careseeker from exploring it.**

Initial presentation of careseeker in relation to wanting help	Pattern of interaction between careseeker and caregiver	Process of engagement by caregiver with careseeker affect	Attachment dynamics in the careseeking system	Attachment dynamics in the caregiving system	Classification of caregiving responses
(Style A) Presents clear account, with sufficient detail. Wants to discuss feelings, issues and concerns and presents with low, medium or high vitality	(Pattern 3) Careseeker introduces issue: caregiver interrupts with questions; careseeker carries on with concerns; caregiver interrupts and diverts; careseeker returns to concerns; caregiver modifies response and orients to the goals of the careseeker; careseeker responds with increased vitality; caregiver continues supporting goal of careseeker.	Initially ineffective purposeful misattunement to the affect of the careseeker. This is then followed by a change in pattern of response based on feedback from careseeker and access to own cognitive learning	Careseeking system is initially over-ridden by the system for self defence, that then subsides in response to effective caregiving and the exploratory system becomes engaged	The caregiving system is activated, becomes infiltrated with the system for self-defence, which is assuaged through a capacity to access methods and techniques that have been learned and are designed to attune to the person of the careseeker.	Initially not-attuned to feedback from affect, and avoidance of engagement with affect; re-orients to goal of caregiver and affect; becomes responsive to feedback; becomes engaged in affect regulation, containment and orientation, correct affect identification, introducing helpful perspectives and supporting exploration **Initial ineffective, purposeful misattunement to careseeker affect. Caregiver then refocuses on careseeker affect, regulates it, and attends to careseeker's goals**
(Style A) Is terse, but clear, and focussed. Wants to discuss feelings, issues and concerns and presents with low, medium or high vitality	(Pattern 4) Careseeker is demanding: caregiver's responses are cognitive and fail to regulate affect; careseeker becomes more demanding, caregiver continues engaging cognitively; careseeker becomes more aroused; caregiver, careseeker, or both, attack or withdraw	Misattunement to the affect of the careseeker. This generally involves failing to match the emotional intensity of the affect of the careseeker, verbally and non-verbally	Careseeking remains active and unassuaged. Careseeker becomes disorganised	Caregiving system is over-ridden by fear system and either takes flight or fights	Does not attune to careseeker affect, avoidance of engagement with affect and capacity for affect regulation disabled **Non attuned to affect, caregiving infiltrated by self defence, becomes disorganised**

Initial presentation of careseeker in relation to wanting help	Pattern of interaction between careseeker and caregiver	Process of engagement by caregiver with careseeker affect	Attachment dynamics in the careseeking system	Attachment dynamics in the caregiving system	Classification of caregiving responses
(Style A) Wants to discuss issues, feelings, conflicts and concerns. Presents with high, low or medium vitality	(Pattern 5) Worries presented with varying degrees of vitality: caregiver provides minimal verbal and non-verbal response; careseeker continues to explore and present worries and concerns; caregiver continues to make little or no response; this continues until careseeker gives up	Non attuned: resists regulating the arousal levels of the careseeker	Careseeking system infiltrated by the systems for self defence (which may take the form of defensive caregiving or other regulating activities)	The system for caregiving infiltrated by the fear system which induces flight	Attuned to affect. Affect regulation and empathic response disabled **Attunes to affect, caregiving infiltrated by self defence, misatrunes to careseeker's goals, becomes immobilised and unresponsive**
(Style B) Is reluctant to discuss feelings, issues, and concerns. Fails to volunteer much information and is mostly monosyllabic in reply	(Pattern 6) Careseeker communicates affect non-verbally and responds minimally to questions: caregiver focuses on verbal communication, avoids emotive messages	Misattunement to the affect of the careseeker. This generally involves failing to engage with the emotional intensity of the affect of the careseeker and withdrawing into cognitive explorations	Careseeking system over-ridden by system for self-defence (deeper in despair)	Caregiving is over-ridden by the fear system and either fights with the careseeker or withdraws	Attuned to affect, own fear system aroused, avoidance of engagement with affect and capacity for affect regulation disabled **Ineffective purposeful misatrunement to careseeker affect in an attempt to deflect careseeker from exploring it.**

Initial presentation of careseeker in relation to wanting help	Pattern of interaction between careseeker and caregiver	Process of engagement by caregiver with careseeker affect	Attachment dynamics in the careseeking system	Attachment dynamics in the caregiving system	Classification of caregiving responses
(Style C) Brings in issues they are concerned about but tangles the caregiver when they try to help	(Pattern 7) After stating initial anxiety careseeker diverts attention to a myriad of seemingly unrelated issues, ambiguously presented and with no focus. Caregiver misses original affect and pursues the detail of the other issues; careseeker gives terse/teasing responses; caregiver keeps engaging; careseeker becomes dismissive	Misattunement to the substantive affective issues being presented by the caregiver. This generally involves misidentifying the critical issues of concern for the careseeker and engaging cognitively	Careseeking system over-ridden by system for self-defence (dismissive)	Caregiving is infiltrated by the fear system and becomes disorganised	Misattunes to affect. Unable to use verbal and non-verbal feedback to sustain an empathic goal-corrected response or regulate affect **Non-attuned to affect, caregiving infiltrated by self defence, becomes disorganised**
(Style D) Brings in issues they are concerned about but dismisses the caregiver when they try to help	(Pattern 8) Careseeker introduces apparently different concerns, caregiver engages with underlying affect; careseeker resists exploration; caregiver continues to pursue; careseeker withdraws or closes the session	Ineffective purposeful misattunement to the substantive cognitive issues being presented. This generally involves misidentifying the critical issues of concern to the careseeker	Careseeking system is infiltrated by the fear system: expressed in the form of attack or withdrawal	Caregiving system becomes disorganised as it fails to reach its goals	Attunes to affect. Unable to use verbal and non-verbal feedback to sustain an empathic goal-corrected response or regulate affect **Attunes to affect, fails to regulate it, caregiving infiltrated by self defence, becomes disorganised**

Initial presentation of careseeker in relation to wanting help	Pattern of interaction between careseeker and caregiver	Process of engagement by caregiver with careseeker affect	Attachment dynamics in the careseeking system	Attachment dynamics in the caregiving system	Classification of caregiving responses
(Style E)	(Pattern 9)	(1)			(1)
Is overwhelmed, incoherent and disorganised in their presentation of feelings, conflicts and concerns	Careseeker presents as highly aroused, and gives an incoherent account of concerns involving a lot of seemingly unconnected detail. Caregiver responds verbally and non-verbally, confirming, containing and encouraging; careseeker continues to expand; caregiver continues to respond - matching vitality affects and verbally focuses; contains and orientates	Effective purposeful misattunement by the caregiver to careseeker affect: comes forward to meet the careseeker and either amplifies their affect or tunes in down. Provides containment, orientation to context, focus and empathy	Careseeking is infiltrated by the fear system. As the fear subsides, careseeking re-establishes, the fear system is triggered, then subsides, careseeking re-establishes and so on	Caregiving is aroused, remains exploratory and is not infiltrated by fear or self defence	Attuned to goals of careseeker using the process of goal-corrected empathic attunement

Effective purposeful misattunement to affect which regulates, contains and attends to careseeker's goals |

The reader can see that there are nine patterns of interaction. What is clear from the patterns is that what is being judged is how each party responds to the other and whether the careseeker is or appears to be reaching their goals as evidenced by their vitality affects.

The three effective careseeking/caregiving patterns (patterns 1, 3 and 9) all involve the caregiver regulating careseeker affect.

The other six patterns in one way or another involve a complete failure to regulate affect. Two involve purposeful misattunement to affect in an attempt to deflect the careseeker from pursuing it (patterns 2 and 6), two involve attunement to affect, followed by a failure to regulate it and the caregiving system being infiltrated by the system for self-defence (patterns 5 and 8) and the last two patterns, (4 and 7) involve the caregiver not attuning to careseeker affect, their caregiving being infiltrated by their system for self-defence and then becoming disorganised.

Patterns 2 and 6 seem to involve a withdrawal from each other, in one it is the caregiver that is withdrawn, (pattern 2) and in the other it is the careseeker. My hypothesis is that the fear system is activated and unregulated.

Patterns 4 and 7 may well be associated with a more ambivalent, resistant careseeking style. For the caregiver who gets entangled in these particular unsatisfying patterns of interaction it may be worth thinking about how one is reading the expressed emotion and whether one is seeing attack where there is in fact distress.

Patterns 5 and 8 seem to be associated with a dismissive caregiving style and a dismissive careseeking style.

As stated in the beginning of this book, adults who seek help when frightened, in pain or facing threat to their lives will adopt one of four typical stances: (i) they will have confidence in their strategies for getting help and be clear and direct in their communication, (ii) they will have no confidence that their needs will be addressed and attended to and so will only seek help in extremis and then in a way that minimises the extent of their problem, thereby giving inadequate information to the potential caregiver, (iii) they will be uncertain, half hopeful, half sceptical, and therefore communicate in contradictory and ambiguous ways, or (iv) they will be bewildered, unclear, uncertain and disorganised about the state they are in and what would relieve it, fearing any response could potentially make things worse, thus avoiding seeking help in the first place and being frightened/angry when in a caregiving context.

Having identified the above patterns, it seems to me the work is only beginning. We need to work out a method for testing the accuracy of these discriminations, to refine and correct them if necessary and to identify in detail the clinical implications.

Example of a successful consultation

English is not the first language of either party.

Caregiver – CG
Careseeker – CS
Vitality affects, affect matching, regulation, attachment dynamics – AD

CS: "I am really troubled by one of the members of my team but I thought I would like some advice or ideas as to how to handle it"
AD: *CG looking at CS, mouth slightly open, chin level, hands resting on inside legs, fingers pointing to floor. CS chin level slightly forward, looking at CG, left hand is clasping his right upper arm.*

CG: "I think we need some background information about your organisation and your role in it"
AD: *One of CG's hands begins to open, CS's hand which is clasping his arm begins to open simultaneously*

CS: "As a vicar I am in charge of the parish, of the church community. I am the boss. There are about 30 people working in different roles in this setting. I am the boss. I think we are working quite well but there is this just one person who is impossible"
AD: *CG moves his right shoulder in exact rhythm to CS's hand and movement. CS leans slightly towards CG and raises his right hand from his leg*

CG: "You are the boss. That is surprising to me because you are also a vicar, how can this be?"
CS: "To be a priest, you have the obligations associated with being a priest; that is your given role, but in the work role where you have to take care of everything, you are not just giving sermons in the church where you are to just doing it"
AD: *Connecting*

CS: "This person is a man, is a colleague, is a priest. He is causing me a lot of trouble and I don't know how to handle him."
AD: *Rising vitality tone in voice*

CG: "What kind of trouble?"
(Moderate even tone of voice, gentle and enquiring. Moves his right shoulder in exact rhythm to CS's hand movement)
CS: (leans slightly towards CG and raises his right hand from his leg)
AD: *Verbally and non-verbally there is both affect attunement (shoulder movement matching hand movement) and purposeful misattunement designed to regulate the affect and to signal proximity and intention to become involved.*

CS: "You see ... he ... he ... I have a system which is that when I am at the office everyone is welcome to come in and take up anything to do with the work and work setting. But ..."

AD: *Momentary disorganisation as careseeking is interrupted by a request for more facts, CS distress (expressed through high voice pitch) continues to rise and responds with more information*

CG: "Sorry, I do not understand you. Do you have an open door is that?"
(Eye brow up, head drawn back and slightly up, mouth slightly open, looks directly at careseeker)

CS: "Well, when I am at the office and the door is open, people are invited to come and talk to me about whatever they want to talk about. And most of the people do that. But this man, this colleague of mine he writes long, long letters to me like four or five or six pages - from the top to the bottom on every side, pointing out what a bad manager I am what a bad leadership style I have"

AD: *Affect rising. One can see in the non-verbal responses of the CG that he reflects the impact of what he is hearing. This is empathic attunement*

CS: "And I don't know what to do with that"
AD: *Careseeking*

CG: "That is awful for you, to get those letters"
AD: *Empathic attunement*

CS: "It is ... I don't know what to do really"
(Rises from his seat and moves forward towards CG then reseats himself.
AD: *Immediate response to the empathy of the CG (draws nearer momentarily) leads to a rise in careseeking*

Picture 25

CS is to the left of the picture in the mirror.
CG: "It must be awful for you to get those letters".
CS: "It is really"

CG: "Yes; no no"
(Matches voice tone and rhythm of speech of careseeker)
CS: "No"
(spoken very softly)
AD: *Affect attunement and empathy*

CG: "So, ah, that must be very distressing?"
(Looking directly at CS, chin level, hands loosely clasped inside thigh)
CS: "And the worst thing about it ..."
(Left hand moves to clasp his right upper arm, moves his hand up and down his arm)

CS: "And the worst thing about it, he has some support in the council, ... that is like ... that is the political elected council. That is the elected council, they have responsibility for the financial management of the Association. And he has some ... he goes to that council when he should go to me"
(right hand reaching forward towards caregiver).
AD: *The pitch of the voice increases and he gets more distressed. Increase in careseeking following empathic attunement. One can also see here an attempt to align the CG (though increasing the affect) to the goal of the CS which is to figure out a way of managing this colleague*

CG: "And, and, you're dependent on this council?"
(Head level, Shoulders down)
AD: *Accurate identification of concerns and purposeful misattunement to affect (through his own relaxed posture) in order to regulate rising distress in CS*

CS: "Yeah" (said very quickly)
AD: *Relief*

CG: "Yes, they are your Board or something"
CS: "They are my Board and they make things hard for me"
AD: *CS speaks quickly, looks distressed and rubs his left arm with his right hand (self comforting behaviour)*

CG: "So it is not only him, its most of the Board?"
CS: "No, I really think that most of the Board would be OK if I just found a way to handle this colleague of mine. That would really loosen things up"

CG: "I assume you have tried to talk to him"
AD: *Assuming competence in the CS, providing an underlying message that this CS can be competent (a very important component of effective caregiving)*

CS: (3 seconds pause – sighs) "Well, I don't know how to do that ... (pause). I Have invited him to some talks, but he never likes to discuss things with me. When I talk to him face to face, he is quite nice, quite smooth really. We have small meetings and everything seems to be quite OK and then two days later I get a long long letter drawing attention to my style of leadership of the organisation"
CG: "What is his complaint?"
AD: *Affect regulation through addressing the facts*

CS: "His complaints are that I am not precise enough, when I am putting proposals or when I am making decisions I am quite vague and that I favorise some of the group"

CG: "Do you feel there is truth in his complaints?"

AD: *CG tests the CS's capacity for self reflection. It is also a way of regulating the affect of the CS through collaborative exploration of the facts of the complaints and not the feelings they give rise to*

CS: "Well now and then I get some kind of shiver, that he might be right, that I might be the wrong person. But honestly when I look at the feedback I get from the other members of the group, I think they are quite happy to have me. And they work quite well with me"

AD: *The capacity for undefended self reflection asserts itself (this is the exploratory system), there is a rise in vitality*

CG: "But if it's right, it won't help to write these letters. I mean he might have a point in some respects, but ..."

CS: (cuts in with vigour) "Well maybe, and I could think about discussing it with him. But it is not my kind of leadership style to negotiate things by letter. For me that is crazy."

AD: *Rise in vitality accompanying sense of self and assertion of self*

CG: "Yes"

CS: "Yes, so that is where it is stuck really"

AD: *Decline in vitality as if CS loses hope*

CG: "I can see how upset you are"
(nods his head in rhythm to CS who is also nodding his head as he responds)

CS: "yes"

AD: *Accurate affect attunement*

CG: "So we must find a way of dealing with it"

AD: *Again, the CG allies himself with the CS and communicates that the CS is not going to be left on their own to deal with the problem they say they can't deal with. This is empathic attunement and attachment-based interaction*

CG: "So ... ah ... do you have any idea of what you would like to do?"

AD: *Momentary disorganisation as CG focuses*

CS: "Well, actually ... I suppose one of the things I did was to come to you!"

AD: *CS able to access own competence in seeking help, mutual laughter and momentary relief*

CG: "Yes, yes, that was a good start"

AD: *Note the image – the expression on both faces is very tender and fluid and they are making eye contact*

CS: "I am really ... I am lost actually"

Picture 26

"Come to you actually"

CG: "Yes, yes, very difficult thing really. Hard to give you any advice just now but maybe if we try to analyse the situation, we can find a way eventually ... so ... ah ..."

AD:*Affect attunement (voice tone, rhythm)*

CG: "I wonder where we should start, because I felt your own feelings about being humilitated and threatened by him were so strong, maybe we should talk some more about your own feelings about being in this hopeless situations"

AD: *The CG by his voice tone (which is serious and entirely focused), his choice of words, the fact that he goes straight for the affect that the CS is experiencing and takes a risk on naming it as well as showing through the expression on his face that he has been affected himself by what the CS has said, provides affect containment and regulation as well as an empathic connection*

CS: (CS answers without a break) 'That is really true'
(Sits back on chair and places right hand over heart)

AD: *Said with incredible tenderness as if the CG had really touched a chord. (See picture over page)*

CS: "He upsets me that much"

CG: "It is some sort of trigger. When I receive the letter, I realise that he touches something that gets me going." (See picture of careseeker with his arm raised and hand in a fist)

AD: *Self-reflective capacity accompanied by vigour and vitality*

Picture 27

"I feel lost actually"

Picture 28

Careseeker is to the left of the picture (in the mirror)
"You feel so humiliated".

Picture 29

"It is really true"

Picture 30

"It upsets me that much"

CS: "But I feel very helpless"
AD: *Note how quickly CS goes from anger and vigour to helplessness and low vitality*

CS: "I don't know really how to deal with this"
AD: *Careseeking*

CG: "Yes. What comes to my mind is that your organisation is a church and my fantasy is that these kinds of things are difficult to cope with in the church because you are supposed to be good to each other. Is that true?"
AD: *Immediate thoughtful response (designed to 'catch the helpless' and to convey he is not leaving him alone with it) ... this again is attachment-based interaction*

CG: Chest drawn slightly back, Hand points to own chest, Head level, Is looking at CS
CS: "That makes sense. That's a ... the Kingdom of God. God's Kingdom is supposed to be nice and polite and very loving. That's perfectly true actually"

CS: "That doesn't give me access ... I am perfectly angry with this"
AD: *Rise in vitality and vigour*

CG: Yes, yes ... is it OK to be that angry for you?"
AD: *Serious, engaged, exploratory tone - empathic containment*

Picture 31

"It is some sort of trigger"

Picture 32

"I am perfectly angry"

CS: "No, no"
AD: *Collapse in vitality*

CG: "Why not?"
AD: *Support for exploration*

CS: "Because one shouldn't be that angry"
CG: "You have that?"
AD: *Support for exploration*

CS: "Of course I know that I can be angry, but not in this setting"
AD: *Rise in vitality as CS explores his situation and his own experiences*

CG: "What would you do ... if you were to forget everything the church teaches ...
what would you like to do to this man"
(CG and CS are already engaged in a smile as CG finishes his sentence)
AD: *Support for exploration. As the CG uses the word 'forget' he draws his right hand level
across his chest in a cutting motion*

CS: "Couple of punches, couple of punches ... on his nose, by God ..."
AD: *Relief in both parties, Shared pleasure, lot of smiling and laughter*

CG: "Well don't do it!"
AD: *Support for containing the impulse*

Picture 33

"If you just forget what your church teaches"

CS: "That is ... very really wonderful. That is really one of the issues that I have. I haven't really thought about ..."
AD: *Brief laugh and lift in mood, then almost immediately his mood changes.*

CG: "How angry you are?"
AD: *Affect identification*

CS: "How angry I am and how difficult it is to find a way to use that anger in this kind of system, because the system and the church is like packing the anger in and you are not allowed access to it"
AD: *Increased liveliness and vitality*

CG: "I can sense that our time is almost up. But I have good hope for our work together because you have so much energy and you really want to solve this problem and I am sure we will find a way to deal with it but we need to meet a couple of times to think about this"
And maybe you need to digest, the fact, that you have discovered how angry you are. How do you feel about that?

CS: "Yeah. It makes sense actually and another piece of reality is that in that setting I don't have anyone to talk to about this business"
AD: *Careseeking*

CG: "So, we will meet again? Next week?"
CS: "Yes, thanks. I look forward to that"

Picture 34

"Couple of punches"

CG: "Yes. so do I"
AD: *Real pleasure and liveliness based on meeting careseeking caregiving goals. The pleasure is associated with experiencing competence*

Picture 35

"Meet again next week?"
"I look forward to that"

In terms of the ways that careseekers present and caregivers respond referred to earlier, clearly in the above example the careseeker wanted to discuss his feelings conflicts and concerns and he was met by a caregiver who was available, was not defensive and was willing to engage with his affect and help him explore what the issues were and what he could do about them.

I mentioned earlier that in terms of judging successful and unsuccessful interactions I paid attention first to the state the careseeker was in at the beginning of the session; their vitality affects, and then to the state they were in at the end. With a digital video camera it is possible to stop the camera at the moment of conclusion and catch the vitality affects of both caregiver and careseeker. As the reader will see in the above shot (in spite of its poor reproductive quality) the pleasure in both parties is clear to see. Thinking back to the research on infant communication referred to in chapter 2, when two people are truly engaged with each other in non defensive ways, there is a rise in vitality and fluid expression of emotion on the face.

Summary

In this chapter I have presented my analysis of the different ways that careseekers and caregivers present and interact together. I classified the nonverbal communication of vitality affects into low, medium and high and gave images from sessions to illustrate what I meant by attunement, misattunement, effective purposeful misattunement, non attunement all of which is in the service of affect regulation as the medium through which one person (in role of caregiver) truly makes contact with another (careseeker) when the instinctive system for careseeking is aroused. Only then can information get transferred between them and collaborative work or engagement begin to happen.

I then went on to classify the way that careseekers approach for help and identified five main styles of careseeking. It looked to me that caregivers tend to typically respond in five different ways. I put all this material together and created a chart which describes the patterns of interaction that evolve from these behaviours. My hope is that my descriptions are sufficiently clear to provide the basis for more rigorous research that can make use of the latest technology in identifying patterns of interaction. One such product on the market yet to be tested in this field is THEME marketed by Noldus.

I will now proceed to the final chapter of this book and conclude my thesis.

CHAPTER TWELVE

Interactions between therapists and patients and their roots in infancy

Introduction

In this final chapter I will summarise the main points from the empirical research and the subsequent analysis. In doing this I will distinguish between the actual development of the concept of goal-corrected empathic attunement and the empirical research I carried out. In practice each influenced the other so that separation is, from a historical point of view, misleading. Nevertheless it is easier to explain my current position in this way.

Theoretical development

I started off in the introduction with an account of failed careseeking leading to despair and inaction. It drew attention to the implications of indirect or complicated patterns of careseeking. The suggestion was that if people cannot express directly what is of utmost concern to them to someone they perceive as being able to help them, then the person who is in role of 'helper' needs to be alert to the indicators that accompany failed careseeking and failed caregiving if they are to provide an effective response. It is this idea that is at the centre of my thesis.

A related idea was that people bring with them their feelings in relation to their experience of previous careseeking, together with the behaviours they have developed to cope with these feelings, into the relationship with potential caregivers. These ideas struck me as having implications for *all* who work in the 'caring professions', whether they be social workers, care staff, medical staff, physiotherapists, psychotherapists, whoever. It seemed to me to be important to examine the processes involved in effective caregiving and to trace the development of careseeking/caregiving patterns from their roots in infancy.

I proceeded in chapter one to introduce the importance of affect attunement between careseekers and caregivers by suggesting that what I had observed as a trainer over many years was that careseekers monitored the reaction of caregivers when they introduced into the conversation an area of some importance to them, and that caregivers often deflected caregivers from the emotion accompanying their concern by distracting them with unrelated questions. In so doing they both bypassed information available to them from the careseeker and deflected the careseeker from information that was potentially available to them. I was curious about how this happened. Did careseekers mis-cue caregivers so that the caregiver was given a message that the careseeker was OK, when that was clearly not the case, or were caregivers responding to some trigger in themselves that served a defensive function?

I had noticed that what the careseeker seemed to do when they got this response from the caregiver was to inhibit their own exploration, change the direction of their flow and follow the lead given by the caregiver. It looked as if one system which had been activated was getting over-ridden by another.

On reflection, this behaviour suggested to me that attachment processes were at work here. By following the lead of the caregiver, the careseeker was not increasing the distance between them and the caregiver; they therefore kept the caregiver within reach, as it were. However, I suggested in line with Heard and Lake (1997) that the *experience* of following the caregiver's lead and giving up on their own agenda could induce the in the careseeker the *affective experience* of anger depression and or despair. A withdrawal by the caregiver from the careseeker's affect could elicit (a) a pattern of behavioural response in the careseeker that had the characteristics of attachment behaviour, and (b) an affective experience that was embedded within the behavioural response.

In this way I drew attention to the fact that failures in caregiving could induce in the careseeker a desire to retain the inadequate caregiver in proximity, or to abandon them altogether. I saw a link between these observations and the attachment concepts of 'set-goal', 'retrieval' and 'proximity'. The concept of 'set-goal' is based on an understanding of instinctive systems which are activated in response to environmental triggers (both internal and external), and cease to be active when certain other conditions are met, at which point that particular system within the organism as a whole remains in a state of quiescence until activated again. Within attachment theory, it is postulated that once the instinctively based careseeking system has been activated it will remain so until it reaches its set-goal, i.e. effective caregiving, when the behaviour will cease having, as it were, been 'goal-corrected'. I agree with Heard and Lake (2003) and other attachment theorists, in the way they differ from Bowlby, that the achievement of proximity to the caregiver is not the goal of careseeking. Careseekers want an effective response from the caregiver that helps them to get back on track and deal more competently with their world.

In seeking to understand these processes I drew first on the understanding of Ainsworth, Bowlby and Heard. These authors suggest an interdependent relationship between the three instinctive goal-corrected systems of careseeking, caregiving and exploration. To the extent that careseeking remains unassuaged, the exploratory system of the careseeker is overridden. Further work by Heard and Lake based on their observations of adults in the clinical context of adult psychotherapy, suggested to them that there were other instinctive systems involved in attachment dynamics – those of sexuality (intra-individual and interpersonal), interest-sharing with peers, and self-defence. In their view, these systems operate together to achieve the optimum levels of vitality, well-being and engagement with the world as is possible.

The implication of this theory is that the consequences of inadequate caregiving can be serious in terms of establishing and maintaining well being alongside social and interpersonal competence. In addition, care-seekers who have a history of inadequate caregiving will present their careseeking needs in ways that are difficult to identify and respond to. Careseekers who continually fail to reach the goal of careseeking experience feelings associated with this phenomenon – anger, depression and despair – and develop adaptive strategies to cope with these feelings, including avoidance of careseeking, ambivalence towards careseeking and disorganisation in relation to careseeking.

The consequences for interpersonal relationships have been well described (see for example the classic study by Mattinson and Sinclair

(1979), as have the consequences for work and relationships in the work place. It is obvious, and therefore hardly needs to be said, that the effect of inadequate caregiving on a person's life is mitigated by social, cultural and environmental factors, such as education, money, health, other people, support networks and cultural norms and expectations. But while for some people the effect of ineffective caregiving might well be mitigated, for many others no such mitigating factors are available.

In working out these ideas I thought it right to look at other psycho-therapy research over the past fifty years. This research has highlighted:

a) the importance of process (Chicago School);
b) the relationship between process and perceptions of and attitude to self (Chicago School);
c) the importance of quality of interaction between therapist and client – affect matching, intensity, depth of empathic input (Carkhuff and Berenson);
d) the need to relate the work of psychotherapy to
    i) measures of process (McLeod)
    ii) early patterns of relating to people (Modern School – e.g. Anstadt, Bucci. Oster, Luborsky).

However, none of the above research had access to recent research into interactions between infants and parents as the prototype of careseeking/caregiving interaction, which has as its goal survival and the development of social and interpersonal competence.

In seeking the sources of an appropriate developmental theory I was particularly struck by the work of Fairbairn, with his emphasis on the way infants are programmed to respond to adults. This was reinforced for me by observational studies such as those of Murray and Trevarthen, and also by brain research. The latter highlights the importance of affect regulation for emotional and cognitive development in infants and shows that this is dependent on inter-action. Infants cannot do this for themselves. The management of vitality affects is dependent on an attuned and sensitive caregiver.

More specifically, I linked the ideas to the work of Daniel Stern on the stages of development in infants as they progress from non-verbal to verbal – he locates the affective core in the pre-verbal infant as the emergent self; the self that is interacting with caregivers. Other research from the developmental psychologists confirmed the way that infants were communicating non-verbally – their understanding of the meaning of affect and their communication of their own affective states.

Attunement to affect is not empathy. Attunement precedes empathy developmentally. Infants are born capable of attuning to the affect of their caregivers, expressed in many ways including the rhythm of their voice (Trevarthen *et al.*, 1998). It is my understanding that attunement to affect transmits information that is necessary for immediate survival. The studies by Meltzhoff, Trevarthen and others suggest that babies are tuned in to the very breath of their caregivers, so that babies literally anticipate the next beat of their mother's voice (see Trevarthen 1999). In contrast, empathy is a metacognitive capacity. It requires the ability to have a sense of other minds, to see things from another's point of view, to understand their emotions, resonate with these emotions and convey in words one's appreciation of the others person's state in a way that is recognisable to them that you have understood them.

The transpositions I made from the world of infancy to the adult world were: (i) to think in terms of the therapist or consultant or clinician as the caregiver in the adult-to-adult context; (ii) to think of the client as careseeker, especially when attachment issues are aroused (as they are when careseeking is active); (iii) to think of the exploratory system, which includes natural curiosity and intelligence, being overridden while careseeking is active; (iv) to think of both careseeker and caregiver resorting to self-defensive strategies when careseeking and caregiving are unsuccessful; (v) to think that insecure caregivers in professional contexts will interact with careseekers in similar ways to the behaviour of the caregiver in the insecure dyads described by the Grossmanns, and will thereby instigate defensive behaviours in the client (careseeker) which will be accompanied by levels of emotional distress.

I then looked at the way these affective states were attuned to by caregivers, and the infant's sense of enjoyment or distress that ensued from different types of caregiving. It became clear from the studies such as those of the Grossmanns that attunement to affect alone is not enough – the play sequences that they describe between secure and insecure interacting dyads show that non-empathic responses from the caregiver trigger distress, as does misattunement to the affective state.

I then linked this work on attunement to affect with research by Ainsworth *et al* (1978) on attachment and noted that sensitive attunement to infants' signals was associated with a secure attachment pattern between infant and caregiver.

I then put together the following ideas: (i) attachment status correlates with sensitive, attuned caregiving (Ainsworth, 1978); (ii) the exploratory system can be overridden by careseeking (Ainsworth, 1978; Heard, 1978); (iii) in insecure careseeker/caregiver dyads, caregivers interfere with the child's play in such a way as to inhibit exploration (Tronick, 1989; Grossmann & Grossmann, 1991a, 1991b). We know from attachment theory that the goal-corrected instinctive system for careseeking remains active until assuaged. It seemed a small step to create the idea that affect regulation and empathic attunement was the crucial ingredients in assuaging careseeking. It seemed to me that attunement and empathy were preconditions for effective caregiving.

Finally, the last extrapolation I made was based on the fact that when instinctive goal-corrected systems reach their goal, the instinctual system for careseeking becomes quiescent and the person experiences relief, and then can proceed to access and express their competence in undefended ways. .

Empirical research

As I mentioned in the introduction to this book all the elements of this theory were not in place when I set out to do my research. The experiments I conducted were not set up to test the theory of goal-corrected empathic attunement. However, I was aware of the research by Ainsworth *et al* (1978) and Haft and Slade (1989) that linked attunement to affect with attachment status in the infant and adult domain. My first experiment therefore was to see whether attunement to affect could be identified in the context of one-to-one psychotherapy with adults.

My first experiment suggested this was possible to some extent. A panel of 9 experts was almost unanimous in identifying one video excerpt of therapy as 'attuned' and another extract as 'non-attuned'. They were not agreed on the status of four others, possibly because what was being shown in these extracts was a process of 'tuning in'. I selected the two excerpts on which there was a very high degree of agreement and presented them to students to see whether they could also identify which was which.

To my surprise students were unable to discriminate attunement from non-attunement. This finding really surprised me. Because the experts were so clear as to what constituted attunement and non-attunement, I almost stopped my experiments at this point; I thought the whole thing was obvious. It was the students' inability to discriminate attunement from non-attunement that woke me up to what was going on in the interaction that they were failing to see. What I found when I examined the experts' response was that when making their judgements they paid attention to the interaction between therapist and client, and took the responses (the feedback client and therapist were giving each other) into account. In particular they took account of what each said to the other, implying that cognitive appreciation of the other's situation was an essential element in their account of attunement. What this signified to me was that they were not just looking at attunement to affect but were also tracking empathic response.

Another aspect that the experts seemed to pay attention to was whether or not the client was enabled to explore their concerns. They were also looking at the client to see whether the response of the therapist had stopped them in some way that was causing them distress. Enabling exploration, therefore, seemed to be a key element in their concept of attunement. The experiment seemed to confirm that paying attention to interaction was a key ingredient in identifying affect attunement, and also that affect attunement on its own was insufficient to promote exploration: empathy was also essential.

I then conducted my second experiment. This was constructed to see whether students' capacity to correctly identify empathic attunement would improve if they were given instructions to pay attention to the interaction between therapist and client. I divided the student group into two groups; a Control Group and an Experimental Group. The Experimental Group were given instructions to pay attention to the interaction between therapist and client. The results indicated that the group which were given instructions to pay attention to the interaction did significantly better at identifying empathic attunement than the Control Group, which was not given instructions. This was a good result and supported the hypothesis that empathic attunement referred to an interactive process based on feedback.

However, qualitative analysis based on debriefing sessions with the students to discuss what they had taken into account when making their rating, revealed that it was not as simple as that. All the students were paying attention to the interaction but were clearly evaluating it differently from each other. The statistical analysis suggested that the students who were given guidance on how to judge the interaction made more accurate ratings. However, in the light of qualitative material, other processes were also at work. Students were affected by what they were observing and were evaluating the same behaviour in very different ways – where one person saw respect for privacy, the other saw abandonment; where one saw intrusion, the other saw support for exploration.

The nature of the students' responses, centring as they did on views about appropriate responses to distress, indicated to me that the observers' own attachment dynamics might have been getting involved and influencing their judgement of the interaction. I wondered whether students who had a more avoidant style themselves in relation to attachment figures were more tuned in to perceiving a therapist as intrusive, irrespective of the information available in the context as a whole (i.e. the feedback that was there for them to observe from the clients' response). In terms of my project, the experiment confirmed for me that paying attention to interaction and feedback were crucial in judging empathic attunement.

This raised for me the question of whether careseekers and caregivers shared a similar evaluation of their experience of caregiving, and whether attunement to feeling and empathy were associated with feeling understood. I constructed self-report measures for caregivers and careseekers. I also set out to see whether students who were given training directed at encouraging them to attune to client affect and respond empathically would subsequently do better than those students who were not given this training. Finally, I set out to see whether the attachment status of the students affected their ability to attune to client affect and to explore the impact of training on this ability.

In order to test for the impact of training I needed independent reliable ratings of the interaction. Through the process of obtaining a reliable rating I realised that the process could not be judged by observing interactive sequences alone – it had to be judged by monitoring a process that went into action when certain responses were triggered in either the careseeker or the caregiver. The interaction then took on a character of either assuagement and exploration, or continued and deepening distress, the affective expression of which was more or less dramatic. This led to the construction of the concept of goal-corrected empathic attunement as set out in chapter five.

The main experiment conducted in the research therefore centered on three issues: (i) whether empathic attunement between adults in a careseeking/caregiving context could be reliably rated; (ii) whether effective caregivers had a secure attachment style; and (iii) whether caregiving could be influenced by training.

The results were related to these questions, and they showed:

1. that it was possible to produce three measures of goal-corrected empathic attunement which were significantly correlated with each other and consistently distinguished between students in a test situation;

2. that one of these measures was significantly correlated with the attachment style of the student, as predicted;

3. that the same measure could be improved by training.

Subsequent work

Drawing on the results of the empirical research, and using the ratings of the videos as a benchmark, I was able to revisit the material frame and by frame in order to get a sense of the detail of the interaction associated with a 'good' or 'poor' rating. With this information I then analysed two further sets of videos; one set created by clinicians in the privacy of their consulting rooms and the other set created during the process of conducing training sessions and workshops with experienced clinicians. From an analysis of this work, and on the basis of the empirical work, some evidence for thinking that successful and unsuccessful meeting of instinctive goals was accompanied by distinctive vitality affects, I identified nine distinct patterns of interaction between careseekers and caregivers, based on careseekers' and caregivers' verbal, non-verbal and emotive messages and their response to each other.

Five styles of careseeking behaviour

(i) Provides clear account of feelings, issues and concerns.

(ii) Is reluctant to discuss feelings, issues and concerns.

(iii) Brings in issues they are concerned about but tangle the caregiver when they try to help.

(iv) Brings in issues they are concerned about but dismisses the caregiver when they try to help.

(v) Is overwhelmed, incoherent and disorganised in their presentation of feelings conflicts and concerns.

In response to these styles of careseeking and the emotive messages that accompany them, caregivers tend to respond in predictable ways that differ from each other. Again , I identified five styles of response.

Caregiver responses

(i) Attunes to careseeker affect, regulates it (through purposeful misattunement) and attends to careseeker's goals.

(ii) Purposefully misatunes to careseeker affect in an attempt to deflect careseeker from exploring it.

(iii) Avoids engaging with affect, becomes disorganised, then refocuses on affect, regulates it and attends to careseeker's goals.

(iv) Misatunes to affect, becomes disorganised.

(v) Attunes to affect, becomes disorganised.

The power of vitality affects to convey emotional states

But more than identifying styles of communication or pattern of interaction and response, what this research has brought home to me is the enormous power people have to convey their innermost state through their emotive messages and their vitality affects. The images presented in chapter eleven surely attest to this. It seems to me we need to get keener in our understanding of emotional expression and our capacity to regulate it in ourselves and others. There is a growing interest in the role of affect regulation in psychotherapy (Beebe & Lachmann, 2003), and it seems to me that extended attachment theory offers a plausible explanation of why affect regulation is so important. Instinctive systems, once aroused, need to reach their goal. The goal of careseeking is effective caregiving, and when this does not happen people withdraw, feel angry or go into despair. These are the feelings that as caregivers we need to learn how to regulate in the here and now through active engagement with the other which does involve our own emotions, intelligence, sensitivity and capacity for reflection and analysis.

Conclusion

Regulating emotions is but the first step as we know. We need to know how to engage with and work with emotion. Dorothy Heard, Brian Lake and myself are currently exploring the clinical implications of extended attachment theory.

It seems to me that we need to understand that careseekers read our faces and respond to what they see there, just as we read other people's faces and respond to their expressions. Reading faces is where emotional arousal and the need for emotional regulation begins (and began in the past). Not having one's face read accurately and responded to empathically is clearly where a lot of pre-verbal pain is located.

To conclude, I want to say that this book is not just for therapists. People get sick, lose their jobs, go into residential care, find themselves one way or another thrust on the care of someone else. What the attachment literature shows is that one's expectations of how one is going to be cared for have been laid down quite early in relation to the actual experiences of care that one has received. What I have got from this research is confirmation that people do tell us (mostly non-verbally) when we (as caregivers) get it wrong and miss them, and they also tell us when we get it right and connect with them – the pleasure is visible and tangible. I started the book with a quotation from Jock Sutherland, "we are born with the expectation of being met as a person". I hope I have shown what vitality and life can be created between two people when that actually happens.

Role play scenarios for day one

Anger

You and your partner are in your early forties. You have a daughter aged 6. Three years ago you lost a baby through having amniocentesis. You are pregnant again and have decided not to have another amniocentesis. This is partly because you could not bear to go through the feelings of loss again. More significantly, in the meantime you have read that when miscarriage follows amniocentesis, it is because the doctor concerned has not undertaken the procedure properly. You are wondering whether to sue. You are worried that, because of your age, there is something the matter with the baby you are carrying. You are furious that you have this dilemma.

Despair

You and Josie have been married for twelve years. You have no children. You have a very intense and stormy relationship. You have separated on at least six occasions, but you have both shared a powerful belief that you are made for each other and that you would always get back together again. The separations usually last about 10 days. Josie goes and stays with her sister. The last time she stayed with a friend in Cornwall and didn't come back for three weeks. This time, you don't know where she is and she has been gone a month. You have given up hope that she is coming back.

You have returned to see a Relate counsellor who has seen you and Josie in the past.

Fear

You are a 37-year-old homosexual male who has been HIV positive for the past 10 years. During this time you have remained in good health, have built up a successful interior design business and have been in a stable relationship. Two months ago your health began to break down and you have had a series of colds, 'flu and recently an attack of pneumonia. You don't seem to be able to shake these things off. At present you are in hospital for investigation and have been seeing the hospital social worker for counselling sessions. This morning, while taking a shower you discovered on your shoulder what you think is Karposi's Sarcoma.

You are extremely frightened ...

Sadness

You are 36, living in the north of England where you have a job that is very important to you. Your family are in Kent where you were brought up. You don't have a partner and despite the geographical distance had a very close relationship with your parents. You thought for years that you would move back down south at some stage, but kept putting it off. Your father died five years ago, leaving your mother alone. She encouraged you to pursue your career rather than to move down to live with her.

You know your mother has been having some memory problems, but you have put this down to recent stresses she has had with her house. However, her GP has contacted you to say that he thinks your mother has Alzheimer's disease.

You are very upset and have contacted social services.

Measure of student attunement to be completed by the actor after each interview

Name of student...Name of actor............................
Role play no.: 1   2   3   4 Date:................Time.............

1. Do you think you conveyed to the client that you understood what they were feeling?

Very Much   Not at All

1   2   3   4   5   6

2. Do you think you conveyed to the client you understood what they were saying

Very Much   Not at All

1   2   3   4   5   6

3. Were you attentive and interested in the client?

Very Much   Not at All

1   2   3   4   5   6

4. Did you think you enabled them to say what they wanted?

Very Much   Not at All

1   2   3   4   5   6

5. Did you feel you enabled them to see things in a new way?

Very Much   Not at All

1   2   3   4   5   6

6. Do you think you said anything helpful?

Very Much   Not at All

1   2   3   4   5   6

Measure of student attunement to be completed by the actor after each interview

Name of student...Name of actor...........................
Role play no.: 1　　　　2　　　3　　　4　Date:.................Time..............

1. Did the student convey to you that they could see how you felt?

Very Much   Not at All

1   2   3   4   5   6

2. Did the student convey they understood what you were saying?

Very Much   Not at All

1   2   3   4   5   6

3. Did you feel the student was interested in you and attentive?

Very Much   Not at All

1   2   3   4   5   6

4. Were you able to say what you wanted?

Very Much   Not at All

1   2   3   4   5   6

5. Did the student enable you to see things in a new way?

Very Much   Not at All

1   2   3   4   5   6

6. Did the student say anything helpful?

Very Much   Not at All

1   2   3   4   5   6

Role play scenarios for day two

Anger

You are 36, living in the north of England where you have a job that is very important to you. Your family are in Kent where you were brought up. You don't have a partner and despite the geographical distance had a very close relationship with your parents. You thought for years that you would move back down south at some stage, but kept putting it off. Your father died five years ago, leaving your mother alone. She encouraged you to pursue your career rather than to move down to live with her.

You know your mother has been having some memory problems, but you have put this down to recent stresses she has had with her house. However, her GP has recently contacted you to say that he thinks your mother has Alzheimer's disease.

Since getting this news, you have spent half term with your mother. You are very distressed by the change in her. You are furious about what is being offered to your mother in the way of 'community care'. Not only is it inadequate but she is having to make a substantial contribution towards the costs of the home help, transport to the day centre and the night sitting service.

Despair

You are a 37-year-old homosexual male who has been HIV positive for the past 10 years. During this time you have remained in good health, have built up a successful interior design business and have been in a stable relationship. Two months ago your health began to break down and you had a series of colds, 'flu and then an attack of pneumonia.

You didn't seem to be able to shake these things off and you went into hospital for investigation. You started seeing a hospital social worker for counselling sessions. You find these sessions extremely helpful as the social worker is someone outside your immediate circle.

While in hospital you began to develop Karposi's sarcoma. You were extremely frightened at this development of your illness. At the moment you are at home. You have begun to sort out your affairs but are losing heart for the whole thing. Friends keep you informed of the latest developments in the treatment of AIDS but you no longer believe anything is going to help.

The social worker has been seeing you at home since your discharge. You get on well together. You are relieved to see them today because you are feeling in the pits.

Fear

You and your partner are in your early forties. You have a daughter aged 6. Three years ago you lost a baby through having amniocentesis. You are pregnant again and decided not to have another amniocentesis. This is partly because you could not bear to go through the feelings of loss again. More significantly, in the meantime you have read that when miscarriage follows amniocentesis, it is because the doctor concerned has not undertaken the procedure properly.

You have been seeing a hospital social worker weekly since your decision not to have an amniocentesis. You have found it helpful to talk over your feelings about losing your baby and your feelings of anger towards the medical profession.

You are now in your seventh month of pregnancy and are overcome with anxiety that the baby you are carrying has got Down's syndrome. If this is true you really don't know whether you and your husband are going to be able to cope. You fear for your marriage.

Sadness

You and Josie were married for twelve years. You have no children. You had a very intense and stormy relationship. You separated on at least six occasions, but you both shared a powerful belief that you were made for each other and that you would always get back together again. The separations usually lasted about 10 days. Josie went and stayed with her sister. Last year she stayed with a friend in Cornwall and didn't come back for three weeks. Recently she disappeared for over a month and you were convinced that she had left you for good. You wondered if she had gone off with someone else, but this didn't quite make sense to you. You saw a Relate counsellor about it at the time.

Last week, the police arrived on your doorstep to tell you that Josie had been killed in a terrible accident on her way back home. You are devastated. You still don't believe it.

REFERENCES

Agass, D. (2000), Containment, Supervision and Abuse, in U. McCluskey & C.A. Hooper (Eds.), *Psychodynamic Perspectives on Abuse: The Cost of Fear* (pp.209–222), London, Philadelphia: Jessica Kingsley.

Agazarian, Y.M. (1997), *Systems-Centered Therapy for Groups*, New York, Guilford.

Agazarian, Y.M. & Gantt, S. (2000), *An Autobiography of a Theory*, London and Philadelphia: Jessica Kingsley.

Ainsworth, M.D.S. (1991), Attachments and other affectional bonds across the life cycle, in C.M. Parkes & J. Stevenson-Hinde & P. Marris (Eds.), *Attachment across the life cycle* (pp.33–51), London and New York: Routledge.

Ainsworth, M.D.S. Bell, S.M. & Stayton, D. (1974), Infant-mother attachment and social development, in M.P. Richards (Ed.), *The Introduction of the Child into a Social World* (pp.99–135), London: Cambridge University Press.

Ainsworth, M.D.S. Blehar, M.C. Waters, E. & Wall, S. (1978), *Patterns of attachment: A Psychological Study of the Strange Situation*. Hillsdale. N.J.: Erlbaum Associates.

Ainsworth, M.D.S. & Wittig, B.A. (1969), Attachment and the exploratory behaviour of one-year-olds in a strange situation, in B.M. Foss (Ed.), *Determinants of Infant behaviour* (Volume 4 ed., pp.113–136), London: Methuen.

Allison, G.H. (1994), On the Homogenization of Psychoanalysis and Psychoanalytic Psychotherapy: A Review of Some of the Issues, in *J. Amer. Psychoanal. Assn.*, 42, 341–362.

Anstadt, T. Merten, J. Ullrich, B. & Krause, R. (1997), Affective Dyadic behaviour, Core Conflictual Relationship Themes, and Success of Treatment, in *Psychotherapy Research*, 7, 397–417.

Balint, M. & Balint, E. (1961), *Psychotherapeutic Techniques in Medicine*, London: Tavistock Publications.

Bartholomew, K. (1990), Avoidance of Intimacy: An attachment Perspective, in *Journal of Social and Personal Relationships*, 7, 147–178.

Bartholomew, K. & Horowitz, L.M. (1991), Attachment styles among young adults: a test of a four category model, in *Journal of Personality and Social Psychology*, 61, 226–244.

Bartholomew, K. & Shaver, P.R. (1998), Methods of Assessing Adult Attachment, Do they Converge? in J.A. Simpson & S.W. Rholes (Eds.), *Attachment Theory and Close Relationships*, (pp.25–45). New York/London: The Guilford Press.

Beebe, B. & Lachman, F.M. (1988), The contribution of mother/infant mutual influence to the origins of self and object relationships, in *Psychoanalytic Psychology*, 5, 305–337.

Beebe, B. & Lachmann, F.M. (2002), *Infant research and adult treatment:Co-constructing interactions*, Hillsdale, NJ: Analytic Press, Inc

Bohart, A.C. & Greenberg, L.S. (1997), *Empathy Reconsidered: New Directions in Psychotherapy*, Washington: American Psychologist.

Bowlby, J. (1969), *Attachment and Loss* (Vol. 1 Attachment), London: Hogarth Press.

Bowlby, J. (1973), *Attachment and Loss* (Vol. 11, Separation, Anxiety and Anger), London, Hogarth Press; New York, Basic Books.

Bowlby, J. (1979), *The Making and Breaking of Affectional Bonds*, London: Tavistock Publications.

Bowlby, J. (1980), *Attachment and Loss* (Vol. 111, Loss: Sadness and Depression), London, Hogarth Press; New York, Basic Books.

Bowlby, J. (1982), *Attachment and Loss* (2 ed. Vol. 1, Attachment), Harmondsworth: Penguin Books.

Bowlby, J. (1988), On knowing what you are not supposed to know and feeling what you are not supposed to feel, *A Secure Base* (pp.99–119), London: Routledge.

Bowlby, J. (1991), Postscript, in C.M. Parkes & J. Stevenson-Hinde & P. Marris (Eds.), *Attachment across the life cycle* (pp.293–297), London and New York: Routledge.

Brazelton, T.B., & Cramer, B.G. (1990), *The earliest relationship*, Reading: Addison-Wesley.

Brazelton, T.B.K.B. & Main, M. (1974), The origins of reciprocity: the early mother/infant interaction, in M. Lewis & L.A. Rosenblum (Eds.), *The effect of the infant on its caregiver* (pp.49–76), New York: Wiley.

Brearley, J. (2000). Working as an Organisational Consultant with Abuse Encountered in the Workplace, in U. McCluskey & C.A. Hooper (Eds.), *Psychodynamic Perspectives on Abuse: The Cost of Fear* (pp.223–239), London, Philadelphia: Jessica Kingsley.

Brennan, K.A. Clark, C.L. & Shaver, P.R. (1998), Self Report Measurement of Adult Attachment; An Integrative Overview, in J.A. Simpson & S.W. Rholes (Eds.), Attachment Theory and Close Relationships (pp.46–76), New York/London: The Guilford Press.

Brennan, K.A. & Shaver, P.R. (1995), Dimensions of Adult Attachment, Affect Regulation, and Romantic Relationship Functioning, Journal of Personality and Social Psychology, 21, 267–283.

Bretherton, I. (1990), Communication patterns, internal working models, and the intergenerational transmission of attachment relationships, *Infant Mental Health Journal*, 11, 237–252.

Bretherton, I. (1991), The roots and growing points of attachment theory, in C.M. Parkes & J. Stevenson-Hinde & P. Marris (Eds.), *Attachment across the life cycle* (pp.9–32), London and New York: Routledge.

Campos, J.J. Barrett, K.C. Lamb, M.E. Goldsmith, H.H. & Stenberg, C. (1983), Socioemotional development, in M.M. Haith & J.J. Campos (Eds.), *Handbook of child psychology* (Vol. 2. Infancy and psychobiology, pp.783–915), New York: Wiley.

Carkhuff, R.R. & Berenson, B.G. (1977), *Beyond Counselling and Therapy*, (Second edition ed.), New York.: Holt, Reinhart and Winston.

Cassidy, J. & Shaver, P.R. (Eds.), (1999), *Handbook of Attachment*, New York: Guilford Press.

Clulow, C. (Ed.) (2001), *Adult Attachment and Couple Psychotherapy*. London: Brunner Routledge.

Cohn, J.T.E.Z. (1987), Mother-infant face-to-face interaction: The sequence of dyadic states at 3, 6, and 9 months. Developmental Psychology, 23: 68–77. (1987), Mother-infant face-to-face interaction: The sequence of dyadic states at 3, 6, and 9 months, in *Developmental Psychology*, 23, 68–77.

Crittenden McKinsey, P. (1995), Attachment and Psychopathology, in S. Goldberg & R. Muir & J. Kerr (Eds.), *Attachment Theory; Social, Developmental and Clinical Perspectives*, London: The Analytic Press.

Dunn, J. (1999), Mindreading, emotion and relationships, in P.D. Zelazo & J.W. Astington & D.R. Olson (Eds.), *Developing theories of intention: social understanding and self control* (pp.229–242.), Mahwah, New Jersey: London.: Lawrence Erlbaum Associates:.

Emde, R.N. (1983), The Prerepresentational self and its affective core, in *Psychoanalytic Study of the Child*, 38, 165–192.

Emde, R.N. (1985), An adaptive view of infants emotions: functions for self and knowing, in *Social Sciences Information*, 24, 237–341.

Emde, R.N. (1990a), Mobilising fundamental modes of development: empathic availability and therapeutic action, in *Int. J. Psycho-Anal*, 69, 881–913.

Emde, R.N. (1990b),. Mobilizing Fundamental Modes of Development: Empathic Availability and Therapeutic Action, *J. Amer. Psychoanal. Assn.*, (APA), 38, 881–913.

Emde, R.N. Biringen, Z. Clyman, R.B. & Oppenheim, D. (1991), The moral self of infancy: affective core and procedural knowledge, *Developmental Review*, 11, 251–270.

Ekman, P. (1993), Expression and the nature of emotion, *American Psychologist*, 48, 384–392.

Ekman, P. & Friesen, W.V. (1975), *Unmasking the face*. Englewood Cliffs, NJ: Prentice-Hall.

Ekman, P. & Oster, H. (1979), Facial expressions of emotions, *Annual Review of Psychology*, 30, 527–554

Ekman, P. & Friesen, W.V. (1986), A new pan-cultural facial expression of emotion, *Motivation and Emotion*, 10, 150–168.

Fairbairn, R. (1952), *Psychoanalytic Studies of the Personality*, London: Tavistock.

Feeney, J.A. Noller, P. & Hanrahan, M. (1994), Assessing Adult Attachment: Developments in the conceptualization of security and insecurity, in M.B. Sperling & W.H. Berman (Eds.), *Attachment in Adults: Theory, Assessment and Treatment* (pp.128–152), New York: Guilford.

Fiedler, F.E. (1953), Quantitative studies on the role of therapists' feelings towards their patients, in O.H. Mowrer (Ed.), *Psychotherapy Theory and Research* (pp.296–315), New York: The Ronald Press Company.

Field, T. (1981), Infant Arousal, Attention and Affect during Early Interactions, in L.P. Lipsitt (Ed.), *Advances in Infancy Research* (Vol. 1): Ablex Publishing Corporation.

Field, T.N. Woodson, R. Greenberg, R. & Cohen, D. (1982), Discrimination and imitation of facial expressions by neonates, *Science*, 218, 179–181.

Fonagy, P. Moran, G.S. Steele, M. & Steele, H. (1992), The integration of psychonalytic theory and work on attachment: The issue of intergenerational psychic processes, in D. Stern & M. Ammaniti (Eds.), *Attacamento E Psiconalis* (pp.19–30), Bari, Italy: Laterza.

Fonagy, P. Steele, M. & Steele, H. (1991), Maternal representations of attachment during pregnancy predict the organisation of infant-mother attachment at one year of age, *Child Development*, 62, 880–893.

Fonagy, P. Steele, M. Steele, H. Leigh, T. Kennedy, R. Mattoon, G. & Target, M. (1995a), Attachment in Adults: clinical and Developmental Perspectives, in S. Goldberg & M. Roy & K. John (Eds.), *Attachment Theory; Social, Developmental and Clinical Perspectives* (pp.233–279), London: The Analytic Press.

Fonagy, P. Steele, M. Steele, H. Leigh, T. Kennedy, R. Mattoon, G. & Target, M. (1995b), Attachment, the Reflective Self, and Borderline States: The predictive specificity of the Adult Attachment Interview and Pathological Emotional Development, in S. Goldberg & R. Muir & J. Kerr (Eds.), *Attachment Theory; Social, Developmental and Clinical Perspectives* (pp.233–279). London: The Analytic Press.

Fraley, R.C. & Waller, N.G. (1998), Adult Attachment Patterns: A Test of the Typological Model, in J.A. Simpson & S.W. Rholes (Eds.), *Attachment Theory and Close Relationships*, New York/London: The Guilford Press.

Friesen, W.V. & Ekman, P. (1984), EMFACS–7 *Emotional facial action coding system*, Unpublished manuscript

George, C. Kaplan, N. & Main, M. (1985), *Adult Attachment Interview.*: Department of Psychology, University of California, Berkeley, Berkeley, California. 94720.

Gergely, G. (1992), Developmental Reconstructions: Infancy from the point of view of psychoanalysis and developmental psychology, *Psychoanalysis and Contemporary Thought*, 15, 3–55.

Gergely, G. (1996), Social Biofeedback Theory of Parental Affect-Mirroring, *Int. J. Psycho-Anal*, 77, 1181–1207.

Gergely, G. & Fonagy, P. (1998), *States of mind.* Paper presented at the International Attachment Network series of seminars on Intersubjectivity, London.

Gopnik, A. Meltzoff, A.N. & Kuhl, P. (1999), *The Scientist in the Crib: minds, brains and how children learn*, New York: W. Morrow.

Graff, H. & Luborsky, L. (1977), Long-Term Trends in Transference and Resistance: A Report on a Quantitative-Analytic Method Applied to Four Psychoanalyses, *J. Amer. Psychoanal. Assn.*, (APA), 25, 471–490.

Grice, P. (1975), Logic and conversation, in P. Cole & J.L. Moran (Eds.) *Syntax and Semantics*: Vol.3 Speech acts (pp41–58), New York, Academic Press.

Grice, P. (1989), *Studies in the way of words*, Cambridge, MA: Harvard University Press

Grossmann, K. Fremmer-Bombik, E. Rudolph, J. & Grossmann, K.E. (1988), Maternal attachment representations as related to child-mother attachment patterns and maternal sensitivity and acceptance of her infant, in R.A. Hinde & J. Stevenson-Hinde (Eds.), *Relations within Families*, Oxford: Oxford University Press.

Grossmann, K. & Grossmann, K.E. (1991a), Newborn behaviour, early parenting quality and later toddler-parent relationships in a group of German infants, in J. Nugent, K. & B.M. Lester & T.B. Brazleton (Eds.), *The Cultural Context of Infancy*, (Vol. 2), Norwood, NJ.: Ablex.

Grossmann, K. Grossmann, K.E. Spangler, G. Suess, G. & Unzner, L. (1985), Maternal sensitivity and newborns' orientation responses as related to quality of attachment in northern Germany, in I. Bretherton & E. Waters (Eds.), *Growing Points in Attachment Theory and Research. Monographs of the Society for Research in Child Development* (Vol. 50, pp.233–278).

Grossmann, K.E. & Grossmann, K. (1991b), Attachment quality as an organiser of emotional and behavioural; responses in a longitudinal perspective, in C.M. Parkes & J. Stevenson-Hinde & P. Marris (Eds.), *Attachment across the life cycle* (pp.93–114), London and New York: Routledge.

Haft, W.L. & Slade, A. (1989), Affect attunement and Maternal attachment: a pilot study, *Infant Mental Health Journal*, 10, 157–171.

Haldane, J.D., McCluskey, U., & Peacey, M. (1980), A residential facility for families in Scotland: developments in prospect and retrospect. *International Journal of Family Therapy*, 1, 357–372

Hardy, G. Aldbridge, J. Davidson, C. Rowe, C. Reilly, S. Shapiro, D. (1999) Therapist responsiveness to client attachment styles and issues observed in client-identified significant events in psychodynamic-interpersonal psychotherapy. *Psychotherapy Research*, 9, 36–53

Hazan, C. & Shaver, P.R. (1987), Romantic love conceptualised as an attachment process, *Journal of Personality and Social Psychology*, 52, 511–524.

Heard, D. & Lake, B. (1986), The attachment dynamic in adult life, *British Journal of Psychiatry*, 149, 430–439.

Heard, D. & Lake, B. (1997), *The challenge of attachment for caregiving*, London.: Routledge:.

Heard, D. & Lake, B. (2000, June 21st.), *The Dynamics of Attachment*, Paper presented at the International Attachment Seminar, London.

Hesse, E. (1996), Discourse, memory and the Adult Attachment Interview: a note with emphasis on the emerging cannot classify category, *Infant Mental Health Journal*, 17, 4–11

Hofer, M.A. (1983), On the relationship between attachment and separation processes in infancy, in R. Plutchik & H. Kellerman (Eds.), *Emotion Theory, Research and Experience* (Vol. 2, pp.199–219), New York: London: Academic Press.

Kiersky, S. & Beebe, B. (1994), The reconstruction of early non-verbal relatedness in the treatment of difficult patients: a special form of empathy, *Psychoanalytic Dialogues* 4, 4, 389–408.

Klinnert, M.D. Campos, J.J. Sorce, J.F. Emde, R.N. & Svejda, M. (1983), Emotions as behaviour regulators: Social referencing in infancy, in R.Plutchik & H.Kellerman (Eds.), *Emotion: Theory, Research and Experience*, (Vol. 2, pp.57–82). New York: Academic Press.

Luborsky, L. & Crits-Christoph, P. (1988), Measures of Psychoanalytic Concepts—The Last Decade of Research from `The Penn Studies', *Int. J. Psycho-Anal.*, 69, 75–86.

Luborsky, L. Papp, C. Luborsky, E. & Mark, D. (1994), The Core Conflictual Relationship Theme, *Psychotherapy Research*, 4, 172–183.

Main, M. Kaplan, N. & Cassidy, J. (1985), Security in infancy, childhood and adulthood: a move to the level of representation, in I. Bretherton and E.Waters (Eds.), Growing points of attachment theory and research, *Monographs of the Society for Research in Child Development*, 50 (1–2, Serial No. 209), 66–104

Main, M. (1991), Metacognitive knowledge, metacognitive monitoring, and singular (coherent). vs. Multiple (incoherent). model of attachment: findings and directions for future research, in C.M. Parkes & J. Stevenson-Hinde & P.Marris (Eds.), *Attachment across the life cycle* (pp.127–159), London: Routledge.

Main, M. & Cassidy, J. (1988), Categories of response to reunion with the parent at age six: Predicted from infant attachment classifications and stable over a one month period, *Developmental Psychology*, 24, 415–426

Main, M. (1995), Recent studies in attachment: overview, with selected implications for clinical work, in S. Goldberg & R. Muir & J. Kerr (Eds.), *Attachment Theory; Social, Developmental and Clinical Perspectives* (pp.407–474.), London: The Analytic Press.

Main, M. (1999), Epilogue. Attachment Theory: Eighteen Points with suggestions for future studies, in J. Cassidy & P.R. Shaver (Eds.), *Handbook of Attachment: Theory Research and Clinical Applications* (pp.845–889), N.Y.: Guilford.

Mattinson, J. (1975), *The Reflection Process in Casework Supervision*, London: Tavistock Marital Studies Institute.

Mattinson, J. & Sinclair, I. (1979), *Mate and Stalemate*, Oxford: Blackwell.

McCluskey, U. & Duerden, S. (1993), Pre-verbal communication: the role of play in establishing rhythms of communication between self and other, *Journal of Social Work Practice*, 7, 17–27.

McCluskey, U. Hooper. C. & Bingley Miller, L. (1999), Goal-corrected empathic attunement, developing and rating the concept, *Psychotherapy, Theory, Research, Training and Practice.*, 80–90.

McCluskey, U. Roger, D. & Nash, P. (1997), A preliminary study of the role of attunement in adult psychotherapy, *Human Relations*, 50, 1261–1273.

McCluskey, U. (2001), A theory of caregiving in adult life: developing and measuring the concept of goal-corrected empathic attunement, Unpublished DPhil Thesis. University of York Library.

McCluskey, U. (2002), The Dynamics of Attachment and Systems-Centered Group Psychotherapy, *Group Dynamics: Theory, Research, and Practice*, APA 6, 131–142.

McCluskey, U (in press), Object Relations and Attachment Dynamics in Group Psychotherapy: the communication, regulation and exploration of affective states.

McLeod, J. (1994), *Doing Counselling Research*, London: Sage.

McLeod, J. (1998), *An introduction to Counselling*, Buckingham & Philadelphia: Open University Press.

Medawer, P.D. (1962), *Hypothesis and Imagination: The Art of the Soluble*, London: Methuen and Co. Ltd.

Meltzoff, A. (1983), Newborn infants imitate adult facial gestures, *Child Development*, 54, 702–709.

Meltzoff, A. (1992), Early imitation within a functional framework: the importance of person, identity, movement, and development, *Infant Behaviour and Development*, 15, 479–505.

Meltzoff, A.N. (1999a), Persons and representations: why infant imitation is important for theories of human development, in J. Nadel & G. Butterworth (Eds.), *Imitation in Infancy* (pp.9–35), Cambridge, UK: Cambridge University Press.

Meltzoff, A.N. Gopnik, A. & Rapacholi, B.M. (1999b), Toddlers' understanding of emotions: explorations of the dark ages, in P.D. Zelazo & J.W. Astington & D. R. Olson (Eds.), *Developing theories of intention: social understanding and self control*, (pp.17–41), Mahwah, New Jersey: London.: Lawrence Erlbaum Associates.

Meltzoff, A.N. & Moore, M.K. (1977), Imitation of facial and manual gestures by human neonates, *Science*, 198, 75–78.

Meltzoff, A.N. & Moore, M.K. (1995), Infants' understanding of people and things: From body imitation to folk psychology, in J. Bermudez & A.J.Marcel & N. Eilan (Eds.), *Body and the self* (pp.43–69.), Cambridge: MIT Press.

Mikulincer, Mario, Shaver, Phillip R. and Pereg, Dana (2003), Attachment Theory and Affect Regulation:The Dynamics, Development, and Cognitive Consequences of Attachment-Related Strategies, *Motivation and Emotion*, Vol. 27, No. 2

Mollon, P. (2000), Dissociative Identity Disorder and Memories of Childhood Abuse, in U. McCluskey & C.A. Hooper (Eds.), *Psychodynamic Perspectives on Abuse: The Cost of Fear* (pp.194–205), London and Philadelphia: Jessica Kingsley.

Murray, L. (1998), Contributions of experimental and clinical perturbations of mother/infant communications to the understanding of infant intersubjectivity, in S. Braten (Ed.), *Intersubjective Communication and Emotion in Early Ontogeny* (pp.127–144.), Cambridge: Cambridge University Press.

Murray, L. & Trevarthen, C. (1985), Emotional regulation of interactions between two month olds and their mothers, in T.M. Field & N.A. Fox (Eds.), *Social Perception in Infants*. New Jersey: Norwood.

Murray, L. & Trevarthen, C. (1986), The infants role in mother/infant communications, *Journal of Child Language*, 13, 15–29.

Nadel, J, Guerini, C., Peze, a., Rivet, C. (1999), The evolving nature of imitation as a means of communication, in J. Nadel & G. Butterworth (Eds.), *Imitation in Infancy* (pp.209–304), Cambridge, UK: Cambridge University Press.

Oster, H. Hegley. D. & Nagel, L. (1992), Adult Judgements And Fine-Grained Analysis of Infant Facial Expressions: Testing the Validity of A Priori Coding Formulas, *Developmental Psychology*, 28, 1115 – 1131.

Papousek, H. & Papousek, M. (1979), Early ontogony of human social interaction: its biological roots and social dimensions, in M.V. Cranach (Ed.), *Human Ethology*, Cambridge, UK: Cambridge University Press.

Papousek, M. (1994), Melodies in caregivers' speech: a species specific guidance towards language, *Early Development and Parentingy*, 3, 5–17.

Rogers, C.R. (1942), *Counseling and Psychotherapy*, Cambridge, Massachusetts: Houghton Mifflin Company, The Riverside Press.

Rogers, C.R. (1953), Some directions and end points in therapy, in O. Hobart Mowrer (Ed.) *Psychotherapy Theory and Research* (pp.44–68), The Ronald Press Company. New York.

Rogers, C.R. & Dymond, R.F. (Eds.), (1954). *Psychotherapy and Personality Change*, Chicago and London.: The University of Chicago Pres.

Roth, A. & Fonagy, P. (1996), *What works for whom? A critical review of psychotherapy research*, New York: London: Guilford.

Rovee-Collier, C.K. & Fagen, J.W. (1981), The retrieval of memory in early infancy, in L.P. Lipsitt (Ed.), *Advances in Infancy Research* (Vol. 1): Ablex.

Rubino, G., Barker, C., Roth, T., Fearon. P. (2000), Therapist empathy and depth of responsiveness in response to potential alliance ruptures: the role of therapist and patient attachment styles, Psychotherapy Research, 10, 408–420.

Rutter, M. (1995), Clinical Implications of Attachment Concepts: Retrospect and Prospect, *Journal of Child Psychology and Psychiatry*, 36, 549–571.

Schore, A.N. (1994), *Affect Regulation and the Origin of the Self: The Neurobiology of Emotional Development*, Hillsdale, New Jersey: Hove UK.: Lawrence Erlbaum Associates.

Schore, A.N. (2000), Attachment and the regulation of the right brain, *Attachment and Human Development*, 2.

Schore, A.N. (2003a), Affect regulation and the repair of the self. New York: W.W. Norton and Co.

Schore, A.N. (2003b), Affect Dysregulation and disorders of the self. New York: W.W. Norton and Co.

Seeman, J. & Raskin, N.J. (1953), Research perspectives in Client-Centered therapy, in O.H. Mowrer (Ed.), *Psychotherapy Theory and Research* (pp.205–234), New York.: The Ronald Press Company.

Segal, L.B. Oster, H. Cohen, M. Caspi, B. Myers, M. & Brown, D. (1995), Smiling and Fussing in Seven-Month-Old Preterm and Full-Term Black Infants in the Still-Face Situation, *Child Development*, 66, 1829–1843.

Siegel, D.J. (1999), *The Developing Mind: Towards a Neurobiology of Interpersonal Experience*, New York: Guilford.

Sroufe, L.A. & Waters, E. (1977), Attachment as an organizational construct, *Child Development*, 48, 1184–1199.

Stern, D.N. (1985), *The Interpersonal World of the Infant*, New York: Basic Books.

Sutherland, J.D. (1993), The autonomous self, *Journal of the Menninger Clinic*.

Suttie, I. (1935), *The origins of Love and Hate*, London: Kegan Paul, Trench, Trubner and Co.

Suttie, I. (1988), *The origins of Love and Hate*, London: Free Association books.

Trevarthen, C. & Hubley, P. (1978), Secondary intersubjectivity: Confidence, confiders and acts of meaning in the first year, in A. Lock (Ed.), *Action, gesture and symbol*, New York: Academic Press.

Trevarthen, C. (1979a), Communication and cooperation in early infancy: A description of primary intersubjectivity, in M. Bullowa (Ed.), *Before Speech* (pp.321–347), New York: Cambridge University Press.

Trevarthen, C. Aitken, K. Papoudi, D. & Roberts, J. (1998), *Children with Autism: Diagnosis and interventions to meet their needs*, London and Philadelphia: Jessica Kingsley.

Trevarthen, C. Kokkinaki, T. & Fiamenghi Jr, G.A. (1999), What infants' imitations communicate with mothers, with fathers and with peers, in J.Nadel & G. Butterworth (Eds.), *Imitation in Infancy* (pp.127–185), Cambridge, UK: Cambridge University Press.

Tronick, E. Als, H. & Brazelton, T.B. (1977), The Infant's capacity to regulate mutuality in face to face communicative interactions, *Journal of Communication*, 27, 74–80.

Tronick, E.Z. (1989), Emotions and Emotional Communication in Infants, *American Psychologist*, 44, 112–119.

Tronick, E.Z. & Cohn, J. (1989), Infant mother face-to face interaction. Age and gender differences in coordination and miscordination, *Child Development*, 59, 85–92

Truckle, S. (Ed.). (2000), *Treatment or torture: working with issues of abuse and torture in the transference*, London and Philadelphia: Jessica Kingsley.

Vas Dias, S. (Ed.). (2000), *Inner silence: one of the impacts of emotional abuse upon the developing self*, in U. McCluskey & C.A. Hooper (Eds.), Psychodynamic Perspectives on Abuse: The Cost of Fear (pp.159–171), London and Philadelphia: Jessica Kingsley

Weil, J.L. (1992), *Early Deprivation of Empathic Care*, Maddison, Connecticut: International Universities Press.

Weinfield, N.S., Sroufe, L. Alan, Egeland, B., & Carlson, E.A. (1999), The nature of individual differences in infant/caregiver attachment, in J.Cassidy & P.R. Shaver (Eds.), *Handbook of Attachment: Theory Research and Clinical Applications* (pp.68–88), N.Y.: Guilford

West, M. & Sheldon-Keller, A. (1992), *The Assessment of Dimensions Relevant to Adult Reciprocal attachment* (Vol. 37).

Winnicott, D.W. (1958a), *The Maturational Processes and the Facilitating Environment*, London.: Hogarth Press and the Institute of Psycho-Analysis.

Winnicott, D.W. (1958b), *Collected Papers Through Paediatrics to Psycho-Analysis*, London: Hogarth Press and the Institute of Psycho-Analysis.

Winnicott, D.W. (1967), *Mirror-role of Mother and Family in Child Development*, in P.Lomas (Ed.), The Predicament of the Family: A Psycho-analytical Symposium. London.: Hogarth Press and the Institute of Psycho-Analysis.

Winnicott, D.W. (1971), *Playing and Reality*, London: Tavistock Publications.

Winnicott, D.W. (1971a), *Playing and Reality*, London.: Tavistock.

Winnicott, D.W. (1971b), *Therapeautic Consultations in Child Psychiatry*, London.: Hogarth Press and the Institute of Psycho-Analysis.

Woodhouse, R. & P. Pengelly. (1986), *Anxiety and the Dynamics of Collaboration*, Aberdeen: AUP.

Index

BF
575
E55
m38
2005
NEAL